ENRICO ACERBI

THE 1799 CAMPAIGN IN ITALY VOL. 2
GENERAL SUVOROV'S ARRIVAL IN ITALY

WAR IN COLOR 008

THE AUTHOR

Dr.Enrico Acerbi born in Valdagno (Vicenza - Italy) on 13.8.1952; graduated in Medicine, expert in Toxicology, worked as Blood Transfusionist in local Hospital, now retired and living in Valdagno (Vicenza), partner of the War Museum of Rovereto, member of the Napoleonic Association of Italy and historiographer of the Great War. Enrico Acerbi developed historical Research during the '90s. For five years he collaborated with the Center for Great War Studies at Asiago. He also collaborated with the "Montane Community" of Arsiero as Teacher at the so called Popular University (historical training courses on the First World War) and with the Montane Community Agno-Chiampo (reconstruction of the fortifications made in the Great War). Partner of the Italian War Museum of Rovereto and founding member of the Great War Historical Research Group of Valdagno, currently entrusted to the study of Napoleonic history in Veneto and Italy. Graphic illustrator of articles on Napoleonic history. He has already published several history subjects.

NOTE EDITORIALI

Tutto il contenuto dei nostri libri, in qualsiasi forma prodotti (cartacei, elettronici o altro) quando non diversamente specificato è copyright soldiershop.com. I diritti di traduzione, riproduzione, memorizzazione con qualsiasi mezzo, digitale, fotografico, fotocopie ecc. Sono riservati per tutti i Paesi. Nessuna delle immagini presenti nei nostri libri può essere riprodotta senza il permesso scritto di soldiershop.com. L'Editore rimane a disposizione degli eventuali aventi diritto per tutte le fonti iconografiche dubbie o non identificate. I marchi Soldiershop Publishing, Bookmoon, Museum s e relative collane sono di proprietà di soldiershop.com o Luca Cristini Editore; di conseguenza qualsiasi uso esterno non è consentito.

PUBLISHING'S NOTES

None of unpublished images or text of our book may be reproduced in any format without the expressed written permission of Soldiershop.com when not indicate as marked with license creative commons 3.0 or 4.0. Soldiershop Publishing has made every reasonable effort to locate, contact and acknowledge rights holders and to correctly apply terms and conditions to Content. In the event that any Content infringes your rights or the rights of any third parties, or Content is not properly identified or acknowledged we would like to hear from you so we may make any necessary alterations. In this event contact: info@soldiershop.com. Our trademark: Soldiershop Publishing @, The names of our series & brand: Museum book, Bookmoon, Soldiers&Weapons, Battlefield, War in colour, Historical Biographies, Darwin's view, Fabula, Altrastoria, Italia Storica Ebook, Witness To History, Soldiers, Weapons & Uniforms, Storia etc. are herein @ by Soldiershop.com.

LICENSES COMMONS

This book may utilize part of material marked with license creative commons 3.0 or 4.0 (CC BY 4.0), (CC BY-ND 4.0), (CC BY-SA 4.0) or (CCo 1.0). Or derived from publication 70 years old or more and recolored from us. We give appropriate attribution credit and indicate if change were made in the acknowledgements field.
All our books utilize only fonts licensed under the SIL Open Font License or other free use license.

ACKNOWLEDGMENT

I would particularly like to thank Robert Burnham of http://www.napoleon-series.org and all the friends, who participate in this very interesting website; above all Mr. Robert Ouvrard and Mr. Leopold Kudma. Thanks also to István Nagy for having send me part of his interesting works and articles (also if reading them in Hungarian language it had been an hard task to perform). Many thanks also to Prof. Vladimir Brnardić of Zagreb for having provided considerable assistance with the Croatian sources. Finally thanks to "The 1809 International Research Society" for the Certificate of Honour they gave to m for this work about the "Kaiserlich-königlich Armée". Naturally, a special thanks to Soldiershop for giving me this beautiful opportunity. A special tanks also to NYPL for his kindly police about the use of the image used in our books.

ISBN: 9788893274531   1st edition May 2019
Title: War in color 008 - **The 1799 campaign in Italy Vol 2** by Enrico Acerbi, iconographic research by Luca Stefano Cristini
Editor: Luca Cristini Editore, for the brand: Soldiershop. Cover & Art Design: Luca S. Cristini.

GENERAL SUVOROV'S ARRIVAL IN ITALY APRIL 14, 1799

"KOSAKEN KOMMEN!"

1799 March, 12th	Suvorov got the command of the Russian Army at St. Petersburg.
1799 March, 25th	Suvorov reached Vienna with Rozenberg and Hermann Corps.
1799 April, 4th	Hermann Corps sent to Galicia (Lemberg) through Pest.
1799 April, 14th	Suvorov reached Verona and Melas. The former General Nummsen Corp had general Rimski-Korsakov as new commander.

The Lion Return [1]

The travel from Vienna was very laborious. On April 8, Suvorov encountered the Rozenberg Russian troops, near Friesach, and unbelievably this eliminated all his fatigue. Applauded with enthusiasm by the soldiers of general Förster avantgarde, Suvorov travelled with them and crossed in their company the Carnia Alps, reaching Italy. From Tarvisio he put himself again on the road in travel towards Udine where he passed the night. The following morning ordered to all to accelerate the march. Knowing the inner situation of the country, upset from the riots against the French domination, already he foresaw that "That war would not have been more a war of the Kings, but a war of the people ...". On April 13, they arrived to Vicenza and stood there for a short stage. The next day, with the sun just waking up, he ordered to dismount the camps to all Russian units, in order to continue the march towards Verona. Frontally opened a valley, included between Tavernelle and the town of Montebello, large and covered by a northern curtain of Alps. Two streams cut the valley. One, the Guà, had flooded out and over the banks during the previous days, and the second, the Chiampo, had made the same some miles forward. In close proximity of that rural area they was able to see one carriageway that, crossing the flooded area, continued beyond the bridge thrown over the Guà.

The field marshal, wanting to save time, determined to use that road for the moves of the army equipment and gave orders to the soldiers to ford the streams. On the road left, elevated on a hill, was found an inn, a grey house which ground floor was equipped with windows secured by iron bars, and there were placed the quarters. Suvorov, riding along the left bank of the Guà, began to encourage everyone who was crossing the torrent. Then he went to the inn in order to pass the night. To the next day, towards 8 hours AM, whith already deployed troops, Suvorov received the visit of general Johann Gabriel de Chasteler, the Austrian Chief of Staff in Italy. The marshal was very pleased to see him, he went towards his coach, shaked his hand and began a fluent chatter like having met an old friend. He pointed out that the destiny intentionally put the two recently coalized armies against the common enemy, as it was already happened during the Russian-Turkish wars and, therefore, he invited Chasteler to lunch together.

While talking together, the waiter carried two italian "polenta" portions with roasted lamb and, as soon as the rapid meal finished, Chasteler put a map on the table, on which were marked the austrian positions and those of the French troops. The Austrian explained the military situation to the Russian field marshal and communicated that in the army of His Imperial Height Franz II were 42,683 combatants, a number inferior to that one of all the French forces scattered in Italy; he stated also that an other Austrian Corps, the general Klenau one strong 4.500 men, was in reserve. After the Verona and Porto Legnago battles against the Austrians, the French army of Schérer numbered alone 28,000 men, without including the two detached republican garrisons in Mantua and Peschiera, a total of 10.000 men. Suvorov, detecting his puzzling and anxious mind, then exclaimed: *"I will add 20,000 Russians to 42,000 Austrians, plus the 8,000 men of Vukassovic and I will defeat them!"*.

On April 14, towards noon, the Russian troops approached the Verona suburbs. Arrived at Porta Vescovo, the Russian field marshal coach, escorted by eight cossacks, under a sparkling sunlight met a copious crowd, which was already waiting for him, behind two Austrian Hussars rows. General Melas went forward on a horse, friendly advancing to embrace Suvorov, but the marshal, correctly, only shaked his hand. From the city door the group proceeded, with some difficulties cutting the way through the enthusiastic city crowd, and, through the via Vescovo, they reached the Adige and crossed it on the Navi bridge; then the "parade" continued through via Cappuccini and finally reached the citadel. Here General Melas had deployed, near the Verona's Arena, some units from the early morning, not being sure of the exact time of the arrival. In the ruined inner part of the ancient

INDEX :

GENERAL SUVOROV'S ARRIVAL IN ITALY APRIL 14, 1799 .... pag. 3

THE ADDA BATTLES OF APRIL 1799 .... pag. 17

FROM MILAN TO THE PO RIVER .... pag. 35

THE SWITZERLAND BORDER COMBATS MAY-JUNE 1799 .... pag. 51

THE PIEDMONT'S INVASION THE FALL OF THE SARDINIAN FORTRESS .... pag. 67

WAITING FOR MACDONALDS ARMY MAY-JUNE 1799 .... pag. 79

roman stadium were exposed the war trophies, conquered after the last combats. In addiction, on the terrace of Mariani palace, waved the captured French flags and, all around, military hymns could be heard.
A citizen, caressing the horses of the marshal, screamed: "Viva il nostro Liberatore ! (Alive our liberator!)". People followed the Suvorov's coach until Villa Emilio, where the marshal, not loving the luxury, had chosen for himself the more unpretentious locations available. During the afternoon, at 3 hours, he received the higher Austrian Staff, come to had the new orders. In the waiting room the officials were received by Prochor, Suvorov's attendant. The marshal complimented the Austrian generals for the recent victories and, after their departure, he received the judges and deputies of the city. Later, in the evening, three Cossacks regiments appeared in the city, provoking great curiosity near the people. Their dressing mode and the eccentric armament were the main arguments of conversation. The Cossacks wore wide long pants "à la brachesse" and brown, red and blue long coats, coloured with incredible verve. They carried all kind of weapons and everyone had two horses to utilize; to their comparison the Russian infantry had more humble uniforms. During the night between April 14 on 15, Suvorov worked without sleeping and sent his orders for the forces forward movement. He sent an Austrian Corps towards Mantova, in whose citadel was the French garrison of general De Foissac, and sent to Goito an other Russian column, the vanguard led by prince Bagration, with whom the field marshal marched. Having reached Goito he decided to give to general Chasteler the task to distribute his new instructions in order to proceed in the advance and, on April 16, he took care personally of the troops reorganization, explaining to the Austrians the principles of his strategy.

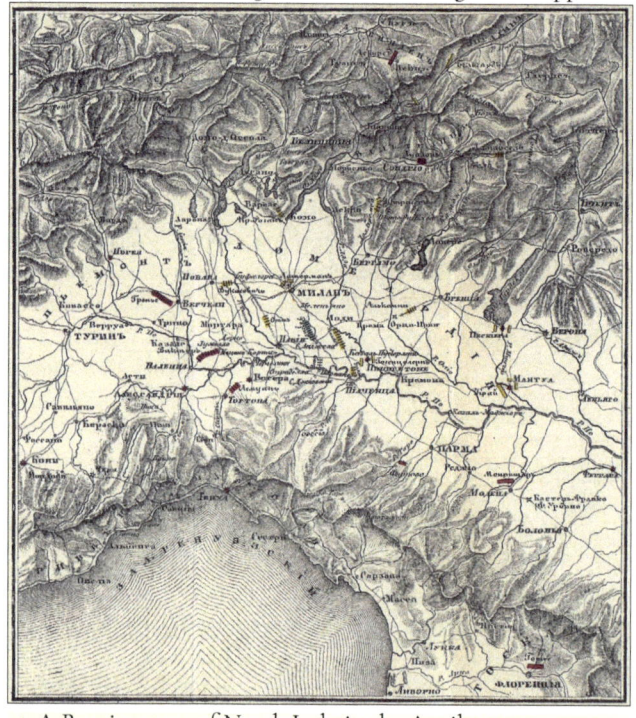

▲ A Russian map of North Italy in the April 1799

THE MARCH TO THE ADDA RIVER DEPLOYMENT OF THE RUSSIAN CORPS

SITUATION OF THE RUSSIAN CORPS IN ITALY ON APRIL 14, 1799

Infantry-general Andrej Grigorjevich Rozenberg Corps	20.247

Rozenberg (Andrej Grigorjevich, 1730 - 1813) - General of Infantry, participated in Seven-years War and in the first Turkish War, was also the Smolensk military governor. From December 3, 1796 until November 29, 1797 (when he was promoted to the rank of General of Infantry) he was the Chief (Inhaber - Entitled to or Owner) of the Vitebsk Musketeers Rgt. From March 12, 1798 to June 8, 1800 he was Chief at the Moscow grenadier Rgt. In 1799 tsar Paul I entrusted Rozenberg with a Corps of 22000 men with the task to move to Italy to support Austrians. Operating under Suvorov's guide, he defeated general Serurier, participated in the battles of Trebbia and Novi. From June 8, 1800 to October 11, 1803 he was the Chief of Vladimir Musketeers Rgt. He was also the governor in Kamienetz- Podolski and Cherson.

Infantry Total	16.013 men
Cavalry Total	2.930 cossacks
Corps Artillery	
Artillery Btn. Lieut. General Ejler	632 men
(with 1st Artillery Coy Ivanov and 2nd Artillery Coy Kuzmin)	
Divisional (regimental) Light Artillery	672 men

Division Lieut. General Jacob Ivanovich Povalo-Shvejkovsky 1st

Povalo-Shvejkovsky the First, Jacob Ivanovich (1750-1807) General of Infantry, in 1799 he was general-lieutenant; from February 6, 1798. Promoted General of Infantry on September 27, 1799, after the Italian Campaign, he maintained the ownership of the the chief Smolensk Musketeers Rgt. (from December 3, 1796 until September 10, 1800 ?); during the later Swiss campaign he was still under the Suvorov's army.

Brigade general-major Mihail Semionovich Baranovsky 2nd

General-major Baranowsky was the Chief of the Nizovski Musketeers Rgt from January 16, 1799 until probably January 28, 1801. From December 14, 1803 until May 29, 1805 he was the Chief of the Tobolsk garrison Rgt. He was excluded from duty on May 29, 1805, the date of his death.

Imperial Russian Grenadier Rgt. GdI Rozenberg or Moskowsky (Moskow) – 2 Btns	1424
cmdr. (until June 10) Colonel Petr Petrovic Passek.	
Imperial Russian Musketeers rgt. GM Baranowsky II or Nizowski Musk. Rgt. – 2 Btns	1590
cmdr Colonel Mihail Aleksejevic Chitrowo	
Imperial Russian 7th Jäger (Jeghersky) Rgt. GM Bagration – 2 Btns	737
cmdr.: Gen. Petr Ivanovic Bagration	
Imperial Russian Grenadier Btn (GB) Lomonosov	606
5th Don Cossacks Rgt. Denissov	490
Denissov Tichon Ivanovich (b. 1749) from 1793 to 1797 Lieutenant Colonel, regiment-commander of Ekateripo-slaw Cossacks Btn.	
6th Don Cossacks Rgt. Pasdejev (written Posdeev)	470

Brigade general-major Mihail Andrejevich Miloradovic 1st

General-lieutenant from November 8, 1800, infantry general from September 29,1809. From May 1, 1813 he was Column Brigadier. From July 27, 1798 to September 1, 1814 he was also the Chief of the Apsheronsky Musketeers Rgt.

Imperial Russian Musketeers rgt. Lieut. General Förster (Ferster) or Tambowski (Tambov)	1503
Cmdr.: Lieut. Colonel Zaltser – 2 Btns	
Imperial Russian Musketeers rgt. GM Mihail Andrejevich Miloradovic or Apsheronsky (Apsheron)	1516
Cmdr. : Podpulkovnik (Lieut. Colonel - from October 3, 1799 pulkovnik or Colonel) Stepan Timofejevich Karlov – 2 Btns	
Imperial Russian Grenadier Btn (GB) Dendrjugyn	623
Don Cossacks Rgt. Molchanov	494

Division Lieut. General Ivan Ivanovich Förster (in Russian Ferster)

Ivan Ivanovich Ferster (Förster, Fershter) Born in 1739. In 1771 was the Second major in the Karlopolsk Carabiniers Rgt. Later Vyatski. General-lieutenant from January 22,1799. From June 4, 1797 to January 24, 1803 he was the Chief of the Tambov Musketeers Rgt. From that date to June 27, 1807 he was Chief of Arkhangelsk garrison Rgt.

Brigade Generalmajor Jacob Ivanovich Tyrtov

Colonel, promoted to general-major on September 14, 1797 in order to became the Chief of the Tula Musketeers Rgt. and probably also commander of the Moscow Musketeers Rgt. On April 30, 1799, after the Cassano battle, he was promoted General-lieutenant. He retired on January 9, 1800 and in 1812 he was Chief of the Tver Home Guard.

Imperial Russian Musketeers rgt. GM Tuyrtov or Tug'lsky (Tula) – 2 btns	1527
Cmdr.: Major Ivan Fjodorovich Golovin	
Imperial Russian Musketeers rgt. GM Baron Ivan Ivanovich Dalheim	1514
or Archangelogorodsky (Archangelsk). Cmdr: Colonel Stepan Nikolajevich Castelli– 2 btns had as Chief, from June 26th, General Major Nikolay Mihailovic Kamensky 2nd	
Imperial Russian 8th Jäger (Jegherski) Rgt. Major General Chubarov	750
Chief from May 13: GM Ivan Ivanovich Miller	
Imperial Russian Grenadier Btn (GB) Kalemin	614
8th Don Cossacks Rgt. Grekov.	494

Brigade Major General Mihail Mihajlovich Veletskij

He was the commander of the Suzdal Musketeers Rgt. He was promoted General-major on October 31, 1798 and commander of the Butyrsk Musketeers Rgt. until June 20, 1799 when he became the Chief of the same regiment until September 16, 1800.

Imperial Russian Musketeers rgt. Young-Baden or molodo-Badensky – 2 Btns	1424
Chief: Lieutenant General Karl Ludwig Prince of Baden. Alias Butyrskowo (Butyrsk) after may 18 renamed as GM Mihail Mihailovich Veletskji Rgt. its former commander	
Imperial Russian Musketeers rgt. LG Povalo-Shveikovsky or Smolensky (Smolensk) – 2 Btns	1510
cmd: Colonel Grigoriy Dimitrjevich Kazakhovsky	
Imperial Russian Grenadier Btn (GB) Sanajev	608
2nd Don Cossacks Rgt. Sujchev	498
Don Cossacks Rgt. Semernikov (Semjornikov)	484

Cavalry Detached from the Austrian Italienisches Armée See also Hohenzollern Brigade

K.k. 1st Light Dragoons Rgt. Kaiser Franz II (6 Sqns)	1000
K.k. 4th Light Dragoons Rgt Karacsay (6 Sqns)	1085
K.k. 2nd Hussars Rgt. Erzherzog Josef Anton (4 Sqns)	650

The French retreat

On April 9, in the evening, Schérer realized that the whole line of the republican outposts between Bormio until lakes Idro and Garda had been attacked by the Austrians and that the French forces withdrew in disorder towards Brescia. This unforeseen news and without no exact knowledge of what was the entity of the enemy force that was trying to encircle his left flank, he immediately ordered to retreat the Army of Italy behind the river Oglio to allow to his troops to reach the bridges on the Adda, with forced marches, in good order and safety. He strengthened moreover the garrison of Mantua leaving there others 6600 men and reorganized the army, disbanding two of the six divisions, raising three new divisions on ten infantry battalions and three cavalry regiments, with an additional avant-guard division on five battalions and two cavalry regiments. The army withdrawn behind the Oglio counted around 28000 men and 60 guns; while performing this reorganization arrived to army HQ, on April 10, the news that also Dessolle had been repulsed from Glurns and that he was marching back to Bormio in Valtelline.

The Austrian outflanking manoeuvre

On April 11, Austrian brigade Vukassovich took the Rocca d'Anfo fortress, the eye over the Idro lake (Brescia), then advanced to Fusine and Lavignano near Brescia. His Avant-Garde, led by colonel Prodanovich, occupied Goito, Roverbella and Marmirolo. On April 12 Vukassovich took Castel Belforte, Bigarella and the right bank of the Molinella channel. General Elsnitz cautiously advanced to the Mantua's plains with 11 btns. and 8 sqns. General Sommariva was ordered to besiege Peschiera and put 3 btns. at Monzambano, with outposts on Garda lake until Goito, deploying 1 btn. and 2 sqns. as garrison in Castelnuovo and Cavalcaselle ... Colonel Schröckinger was sent from Mozambano to Ponti to block Peschiera Fortress on the Mincio's right bank. In the meantime, the Austrians hap pulled forward their vanguards to attack the French Lines of Communications. Before the cities of Brescia and Bergamo there were two vital military structures which had the task to ensure supplies to the Mincio line: fortress Orzinuovi (see also the Sieges part) and the large Monte Chiaro Depot camp (today Montichiari near Brescia). Orzinuovi resisted until April 30, when it was occupied by general Alcaini detachment, Monte Chiaro, instead, was cleared by Vukassovich troops. These events forced the French to forget the hypothetical river Oglio line and to reach, in hurry, the more defensible Adda line; this, however, had a major problem: it was too long for only 30.000 demoralized French.

If the river Po was the principal line of defence southwards, the only way to protect the capital city of Milano (Milan) was a deployment along the Adda river, coming north direclty from the Como lake at Lecco, and ending into the Po. The French could have had for their projects the Po line or the so-called Pizzighettone-Cremona-Piacenza triangle, with Alessandria to the left and Mantua to the right. This would had provided effective defence and would had enabled the army either to wait in safety for the arrival of distant allies or, eventually, to advance offensively in the plains between the Sesia and the Adige rivers. However, in this case, Milano had to be lost. The Cordon defensive system was too vulnerable, because it allowed a wide advancing initiative with the possibility to concentrate the forces where wanted.

While concentrating troops near the bridges seemed an adequate tactic for that times (streams were very dif-

The French had constituted fortified bridgeheads dividing the Army in a defensive Cordon that lead from Lecco, where was Sérurier till Pizzighettone fortress, held by Laboissiére Rearguard, a line of about 90 km as the crow flies from North until river Po

ficult to ford through), this deployment left too many gaps to be considered safe. Moreover the defender had to foresee, in due course, where the enemy main endeavour would have applied, succeeding to detect the several gambits that this situation could had put in action. Consider als that this strategic defensive disposition had payed Austrians with many defeats in the Bonaparte previous italian epoch (and others will cost they in future), definitevely a signal not learned by Schérer from the historical experience.

So what could had be done by an other Chief, like Bonaparte? History does not teach us. The situation was bad in numbers and worse in moral, by the French. It is allowed to think that, with Napoleon, the events would had followed an other development. Probably we could not had assisted to Magnano battle and, so, neither to the Cassano. Taking a defensive behaviour while waiting for the armée de Naples and outflanking Verona from the South (Ferrara) had to be a better way to get out from that problem.

The Coalition Advance

On April 19, the army advanced to the Chiese river and on 20 (Ferrara, Peschiera and Mantua being blockaded) broke up from that river; the right under Kray advancing on Brescia, the left under Melas, on Chiari, while the Vukassovich detached Corps, towards the mountains and Hohenzollern on the lower Oglio threatened the flank of Scherer's army. Suvarov studied the situation: *"the French are behind the Oglio, either scattered along his course, or massed at the most advantageos point. Well! What matter? Let us make our main effort on a point conforming to strategic rule, and be satisfied with a strong demonstration on the rest of the line. If we find the enemy scattered, the demonstration will keep him so, and the mass will crush him. If, on the contrary, we find him massed in face of our main attack, the demonstration will act on its side, and become a column of manoeuvre to take the enemy in flank."*

The field marshal analysis pointed on Soncino town, from where it will be very easy to drive the beaten enemy towards the Po. Kray, left Elsnitz at Mantua, prepared to escalade Brescia citadel. The surrounded city surrendered on April 21 with its garrison of 1200 men. Melas, delayed by bad roads and swollen streams, halted on the Mella creek. Suvorov wrote to him:

"I hear people complain that the infantry have their feet wet. It was the fault of the weather. The march was ordered for the service of the Emperor. Women, coxcombs and idlers alone require fine weather. Your chatterers, who grumble at their sovereign's service, must be treated henceforth as egotist, and put out of command..."

The weather had been severe, and on April 24, the Coalition's army crossed the Oglio without finding any French; their right moving on Bergamo, their left on Trivulgio (or Treviglio). Hohenzollern Gruppe entered Cremona on the following day, after poor resistance. Almost simultaneously Bergamo opened its gates, after a sharp engagement [2]. The Allies approached the Adda river in three columns towards Lecco, Vaprio and Cassano. On April 25 the headquarters were put at Treviglio while Kray was recalled back to direct the sieges of the French fortresses.

Coalition's Army Advance Table	Date	Corps	Position
APRIL	19	Main Army	River Chiese
	19	Ott and Bagration Vanguards	Castenedolo
	20	Main Army	Camps by river Chiese
	20	1st Division Zopf	Ponte San Marco Camp
	20	2nd Division Fröhlich (under Lusignan)	Calcinato
	20	Right Wing – Div. Kaim and Shvejkowsky	Monte Chiaro
	20	Vanguards	Castenedolo
	21	Ott and Bagration Vanguards	Attack Vs Brescia Citadel
	21	Main division	Roncadelle e Fornace on river Mella
	22	Army gathering and fording	Through river Mella
	23	Main division	By river Oglio
	23	Vanguards	Clash at Palazzolo
	24	Main division fording	Through Oglio river
	24	Cossacks Vanguard	Deployed at Bergamo
	25	Main Army	Approaching the Adda
	25	Right Wing	Through Caprino
	25	Center	To San Gervasio and Treviglio
	25	Left Wing	To Crema and Pizzighettone

The Coalition's Rearguard
Austrian Reserves and garrisons

Brescia and Bergamo citadels

III Btn. K.k. IR 40 hungarian Rifle Line Inf. Rgt. FZM Graf Joseph Mittrowsky	723

Verona citadel

K.k. IR 26 Rifle Line Inf. Rgt. Freiherr Wilhelm Schröder von Lilienhoff	1162
Cdr.: Oberst Rudolph Avemann - (had three battalions I, II and III)	

Legnago citadel

III Btn. K.k. IR 45 Rifle Line Inf. Rgt. Freiherr Franz von Lattermann	517

Venice

IV Btn K.k. IR 18 Rifle Line Inf. Rgt. Graf Patrick Stuart	928
K.k. IR 10 Rifle Line Inf. Rgt. (former IR Rgt Kheul)	2514
(Three battalion in Venice. They will be sent later to Mantua) Cdr.: Oberst Freiherr Ferdinand Beulwitz	

Friuli, Trieste and Istria

K.k. IR 44 Rifle Line Inf. Rgt.(no Inhaber) The former italian regiment Belgiojoso. Cdr.: Freiherr Philipp von Brentano-Cimaroli. I and II Btns. reorganizing.	822
I Btn 1st Grenzregiment Carlstädt-Liccaner (Lika)	1011
I Btn 2nd Grenzregiment Carlstädt-Otoschatz (Otočac) former 2nd Carlstadt Btn.	1151
II Btn 2nd Grenzregiment Carlstädt-Otoschatz (Otočac) former 3rd Carlstadt Btn.	1151
III Btn 3rd Grenzregiment Carlstädt-Oguliner (Ogulin) former 7th Carlstadt Btn.	961
IV Btn Banal Grenzregiment or II Btn 10th Grenzrgt. of Glina	765
K.k. Grenadier battalion Freiherr Franz von Neny	265

Clearing Lombardy fortresses and Sieges

MANTUA

As a fortress Mantua was long one of the most formidable in Europe, a force of thirty to forty thousand men finding accommodation within its walls; but it had two serious defects: the marshy climate told heavily on the health of the garrison, and effective sorties were almost impossible. A detailed account about the long Mantua siege will be planned within a separate dedicated file. After Magnano general Kray was charged of the besieging operations. Initially he detached, with a small force, general Elsnitz in order to organize the necessary siege camp around the city, later, and before the beginning of the Adda's combats, he reached that camp leading the siege until its end, in Summer 1799. From that moment, the Austrian Mantua's siege army became the real Rearguard of the Italienische Armée, a kind of very large reserve unit for the campaign.

From a strategical point of view, we can say that Mantua, in 1799, had not the same essential impact of 1796 campaign regarding the evolution of the military operations. In the Suvorov's campaign the Coalition armies had always a numerical supremacy over the French, like happened to Austria during the last 1796 months. However Mantua blockade was not so crucial in 1799 as it

▲ Mantova fortress

had been three years before (when the blockades of the two fortress of Mantua and Kehl, in Germany, decided all the operations development). Probably the French had had, then, more motivated soldiers, almost certainly they did not fight, in 1796, also against the Italian people resentment, but, above all, they actually did not have either Bonaparte as commander, either Massena and Augereau as "executives".

PESCHIERA

With the Medieval Lord Mastino della Scala it beginned the town fortification works: the castle (Rocca) was constructed over a Roman building and, in XV century, the Fortress was finally composed by a group of civil houses,

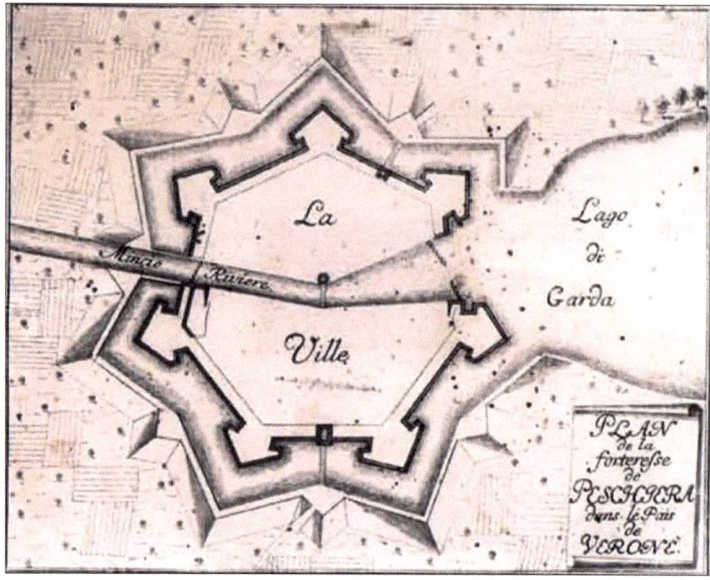

▲ Peschiera fortress

surrounded by walls with towers disposed on five sides. and, in the southern corner, the Rocchetta, the witness of the position of the ancient Rocca. In 1439 Peschiera was part of the Serenissima Republic of Venice. With its participation, the town in 1549 had a new fortress which assumed a pentagonal shape. The town-walls were substituted with bastions, made with stones and earth, placed on the pentagonal basement. That system of town-walls fortification knitted the two ancient islands with singular and powerful fortified bridges, connecting together the two Fortress inner fields, crossed by the main branch of the Mincio river. This fortress configuration remained unchanged until the French arrival in 1796, after the fall of the Venice Republic. Initially the fortress was kept as originally, a border watch building. From 1800 and during the French domination (1801-1814) it was partially dismantled in order to realize a new defensive fortified Camp, as the main place of a system of separate forts, which surrounded the town, on dominant positions, within the countryside. That plan put into effect only partially, like the only two napoleonic forts witness: Forte Salvi vecchio against Brescia, Forte Mandella vecchio against Verona. Peschiera surrendered on May 7, 1799.

CISALPINE GARRISON

Peschiera Fortress: Adjudant général Couthieux (French)

Infantry	1000
Guns	75
Gunboats	19

Chief-of-Engineers Staff (Army of Italy)
Marquis François de Chasseloup-Laubat [3]
Organized Peschiera fortifications.

II Btn. 21st Line Demi Brigade	600

On May 6, 1799, Peschiera surrendered and Austrian captured a flag of the 21e demi-brigade, which was there with one battalion

Coalition Siege Group

First deployment
Kolonne Marquis Hannibal Sommariva

K.k. IR 34 Rifle Rgt.	1528
(the former Esterházy regiment) I and II Btns Cmdr.: Oberst Johann Hillinger	
K.k. IR 19 Rifle Rgt. Freiherr Jozsef Alvinczy de Berberek	1476

▲ French chasseur 5th regiment

I and II Btns. – Cmdr. Barone Lelio Spannocchi	
K.k. 10th Dragoons Rgt. GdC Joseph Fürst Lobkowitz	368
(2 Sqn) – Cdr. Marquis Hannibal Sommariva	

Second deployment

Siege Group Obst Johann Schröckinger von Neudenberg 4	
K.k. IR 8 Rifle Rgt. (former Huff Rgt)	1805
Cmdr. Obst Johann Schröckinger von Neudenberg (I-II Btns) – III Btn coming later at Mantua siege.	

Brigade Generalmajor Graf Johann Franz de Saint Julien	3176
l Jäger-Kompanie d'Aspre	130
K.k. IR 48 Rifle Rgt. (no Inhaber)	1402
It will became the Rgt. Freiherr Philipp von Vukassovic . Cdr.: Oblt Franz De Baut I – II – III btns.	
K.k. IR 14 Rifle Rgt. Freiherr Wilhelm von Klebek	1644
I – II – III btns. Cdr.: Oberst Freiherr Franz Kottulinsky	

FLANKING UNITS FROM TYROLER ARMÉE
Rocca d'Anfo

Cisalpine Infantry	300
Guns	??

The Anfo fortress, a military structure re-built by Napoleon on a precedent structure, is a reminder of ancient times. It is a unique example of its kind in Europe, with its eight camouflaged and interconnected forts dug out in the mountain at various heights dominating the road between Trento and Brescia over the Lake Idro (Brescia province). On April 11, Vukassovich took the Rocca d'Anfo on Idro lake, then advanced to Fusine and Lavignano near Brescia. His Avant-Garde led by colonel Prodanovich occupied Goito, Roverbella and Marmirolo. On April 12, Vukassovich took Castel Belforte, Bigarella and the right bank of the Molinella. General Elsnitz cautiously advanced in the Mantua's plains with 11 btns. And 8 sqns. General Sommariva was ordered to siege Peschiera and put 3 btns. at Monzambano, with outposts on Garda lake until Goito, deploying 1 btn. And 2 sqns. as garrison in Castelnuovo and Cavalcaselle …. Colonel Schröckinger was sent from Mozambano to Ponti to block Peschiera on the Mincio's right bank.

Brigade Generalmajor Freiherr Josef Philipp von Vukassovich	6938
The Verona OoB's numbers were the Clausewitz hypothetical datas. These are Miljutin's datas.	
Right Kolonne Avant Garde (Oberst) Generalmajor Sebastian Prodanovich	
Jäger Freikorps Mjr Johann Le Loup (dutch Btn. -3 coys)	394
K.k. Light Btn. N. 14 Oberst Prince Ludwig (Louis) Rohan (italian Btn.)	649
K.k. Light Btn. N. 15 Oberst Bonaventura Mihanovic (croat-slavonian)	800
K.k. Light Btn. N. 2 Oberst Carl Prince of Rohan (Italian Btn)	580
II Btn Grenzregiment of Banat (or I btn. 13th GrenzRgt)	1005
On April 8, 1799 Oberst Carl Rohan personally led the attack against the French outpost of San Antonio (lake Idro) supporting the successive attack up to the steep rocky climb of Rocca d'Anfo. Carl Rohan, then, was charged to secure the right flank of the Vukassovich main column which was marching towards Brescia.	
Left (Haupt)Kolonne von Vukassovich	
V Btn Grenzregiment of Banat	600
KK IR 52 Rifle Rgt. Erzherzog Palatin Anton Viktor	2700
I – II –III btns. cdr.: Graf Johann Nepomuk Khuen de Belasi	
K.k. 9th Hussar Rgt. FML Johann Nepomuk Graf Erdödy de Monyorókerek (Erdödy Husaren)	210

Fortress Orzinuovi or San Giorgio   Cisalpine garrison

Infantry	517
Guns	40

Orzinuovi has a date of birth: in 1193 Brescia's people decided to erect a fortress in this strategic location near the Oglio River. In 1520, Venice entrusted the architect Sammicheli with the task of making the citadel invulnerable; it took the form of a five-pointed star with seven ramparts. Of that powerful complex, today there remains only the Rocca (1477), a work of the military architect Giovanni Borella; now in restoration.
It was attacked by count Alcaini Gruppe on May 1, 1799. During the same day the Garrison (Cisalpines and some French) surrendered (500 men + 100 wounded, recovered in hospital). Graf Alcaini took the 40 guns of the fortress. Alcaini had 7 btns. And 2 Sqns. He spent the rest of the campaign with troops of Vukassovich, Strauch and Rohan. Another commander from Tirol's Army: Generalmajor Johann (Giovanni) Graf Alcaini 5

Pizzighettone

Pizzighettone Fortress Cdr. Capt. Jacquet	
Infantry	630
Guns	96

If the river Po was the principal line of defence, the Pizzighettone-Cremona-Piacenza triangle, with Alessandria to the left and Mantua to the right, would provide effective defence of this line and enable the army either to wait in security for the arrival of distant allies or if need be to advance offensively in the decisive plain between the Sesia and the Adige. The base of the "Gera public square" was constituted in the period of half XVII century, in 1654, during the 30 Years War, when Lombardy was an Habsburg of Spain dominion. Planned by the

▲ French drum major and musicians of light infantry

mathematician Alexander Champion, at the service of the Governor Luis de Benavidez Marquis of Caracena, the fortress of Gera had to serve like complement of the fortress Pizzighettone, a bridgehead erected in order to control the passage on river Adda and the ways of communication that joined Cremona with the rest of the "Milanesado". The fort was rebuilt many times in the 1600s years and the 1700s: in particular, during the Austrian dominion, between 1720 and 1725, under Emperor Carl of Habsburg, when it obtained the current conformation. On May 11, 1799, the fortress was bombarded by Austrian artillery during a full day (daylight) and surrendered in the early evening.

Pizzighettone Siege Corps – May 1, 1799	
Brigade Gen.Major Friedrich Xavier Fürst Hohenzollern-Hechingen	
K.k. IR 36 Rifle Rgt. Fürst Carl Fürstenberg I – II -III btns	2576
K.k. IR 32 Rifle Rgt. Graf Samuel Gyulai I - II Btns.	1482
Brigade Generalmajor Friedrich Freiherr von Seckendorf 6	
K.k. 5th Hussar Regiment 6 Sqn. Cdr. Freiherr Andreas Szörenyi	826
Pizzighettone Siege Corps – May 6-7, 1799	
Division Generalmajor Konrad Valentin Kaim	
K.k. hungarian Grenadier Btn Oberleutnant Ferdinand Pers garrison at Lodi and Pizzighettone	199
K.k. IR 24 Rifle Rgt (former Preiss)	1424
(btns I – II – III) - Cmdr Oberst Carl Philipp von Weidenfeld	
K.k. IR 32 Rifle Rgt. Graf Samuel Gyulai	1482
Cmdr. Oberst Franz Posztrehowsky von Millenburg - (I-II-Btns) III btn to Mantua	
K.k. IR 36 Rifle Rgt. Fürst Carl Fürstenberg	2576
(I-II-III Btn) Cmdr. Oberst Conrad von Thelen	
VII Combined Btn Grenzregiment Warasdiner of Varazdin	627
K.k. 5th Hussar Regiment 6 Sqn. Cdr. ObstLt. Freiherr Andreas Szörenyi	826
Pizzighettone garrison after the conquer– May 20, 1799	
K.k. hungarian Grenadier Btn Oberleutnant Ferdinand Pers garrison in Lodi and in Pizzighettone	199

NOTES

1 **Aleksandr Vassiljevic Suvorov Graf Rimniksky**, Prince Italysky (1729-1800), was born at Moscow on November 24, 1729, descending of a Swede named Suvor who emigrated to Russia in 1622. He entered the army as a boy, served against the Swedes in Finland and against the Prussians during the Seven Years' War. After repeatedly distinguishing, himself in battle he was made colonel in 1762. He next served in Poland, dispersed the Polish forces under Pulawski, stormed Cracow (1768) and was made generalmajor. In his first campaigns against the Turks in 1773-74, and particularly in the battle of Kosludski in the latter year, he laid the basics of his reputation. In 1775 he suppressed the rebellion of Pugachov. From 1777 to 1783 he served in Crimea and Caucasus, becoming lieutenant-general in 1780, and general of infantry in 1783. From 1787 to 1791 he was again fighting the Turks and won many combats; he was wounded at Kinburn (1787), took part in the siege of Ochakov, and in 1788 won two great clashes around Focsani and on the Rimnik river. For the latter victory, in which he was flanked by an Austrian corps under Prince Josias of Saxe-Coburg, Empress Catherine II made him a count with the name Rimniksky in addition to his own name, and the austrian emperor Joseph II created him count of the Holy Roman Empire. On December 22, 1790, Suvarov stormed Ismail in Bessarabia. He was next placed at the head of the army which subdued the Poles, repeating the former triumph. He was now made field marshal, and was in Poland until 1795, when he returned to St.Petersburg. But his sovereign and friend Catherine died in 1796, and her successor Paul dismissed the veteran in disgrace. Suvarov then lived for some years in retirement on his estate of Konchauskoy, near Moscow. He criticized the new military tactics and dress introduced by the emperor, and some of his acid words reached the ears of the Emperor. His conduct was therefore more cautious and his correspondence with his wife, who had remained at Moscow - for his marriage relations had not been happy - was censored. On Sundays he tolled the bell for church and sang among the rustics in the village choir. On week days he worked among them in a smock frock. But in February 1799 he was summoned by the tsar to take the field again, this time against the French Revolutionary armies in Italy.

The campaign opened with a series of victories (Cassano, Trebbia, Novi) which reduced the French government to dire straits and drove every French soldier from Italy, save for the few under Moreau, which maintained a base in the Maritime Alps and around Genoa. Suvarov himself was made prince of Italy (kniaz Italijnski). But the later events of the busy year went consistently against the Coalition. Suvarov's lieutenant Korsakov was defeated by Massena at Zurich, and the old field marshal, seeking to make his way over the Swiss passes to the Upper Rhine, had to retreat to the Vorarlberg, where the army, much shattered and almost destitute of horses and artillery, went into winter quarters. Early in 1800 Suvarov returned to St Petersburg again in discredit. Paul refused to give him an audience, and, worn out and ill, he died a few days afterwards on the 18th of May 1800 at St Petersburg. Lord Whitworth, the English ambassador, was the only person of distinction present at the funeral. Suvarov lies buried in the church of the Annunciation in the Aleksandr-Nevskii monastery, the simple inscrip-

▲ Aleksandr Vassiljevic Suvorov Graf Rimniksky, Prince Italysky (1729-1800)

tion on his grave being, according to his own direction, "Here lies Suvarov." But within a year of his death the tsar Alexander I. erected a statue to his memory in the Field of Mars, St Petersburg.

His son Arkadi (1783-1811) was a general officer in the Russian army during the Napoleonic and Turkish wars of the early 19th century, and was drowned in the river Rimnik. His grandson Aleksandr Arkadievich (1804-1882) was also a Russian general. He was a great captain, viewed from the standpoint of any age of military history, specially the great commander of the Russian nation, for his leadership character responded to the character of the Russian soldier. In an age when war had become an act of diplomacy he restored its true significance as an act of force. He was reckless of human life, bent only on the achievement of the object in hand, and he spared his own soldiers as little as he showed mercy to the population of a fallen city. He was a man of great simplicity of manners, and while on a campaign lived as a private soldier, sleeping on straw and contenting himself with the humblest fare. But he had himself passed through all the gradations of military service; moreover, his education had been of the rudest kind. His acid tongue procured him many enemies. He had all the contempt of a man of ability and action for ignorant favourites Officers and politicians. In Italy seemed to be moved by a deep religious impulse; however his frequent announcements, claiming God and the Catholic religion at his side, seemed more smart tricks of a fervid political mind. But his passion served, sometimes to hide, more often to express, a military genius, the effect of which the Russian army has not outgrown. Some of the maxims of Suvarov's Turkish wars were universally followed: the spirit of self-sacrifice, resolution and indifference to losses.

2 Marching from Palazzolo to Bergamo, Sérurier had to invert his march to engage the Russian avantgarde. In the attack Prince Bagration lost 500 men. It was the first official time in which French infantry fought against the Cossacks. The Sérurier "grognards" deployed in a large square, repulsed the Cossacks charge of Grekov riders, who were countercharged on the flanks by the French (and Piedmontese) light cavalry. After the combat the French 1st division du Tyrol continued its march and the city of Bergamo surrendered.

3 **Marquis François de Chasseloup-Laubat** (August 18, 1754 - October 3, 1833), , was born at St Semi. (Lower Charente), of a noble family, and entered the French engineers in 1774. He was still a subaltern at the outbreak of the Revolution, becoming captain in 1791. His ability as a military engineer was recognized in the campaigns of 1792 and 1793. In the following year he won distinction in various actions and was promoted successively chef-de-bataillon and colonel. He was Engineers chief at the Mainz siege in 1796, after which he was sent to Italy. There he commanded and organized the lines' positions of Bonaparte. He was promoted general-de-brigade before the end of the campaign, and was subsequently employed in fortifying the new French Rhine border. His work as Engineers' Chief in the army of Italy (1799) had good results, and he was made general-de-division after the Novi battle. When Napoleon began his new campaign (1800) to retrieve 1799 disasters, Chasseloup was again chosen as Engineer Chief. During the peace period (1801-1805) he was mainly ordered to reorganize the northern Italy, and, in particular, the Mantua's area. His masterpiece was the large Alessandria fortress by the Tanaro river.

In 1805 he remained in Italy with André Masséna, but at the end of 1806, Napoleon, leading the Polish campaign, called him to his Grande Armée, with which he served during the campaign of 1806-07, directing sieges at Colberg, Danzig and Stralsund. During the Napoleonic domination in Germany, Chasseloup reconstructed many fortresses, in particular Magdeburg. In the 1809 campaign he was again in Italy. In 1810 Napoleon made him a State Advisor. His last active campaign was the Russian of 1812.

Retired from active service, in 1814 he was occasionally engaged for inspections and construction of fortifications. Louis XVIII made him a peer of France and a knight of St Louis. He refused to join Napoleon during the Hundred Days, but after the second Restoration he voted in the chamber of peers against the condemnation of Marshal Ney. As an Engineer, Chasseloup was a supporter of the old bastioned system, though with some modern views,. He followed in many respects the works of the Engineer Bousmard, published in 1797 and who fell, as a Prussian officer, during the Danzig defence of 1807 against Chasseloup's own attack. His ideas were applied at Alessandria, which had many upgrades of the bastion outline, with, in particular, the masked tenaille flanks, which served as extra flanks of the bastions. The bastions themselves were carefully entrenched. The usual "Rivellino" (ravelin) was replaced with an heavy casemated caponier (à la Montalembert), and, like Bousmard's, the true ravelin became a large and powerful fort built outer, beyond the glacis.

4 **Oberst Johann Schröckinger von Neudenberg**, (dead 26.7.1808), provisional Generamajor on March 6 (26?)1800, confirmed on 22.4.1800, retired in 1805.

5 A brigade from Tyroler armée attached as Armée Reserve. **(Johann Baptist) Giovanni Battista Reichsgraf von Alcaini** was born in Venice on August 18, 1748. On January 24, 1794 he was named provisional Generalmajor and confirmed in that rank on February 12, 1794. In 1799 he was 55 years old; from September, 1, had the provisional rank of Field Marshal Lieutenant and was confirmed on October 2, 1799. He died on October 8, 1800, for the severe wounds suffered during Tortona siege.

6 **Generalmajor Friedrich Alexander Wilhelm Freiherr von Seckendorf-Aberdar**, (2.8.1743 -11.6.1814). Had the provisional nomination to Generalmajor from May 1, 1794 but on May 30 his promotion was official. He followed FML Wurmser in Italy often employed as Staff organizer, cavalry reserve commander and adjudant. He did not stay in Mantua, but remained in Tirol where he participated to the deployment of the right wing at Rivoli, January 14, 1797, in the place of FML Davidovich. He was with Mélas during the 1799 campaign often performing rearguard or siege tasks. On September 12, 1799 he was provisionally named Feldmarschalleutnant, rank confirmed a month later, October 2, 1799.

BATTLES AT LECCO, BRIVIO, TREZZO, VAPRIO AND CASSANO APRIL 25 TO 27, 1799
THE ADDA BATTLE(S) ALSO KNOWN AS THE BATTLE OF CASSANO

Coalition's Army positions before the battles

Unit	Location	Infantry	Cavalry	total
Avantgarde Prince Bagration	at Lecco	3 btns	3 Cossacks Rgts.	3000
Rozemberg Corps	Road from Caprino to Lecco	9 btns	1 Coss.Rgt. - 9 sqns	9000
Vukassovich Av.Guard Corps	at Brivio	8 btns + 2 coys	2 squadrons	7000
Avantgarde Division Ott	at San Gervasio	6 btns	8 squadrons	5000
1st Division Zopf	at Canonica	6 btns	8 squadrons	5000
2nd Division Fröhlich (under Lusignan)	at Treviglio	16 btns	16 squadrons	13000
Left wing Division Kaim	"	together	together	together
Feldbrigade Seckendorff	at Lodi	2 btns	2 sqns	1500
Gruppe Hohenzollern	at Pizzighettone	5 btns	6 sqns	5000
TOTALS		55 btns +2 coys	50 sqns +4 Coss.Rgts	48500

French Army positions before the battles

Unit	Location	Infantry	Cavalry	total
Left Division Sèrurier	from Lecco until Trezzo	10 btns	10 squadrons	8000
1st Center Division Grenier	from Vaprio until Villa Pompeiana	10 btns	10 squadrons	8000
2nd Center Division Victor	from Villa Pompeiana until Robecco	10 btns	10 squadrons	8000
Avantgarde Division Laboissiére	from Robecco until river Po	5 btns	7 squadrons	4000
TOTALS		35 btns	37 sqns	28000

ARMÉE D'ITALIE HQ AT INZAGO
Comm. In Chief: General de Division Jean Victor Marie Moreau
Adjudant : General Jacques Maurice Hatry

On April 25, 1799 all the French army was behind the Adda. General Jean Marie Moreau had the task to defend Lodi while the other divisions took positions along the right bank of the river. The headquarters, initially placed at Lodi, were transferred to Inzago, in more central position. Having received the new the Cisalpine Directory had abandoned Milano, General Barthélémy Louis Joseph Schérer decided to reach the city. Moreau was sent to Inzago to take the provisional command of army HQs. Escorted by 20 guides Schérer reached the Lombardy capital city. There he did not found the authorities he hoped to see, but he met Rivaud who gave him the French Directory's letter of his dischargement. Schérer immediately resigned, he did not made the inverse voyage to Inzago where Moreau agreed to substitute him. [1]

Bagration, repulsed on 25 near Bergamo, rallied his troops. Suvorov and Rozenberg organized a three columns formation near Ponte San Pietro: the first was a Rozenberg regiment battalion, the second the Dendrjugyn Grenadiers, the third was the Miloradovich brigade deployed as a second line. Between the infantry were Cossacks echelons. The remaining Rozenberg's troops followed as a reserve.

April 26, afternoon. At 2.00 PM hours, the Moskovite vanguard contacted the Soyez demi-brigade, just replenished with fresh recruits which had the Sérurier rearguard task. Soyez's Chasseurs fought and disengaged but, at 4.00 PM a French guard of about 150 chasseurs was ovverrun by Cossacks, who ran against a small redoubt in front of Lecco. They were met with a Salvo of 25 cannister shots which made thinner the riders' rows and caused great disorder. Too late to engage the infantry, the night incoming, Bagration resolved to wait for the next day.

THE LECCO BATTLE
LECCO. The alternative, and more difficult, way to reach Milano from Bergamo passed through Lecco, on the lower right branch of the lake of Como. In the IV Century an important military way crossed Lecco; coming from Aquileia in Friuli, it continued through Bergamo, directed to the Alps passes after Como. There was an an-

cient bridge near Olginate (some ruins of semi submerged columns are currently visible) which allowed to cross the Adda. Nearby two roads surely existed: one to Milan and one to Como. In 1784 Joseph II of Austria visite the town and decided the definitive demolition of the town walls. With the arrival of Bonaparte and the birth of the Cisalpine republic, in 1797, the Lecco land was enclosed in the Mountain Lombardy Department (Lecco became the chief town). In 1799 the bridge over the Adda, south of Caldone stream, was near the village of Pescarenico, where the battle enraged.

Division de gauche - General Jean-Mathieu-Philibert Sérurier	7636
* Numbers and dislocations are estimated.	

Detachment Louis-Stanislas-Xavier Soyez at Lecco
Staff: Aides Bernard, Delort and Willot

Artillery Mount Barro Heavy Bty	6 heavy (4 guns – 2 How.	60
Lecco position artillery	12 guns (4 on bastions)	8 redoubt
Lake gunboats		2
2 Grenadiers Coys – Line Infantry		150
18th Light Demi-Brigade Carabiniers Btn		430
30th Light infantry Demi-Brigade I Btn.		650
1st Piedmontese Light Demi-Brigade Guards Btn. (retreating, merged with Fresia Brigade)		470
9e Régiment Dragons 1 sqn.		100

At BRIVIO. It is a village built on the Adda river where the hills leave the land to the plains, dominated by an old square medieval castle and situated 15 km far from (south of) Lecco.

Brigade Adj-Gen Pierre-Joseph Guillet (Guillot ?) from Lecco until the Brivio passage

29th Light infantry Demi-Brigade III btn Pierre-François Mont-Serraz	670
18th Light Demi-Brigade I – II and III Btn	1170
9e Régiment Dragons 1 sqn.	100

At Verderio. The name of the village derived from the Latin word 'viridarium' that it means 'garden'. It was a remarkable town between the XII and XIV centuries because of the presence of Temple's Knights (Templars), who had one district in that territory (Commenda, Castel Negrino, Brugarola). This substantially agricultural country location had two hamlets, Inferior and Superior Verderio, of which one can find trace from documents dated 1412. On April 1799, the French division Sérurier entrenched into the Villa Confalonieri (today Villa Gnecchi-Ruscone), into the Castle and the cemetery. Therefore surrounded by the Austrians it was defeated and cancelled from the rosters.

General de Division Jean-Mathieu-Philibert Sérurier
Adj-Gen Louis Garreau

30th Light infantry Demi-Brigade II – III Btns.	1300
21st Line Demi-Brigade Chef de Brigade Robert I Btn.	670
The I Btn. Lost its flag after the Vaprio battle. On May 6, 1799, Peschiera surrendered and Austrian captured a flag of the 21e demi-brigade, which was there with another battalion	
1 Foot artillery battery (7th regiment)	3 guns
9e Régiment Dragons Chef-de-Brigade Prov. Sebastiani 2 sqns.	376
Brigade Général Maurizio Ignazio Frésia baron of Oglianico	1850 [2]
1st Piedmontese Light Demi-Brigade the Light Btn.	560
2nd Piedmontese Dragoons Regiment	480
4th Piedmontese Dragoons Regiment	510

Coalition's Army
Commander in chief: Field Marshal Aleksandr Vassiljevic Suvorov Graf Rimniksky

Russian Avantgarde Brigade General Prince Petr Ivanovich Bagration [3]	2822

Prince Bagration took part in many campaigns, wars and battles. In the campaign of 1794 year Bargation showed himself as a brave cavalry commander. Suvorov thought highly of his skills, bravery, enterprise and accuracy of his command, he noted at once his the military talent of the young officer. The military service under the command of Suvorov had big influence on forming of military skills of Bagration. In the rank of General-Major Bagration took part in the Italian campaign of Suvorov in 1799. He commanded the vanguard of the Russian troops. He stormed and seized towns of Brescia and Lecco and executed the most important missions in the battles at Trebbia and Novi. In the well-known Swiss campaign of Suvorov in 1799 Bagration commanded the Russian vanguard, he was the first who accepted the enemy blows when the Russian troops crossed St. Gotthard, the Devil Bridge and others. Then during the retreat of the Russian Army he commanded the rear-guard, covered the retreat of the main forces and contained the attacks of the outnumbered enemy forces (the Panix mountain ridge). In the Swiss campaign Bagration was Suvorov's most reliable support. For his courage, bravery and military skills he was rewarded with many Russian and foreign Orders and arms: the gold sword decorated with diamonds with the inscription "For courage".

▲ Pyotr I. Bagration (1765-1812) by George Dawe

5th Don Cossacks Rgt. Denissov	490
Denissov T. Ivanovich (b. 1749) from 1793 to 1797 Lieutenant Colonel, regiment-commander of Ekaterinoslaw Cossacks Btn.	
Don Cossacks Rgt. Molchanov	495
8th Don Cossacks Rgt. Grekov.	494
Imperial Russian Grenadier Btn (GB) Lomonosov	606
Imperial Russian 7th Jäger (Jeghersky) Rgt. GM Bagration – 2 Btns	737
cmdr.: Gen. Petr Ivanovic Bagration	
Main Corps 1st line	
Imperial Russian Grenadier Rgt. GdI Rozenberg or Moskow – I Btn	778
Imperial Russian Grenadier Btn (GB) Dendrjugyn	589
Main Corps 2nd line	
Imperial Russian Musketeers rgt. LG Povalo-Shveikovsky or Smolensky (Smolensk) – I Btn	785
cmd: Colonel Grigoriy Dimitrjevich Kazakhovsky	
K.k. 4th Light Dragoons Rgt Karacsay (2 Sqns)	310
Right Wing Brigade general-major Mihail Andrejevich Miloradovich 1st 4	2462
Main Corps	
Left Brigade Infantry-general Andrej Grigorjevich Rozenberg	3317
Imperial Russian Grenadier Btn (GB) Sanajev	608
Imperial Russian Musketeers rgt. Young-Baden or molodo-Badensky – II Btn	712
Imperial Russian Musketeers rgt. GM Tuyrtov or Tug'lsky (Tula) – I btn	763
Don Cossacks Rgt. Semernikov (Semjornikov)	484
Reserve Brigade general-major Nikolaj Andrejevic Chubarov 5	
Imperial Russian 8th Jäger (Jegherski) Rgt. Major General Chubarov	750
Chief from May 13: GM Ivan Ivanovich Miller	
Imperial Russian Musketeers rgt. GM Baranowsky II - I Btn	804

April 26, Night. The Russian were masters of the left Adda's bank. Sérurier, seeing a threat at the Brivio passage, detached Adjudant général Guillet to cover his northern flank.

April 27, Dawn. Soyez is in Lecco. The walled town of 4000 inhabitants is at a distance of 400 mt from the Adda's stone bridge, a fortified structure long 100 mt. The Russian moved forward at 8.00 AM but their advance was harassed by the Lecco's pieces and definitively halted at 10.00 AM. Bagration decided to wait for the programmed Austrian diversionary attack at Brivio. Soyez sent the two Grenadiers coy south, to cover his right flank in direction of Olginate.

April 27, 2.00 PM. Rozenberg Grenadiers advanced against Lecco but were sent back by the Carabiniers of 18th demi-brigade. The melée assault was very bloody (Rozenberg battalion lost 150 men dead and 360 hevily wounded). The victory is French, however they began very shortened of ammunitions and withdrawn into the town walls. At 9.00 PM in the evening a courier arrived by Soyez bringing a message from Guillet. It was the news of the massive Austrian deployment along the Adda; Guillet said he had to withdraw to Como leaving Soyez free to decide to do whatever he wanted. Sérurier was missing without any reason, after his visit to HQs, on April 26, where he thought to find still Schérer. Soyez realized that his right flank was cut off from the Army center and ordered the retreat, in echelons, in order to save as many troops as possible.

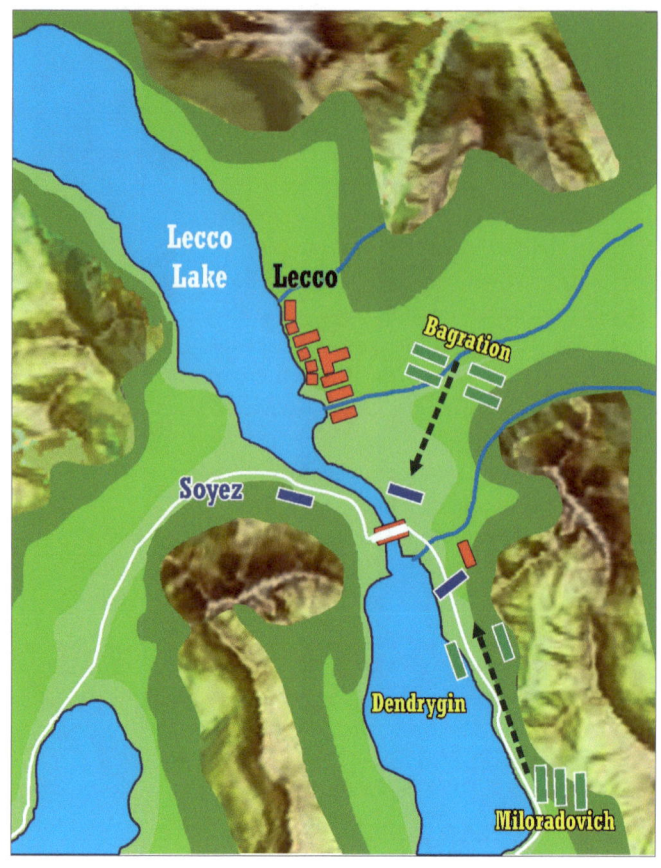

At 11.00 PM during the night only the 18th légère remained to guard the Adda bridge, the others all were already retreating towards Erba and Como. Before dawn the demi-brigade was embarked on 28 boats and bridge was mined and destroyed by Soyez sappers. (The 18th demi-brigade crossed all the Como lake and continued its march towards Lugano in Switzerland without any losses in men, materials and guns). From Lugano, where they blocked a people uprising, the demi-brigade took the way of Lake Maggiore; other boats were requisitioned and the French disembarked at Arona, on April 30. There Soyez had orders to reach Lavino, on the road to Novara and there he got the new, on May 1, of the Moreau defeat at Cassano.

The Suvorov's Plan of April 26

The impatient Field Marshal, on April 26, had planned that, while Bagration had to attack Lecco forcing the Adda passage and sending a strong Avantguard to Como, general Vukassovich would have gathered as many boats he could had found in order to pass the river at Brivio, during the incoming night. Ott and Zoph division, with a 3-days food reserve, had to reach San Gervasio and San Pietro to found a good position to install a pontoon, near Trezzo. The avant-guard had to direct itself north, from Trezzo to Vaprio and to join with Vukassovich. The

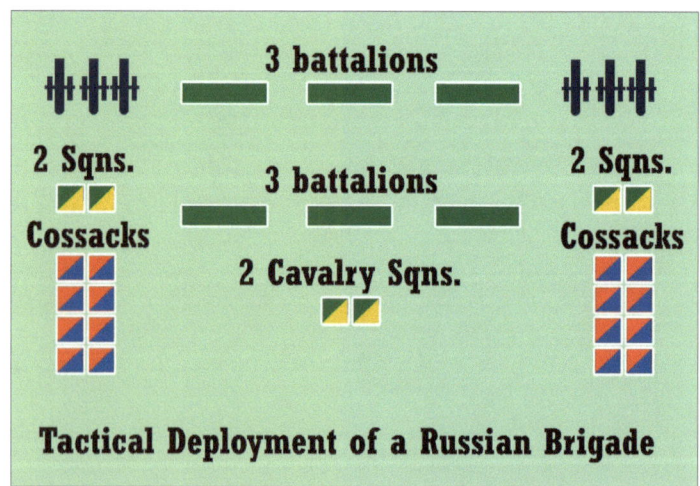

main columns and the rear-guard had to go south towards Cassano. Melas, with the Fröhlich division, had to take contact with the French Cassano bridgehead or Pritorto entrenchments at Cascina Franca and attck them. Count Seckendorff had to move, on 26 evening, towards Lodi attacking that bridge and trying to concentrate the French attention on that city while Prince Hohenzollern, after sunset, had to send patrols under Pizzighettone walls, reaching himself the meeting point of rivers Adda and Po. There he had to send spies with the fake gossip of the Austrian will to conquer Piacenza and, at April 27 dawn, had to bombard the Adda fords and the right Po river bank from Monticelli to San Nazzaro. Suvorov marched with the Austrian II Kolonne (Ott), masked by a very dark night in which the wind hampered to hear noise or the sound of moving troops.

1st Austrian Avant-Guard Corps Generalmajor Freiherr Josef Philipp von Vukassovich		7693
7 btns + 3 coys	2 squadrons;	
After having gathered many river boats, Vukassovich sent his vanguards on the other river side and found the parts of a French pontoon bridge equipment, abandoned by Sérurier. Hastily Austrian Pioneers reconstructed the pontoon definitively opening the way to the right Adda bank. Vukassovich patrols went north towards Como; a detachment led by Major Lettnitz engaged the French rear-guard at Olginate and repulsed it.		

Avant Garde (Oberst) Generalmajor Sebastian Prodanovich

Dutch Light Volunteers - Freikorps Mjr Johann Le Loup (3 coys)	359
K.k. 14th Light Infantry Btn. (Italian) Oberst Prince Ludwig (Louis) Rohan	590
II Btn Banater Grenzregiment (or I btn. 13th GrenzRgt)	1005
V Btn Banater Grenzregiment	596
K.k. 2nd Light Infantry Btn. (Italian) Oberst Carl Prince of Rohan	578
K.k. IR 52 hungarian Rifle Line Inf. Rgt. Erzherzog Palatin Anton Viktor	2702
I – II –III btns. cdr.: Graf Johann Nepomuk Khuen de Belasi	
K.k. 9th Hussar Regiment FML Johann Nepomuk Graf Erdödy de Monyorókerek	210

(Erdödy Hussaren) Cdr. Oberst Franz Freiherr von Stephaics, not with Vukassovic. Had 2 sqns.

THE ADDA BATTLE. COMBATS OF TREZZO AND VAPRIO

The Adda River is only a small mountain creek when it leaves the small lakes of Alpisella, just over Livigno, at 2235 metres above sea level, and pass through Valtelline, from Bormio to Colico. After having crossed Como Lake for 42 kilometres, it takes the form of a large river in Lecco, south of which it forms two small lakes; Garlate and then Olginate. The Adda River slopes steeply among rocks below Brivio. After Paderno the river enters a sort of "canyon" washed between banks of stone and then enters the Lombardy plains.

The Adda River has a gentle bend in Trezzo, an S shaped outline which limits the promontory of the old Visconti castle (at the time fortified by the French). After the town, on the right bank, the river generates the waterway Martesana, an ancient artificial canal which takes the river waters merging them with the internal Milan channels (Navigli). Become the official major left tributary of the river Po in Lombardy, the flow of the Adda River becomes more regular after Cassano, with some irregularities extending in wide areas and, today, in banks of gravel (actually there were large swampy areas) as far as the confluence in the river Po, in Castelnuovo Bocca d'Adda, near Cremona.

Battles for the bridges

The first Adda bridges' battle was fought around the 268 b.C., a clash between the Roman factions of Mark Acilio Aureolo and of Galliano. Close to the bridge that connected Vaprio with Canonica on the other side, met the rebel army and the regular army. Aureolo was then killed in Milan from his own soldiers and buried near that bridge which became the bridge (Pons) of Aureolus, name after evolved in Pontirolo. The "pax romana" was short and the invasions from the north followed. In 1158 Brescia and Bergamo claimed the Emperor's Frederick the Barbarossa help against Milano. The Holy Roman Empire Chief picked the pretest in order to reach Italy in forces. In occasion of this second coming (1158) that the Adda banks were fortified as the natural defensive Milanese, reinforced between Trezzo and Cassano which guaranteed commercial traffics towards Bergamo, Brescia and, therefore, Venice. In correspondence of Cassano, which famous (and alone) bridge was defended by a castle since IX Century, the passage of the river seemed easier. So Barbarossa first captured Cassano, along with his strategy to control all ways that could have guaranteed his return in Germany, and then ruined the castle.

The "Condottiere" Ezzelino III of Romano, who cultivated the dream to constitute a large Lordship over northern Italy, found just on the river an invalicabile stop. After having crossed the Adda on the Canonica bridge, he occupied Vaprio, then heading directly to Milan. At that city he was repulsed and forced to withdraw towards Trezzo which was burned out. The final battle occurred on the bridge of Cassano in order to decide if he had definitivel to withdraw or not.

It was a bloody battle. Ezzelino was wounded and taken prisoner by Milanese.

During the Spanish Succession War there was the first battle of Cassano between Spain and Austria, in 1705. That Italian campaign concluded with the peace of Utrecht which assigned the Milan Duchy to Austria. From then begun a long period of Austrian dominion that lasted until the arrival of Bonaparte in 1796. With the first Advance of Bonaparte in Italy, the French repulsed the Austrians towards Milan and defeated them on the bridge of Lodi. The campaign was very difficult for the natural obstacles of the land. Napoleon himself stated that the Adda was the more defensible river of Italy.

Division General de Division Paul Grenier * (numbers estimated)		8120
ADC- Adjudant-généraux : Adj-Gen Leonard-Nicholas Becker comte de Mons (uncertain his presence)		
Light foot artillery (2 coys)		100
Horse artillery	2 Btys	
Heavy foot artillery	4 Btys.	200
Sappers	1 ½ platoon	180
At Trezzo		
II Btn 33rd Line Demi Brigade		680

Trezzo. The town of Trezzo (on the Adda) is firmly linked with Leonardo da Vinci, who lived in there. The Master designed the projects of the Adda's locks and calculated the flow of the Martesana channel to allow the boats from Lecco to reach Milano. The Visconti's Castle is the symbol of the town, a village of ancient origins (IV-III century a.C.) situated northeast of Milan. It was constructed in 1300, by count Bernabò Visconti, near the mansion which the tradition assigns to Longobard Queen Teodolinda. This fortification has been witness of a tormented history, fights and sieges, with "starrings" as Barbarossa, Torriani and Visconti. Today, among the impressive castle ruins, remain the square tower, 42 meters high, and suggestive basements. Here there was also a bridge over the Adda, destroyed in 1416 by Carmagnola, with its shoulder still visible. In 1799 no bridge was there.

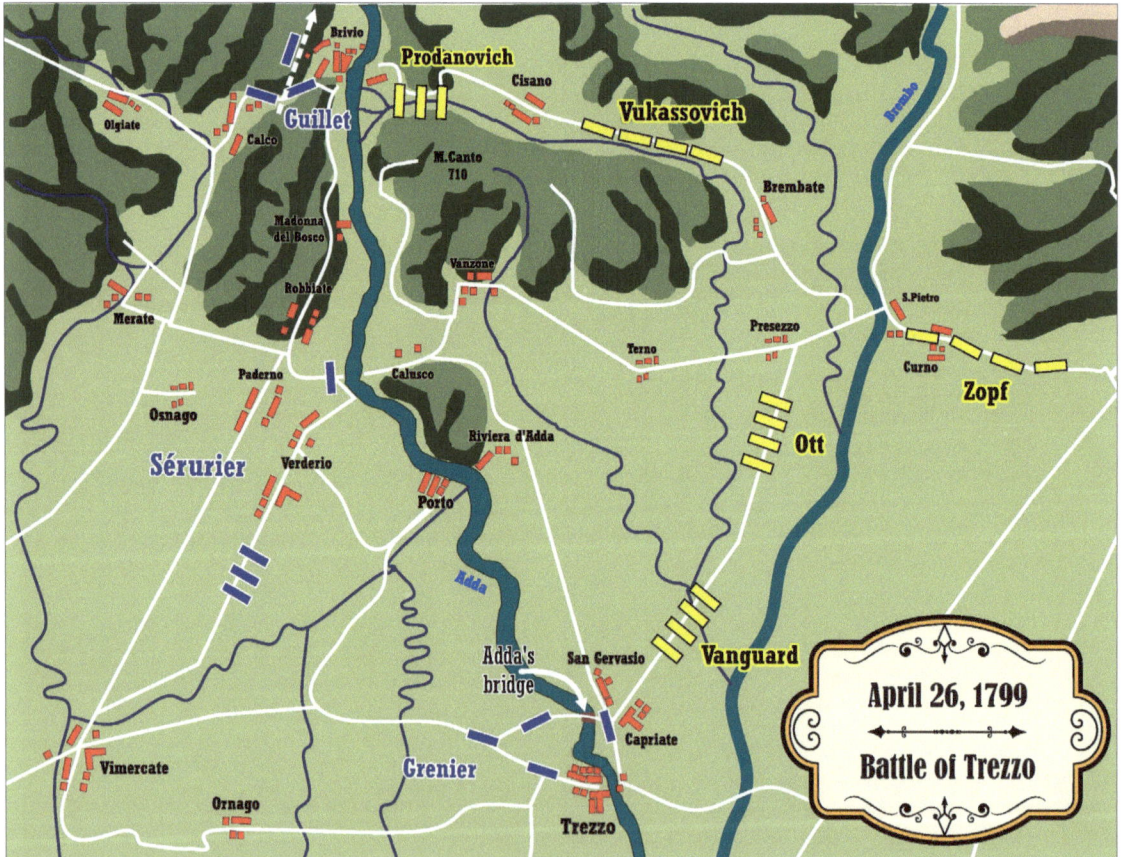

At Vaprio
Brigade Général de brigade George Kister

III Btn. 33rd Line Demi Brigade	670
63rd Line Demi Brigade Chef Antoine-Francois Brenier de Montmorand (wounded on April 27) I-II-III btns	1280
The II Btn lost its flag at Vaprio	
24th Rgt Chasseurs à Cheval	180

THE BATTLE OF VAPRIO.

The Lombardy country land, where Vaprio is touched by the Adda river, was defined, in the past centuries, as "the most beautiful garden in Italy". Probably, from the 1400's years, one can easy believe to such affirmation; there were many luxury estates (Villas) such as Villa Melzi, splendid example of a "rustic country estate". Vaprio was crossed by the Naviglio (Channel) Martesana, a navigable water-way to Milano, like other hamlets of that land. Milanese gentlemen, attracted by the land serenity and the surrounding forests, were often there moving along the water-channels by boats. Austrian Empress Maria Theresia, in 1763, declared the beautiful environs of Vaprio as personal (secret) hunting place, above all because the Duke of Modena, in those times Austrian Lombardy administrator, had set Vaprio village as the own holiday place. Near the ruins of an old Roman stone bridge (they say erected by the Emperor Claudius) Vaprio had a wooden bridge to cross the Adda river, at that time damaged by the French. The Martesana channel ran approximately forty meters south of the village and had high banks to protect houses from floods.

Brigade François-Jean-Baptiste baron de Quesnel du Torpt

17th Demi Brigade Légère Chef de brigade Henry-François Fornésy I-II-III Btns.	1100
24th Line Demi Brigade Général de brigade George Kister – I and II Btns.	1200
Had only two battalions, the third was in Piedmont	
3th Rgt Chasseurs à Cheval Chef Bouquet (?)	200

Reserve Adjudant-général Leonard-Nicholas Becker comte de Mons (??) [6]

I Btn. 33rd Line Demi Brigade - Chef Roguet	710
106th Line Demi Brigade at Cassano Redoubt - Chef Jean Claude Roussel	1200
24th Rgt Chasseurs à Cheval 3 Sqns.	450

Brigade General Gaspard-Amédée Gardanne

3e Demi Brigade de Ligne [7] (one battalion) Chef Pierre Martilliere	1104
3rd Régiment Chasseurs à Cheval Chef François-Alexandre Grosjean	450

A self-made new Bridge

After a reconnoissance with Jäger Colonel D'Aspre, Chasteler, who was with Suvorov in the second Austrian avantgarde, decided to build a pontoon in front of San Gervasio (north of Trezzo). Here, between San Gervasio and Trezzo, the river squeezed resulting in a 50 m large flood (but 6 feet deep) which presented a double curved course (like an "S" letter). On a promontory, emerging out of Trezzo, was the renowned Visconti castle.

20 german Jägers passed the river on boats deploying on the opposite bank to secure the works. The pontoons convoy arrived late, at 11 PM by night, from San Pietro; it was stopped far from the river and the transports were carried on by Banater croats and D'Aspre Jägern troops. Chasteler ordered to secure the bridge with strong ropes fixed in the rocky bank of Adda, because the river was, there, not large but deep, so the anchors did not touch its bottom. Before it was finished, 4 boats long 20 feet crossed the waters carrying 200 croats and 2 Nadasdy regiment's coys, who advanced cautiously till the first houses of Trezzo (were French slept in whole peacefulness). An horrible night that of April 26. Strong winds continually made obstacles to works, gusts of heavy rain beating the tired sappers. At dawn, 4 AM hours in the morning, the bridge was not ready, beginning to be passable only at 5.00 AM, when rain ceased and Adda flood became lower. The first to pass was colonel Constantin d'Aspre with his 6 Jägern coys, which took position in front of a French outpost cleared with rifles fire. Then followed 1 batallion of the Nadasdy regiment under Major Pretzer, 600 Cossacks and 1 squadron of the 7th Hussars. After 300 mt. followed the main troops of general Ott with Suvorov.

▲ Russian army in 1799. Grenadier, musketeer and jager.

Avantguard Division Generalmajor Carl Peter Ott de Batorkéz			7245
at San Gervasio	6 btns	8 squadrons	5000 ?
Avantguard Kolonne Oberst Bidegkuty			
III Btn. K.k. IR 39 Rifle Line hungarian Inf. Rgt. Graf Támas Nádasdy - Major Pretzer			876
On May 27 the III Btn. was in front of Trezzo. Second lieutenant Ritzko with 50 volunteers and 80 Jägern fortified the hamlet of Posto (Pozzo?). After the boat-bridge was completed the Austrian attacked the French outposts at Trezzo and captured the old Castle advancing against Vaprio to engage Grenier's division. The III Btn. took the village with a fast assault with the help of Zoph division troops. In that occurrence the battalion took 200 French prisoners and had a Captain plus 50 men dead while other 141 were wounded.			
Freiwillige Jäger Korps Freiherr Constantin d'Aspre (6 coys)			860
6th Don Cossacks Rgt. Pasdejev			470
K.k. 7th Hussar Régiment 2 sqns. II Div. (Obstlt.) Major Franz Szabo			204
Main Kolonne			
K.k. 15th Light Infantry Btn. (croatian-slavonian) Oberst Bonaventura Mihanovic			795
VI Btn. of Banater Grenzregiment			888
K.k. Grenadier battalion Freiherr Georg von Stentsch Graf Anton Schiaffinati			613
Count Freiherr Georg von Stentsch was wounded during the combats at Pastrengo-Verona. He died later, in April, for the wounds suffered. The leadership was taken by Count Anton Schiaffinati.			
K.k. Grenadier battalion FML Karl Graf von Mercandin Graf Carl Paar			623
K.k. IR 34 hungarian Rifle Line Inf. Rgt. (the former Rgt Esterházy)			1528
(no Inhaber. The future IR Frh. Kraj de Kraiova) (had the I and II Btn). Cdr.: Oberst Johann Hillinger			
K.k. 7th Hussar regiment (no Inhaber)			388

Cdr.: Oberst Carl Freiherr von Schauroth. With 4 Sqns.
II Div. (see after) Obstlt. Graf Thomas Dessöffy (dead at Parona) then Major Franz Szabo – III Div. 1st Major Szabo then Major Joszef Meszko – IV div. 2nd Major Joszef Meszko then Major Felix Graf Montecuccoli

General Moreau, on April 27 at 9.00 AM, ordered immediately to gather his three divisions north of Cassano. The alarm had been given by the II btn of 33rd demi-brigade the first to be repulsed by Austrians. The bataillon retreated on the road for Vaprio maintaining the contact with the river bank. Left of the 70 houses of Vaprio deployed the 63rd demi-brigade, the first squadron of 24th Chasseurs and 2 guns. Hearing the first gunshots, Moreau jumped on his horse leaving Inzago, during his speed ride was attacked by a Cossacks squadron (sotnya), but fled away reaching Grenier.

At 10.00 AM the Zoph division pessed the boats-bridge at Trezzo and the Austrian reformed their long Columns for the Advance with 25 guns for support.

1st hungarian Division FML Johann Zoph				4721
1st Division Zopf	at Canonica	6 btns	8 squadrons	
K.k. IR 39 Rifle Line hungarian Inf. Rgt. Graf Thomas (Támas) Nádasdy				1753
(I and II Btns.) – Cdr.: Freiherr Johann Nepomuk Abfaltern				
The two battalions were committed to attack the French bridgehead of Cassano. After the success they chased the enemies until the incoming night reaching Gorgonzola town. The commander Oberst Abfaltern and the Oberstlieutenant Pértussy distinguished themselves, the latter commanding the former Korherr Grenadier battalion.				
K.k. hungarian Grenadier Btn Oberleutnant Ferdinand Pers				600
K.k. hungarian Grenadier battalion Major Joseph Korherr				477
(Major Joseph Korherr died at Magnano. The battalion was led by Nadasdy's OberstLeutnant Johann Pértussy)				
K.k. IR 40 hungarian Rifle Line Inf. Rgt. FZM Graf Joseph Mittrowsky				1279
I and II btns. Cdr.: Oberst Franz Kreyssern.				
K.k. 2nd Hussar regiment Erzherzog Joseph Anton – 8 Sqns				612
The «Light Blue Hussars» had 8 sqns. And four divisions. Cdr.: Oberst Vincenz Freiherr Knesevich II Div. ObstLt. Gabriel von Hertellendy – III Div. 1st Major Emmerich Dobay – IV Div. 2nd Major Ignaz baron Splenyi				

About the 2nd Hussars, Major Dobay with his Division was Vs. the left French wing near Vaprio. Oberstltn. Von Hertellendy was with his Division (II) against the right French wing. The latter made three consecutive attacks together with other two divisions of the regiment. The joint attack of the six squadrons pierced the French line (200 French out of combat and 300 prisoners). They advanced until Inzago capturing Moreau HQs clearing Vaprio and Pozzo. The final booty was great: one flag, 12 guns, 1 howitzer, 6 ammunition wagons and about 2800 prisoners. Oberstltn. Von Hertellendy and the commander baron von was awarded with the Maria-Theresia Cross. The regiment's losses were: 153 hussars and 171 horses dead, many the wounded.

After the Austrian reorganization on the battlefield the little French contingent had no hope to resist. Moreau ordered the retreat towards the Milano road. Kister and Becker directed towards Gorgonzola, while Quesnel withdrawn to Inzago, having the road to Milano cut off by Austrian cavalry. During that retreat came to help the first Victor's unit: Argod. After a short combat, in which general Argod was killed, the French army continued the retreat. Grenier camped at Lambrate, near Milano, where he found the 106e demi-brigade with other 500 men of all the branches of Service (mainly sappers). Victor's division, threatened by its left flank, was not able to avoid the Austrian seize of the Cassano bridge; so it followed Grenier on the Milano road where it was reached by Laboissiere, who, while having forced his march, was too late to participate at the battle. Some authors refer also the participation of the Cossacks group of Bagration during the final phases of the Austrian Advance, in order to harass the left French flank and to clear the hamlet of Pozzo.

* Victor's and Laboissiere's units and numbers are estimated

Division du Centre General Claude-Victor Perrin	8131

Chief of Staff : Gén. Jacques Blondeau
Foot artillery 1 battery

Brigade Adjudant général François Argod (killed during the combats of April 27)

14th Line Demi Brigade Chef Jean-Claude Moreau I and II Btns.	1250
99th Line Demi Brigade de Ligne Chef Georges Mouton - I II III Btns.	2000

Brigade Général Baron Jacques-Antoine Chambarlhac de Laubespin

92nd Line Demi Brigade Chef Bruno-Albert-Joseph Duplouy - I II III Btns.	1970
5th Line Demi-brigade I Btn. Chef Louis-Hyacinthe Le Feron I and II Btns.	1300

15th Rgt Chasseurs à Cheval (4 sqns) Chef Louis Lepic	488
18th Rgt. de Cavalerie (4 sqns) Chef Denis Terreyre	453
Division de droit Pierre Garnier de Laboissière 8	4206

5e Demi-brigade légère I Btn. Chef-de-Brigade Antoine Chatagnier	950
45th Line Demi Brigade I and II Btns. Chef Jean Baptist Philip	1210
93rd Line Demi-brigade I and II Btns.	1230

9th Régiment Chasseurs à Cheval Chef Claude Matthieu Gardane	410
3rd Régiment de Cavalerie - Chef de Brigade Jean-Baptiste Meunier	406

THE BATTLE (?) OF CASSANO

Since the most important tactical location along the middle Adda river was the Cassano bridge (road from Milano to Bergamo), historians called the Adda battle as the Cassano battle. However they, more correctly, had to rename the fight as the Vaprio battle or the Adda battles.

CASSANO Placed on the right bank of the Adda, Cassano is today part of the Milan province, that city being approximately thirty kilometers far away. The Martesana Channel, established in 1457, determined its northern borders with the Vaprio lands. Also there, many Villas (Borromeo, Brambilla….), of important Milanese families, witnessed the history of its countryside utilized for weekends holidays, farms and estates from which bore the village core. The south-eastern Adda channel called Muzza, built with the twin scope to protect the ancient castle and to carry the necessary water for the local hospital, had fortifications which defended the bridge over the Adda, the main way to reach Bergamo from Milano. On the left Adda's bank was the village of Cascina Franca, after San Pietro on the Muzza channel. Since 1323, in order to pass the only one bridge over the Adda at Cassano, one would have had to paid a tax called "Thelonius", specific for the passage on the bridges. From this period the two hamlets, on the opposite river banks, begun to compete one against the other: Cassano on the Milanese side and the Cascina Franca on the Bergamo side, the former Celtic village Bergias (Cascina Franca as Farm "duty-free" regarding the toll to pass the bridge and to use the port of Cassano.

The bridgehead was controlled by Grenier troops and, after, from the Victor's vanguards. On the opposite side the Muzza channel (and the island) were occupied by the Austrian vanguards of Melas Gruppe. Some fire combats occurred along the Ritorto Channel, south of Cassano, but not more than a "scaramouche". On April 27, Cassano was abandoned by Victor's troops which retreated towards Gorgonzola and Melzo.

"The odds here were overwhelmingly against the French" say Christopher Duffy in his masterpiece *"even after the 106th demi-brigade was reinforced from the corps of Victor, for they confronted Melas and the two Austrian divisions of Kaim and Frelich. However the 106th had an outer defence in form of a bridgehead fortification on the left (eastern) bank of the Adda, and this in turn was covered by the outlying Canale Ritorto.*

For most of the day Melas had contented himself with cannonading the French works until, under pressure from Suvorov, his pioneers braved heavy fire to make a trestle bridge across the canal. once the passage was complete, the regiment of Reysky doubled across with such speed that the French at once abandoned the bridgehead along with three pieces, and did not have the time to set fire to the combustible materials which they had heaped upon on the Adda bridge behind. The main Austrian force now crossed the intact bridge, and encountered little more than a token resistance on the far side, for Ott, Zoph and the Russians had already broken through further to the north in the way already described."

And this was the Cassano battle

Österreichische Italienische-Armée

Hauptarmée Feld Marshal Leut. Michael Friedrich Benedikt Mélas
Generalquartiermeister: GM. Johann Gabriel Chasteler Marquis de Courcelles (Chasteler was with Suvorov at Trezzo and Vaprio)

2nd Division Generalmajor Freiherr Michael von Fröhlich Under provisional command of Generalmajor Franz Joseph Marquis de Lusignan		11941
2nd Division Fröhlich	HQs at Treviglio	

Feldbrigade Generalmajor Franz Joseph Marquis de Lusignan	2894
K.k. Grenadier battalion Oblt Franz Xavier Weber von Treuenfeld (called Weber Btn.)	347
K.k. Grenadier battalion Graf Joseph Fiquelmont Count Johann Morzin	577
K.k. 14th Light Dragoons Rgt. Franz Freiherr von Levenehr	870
Cdr.: Oberst Joseph Zinn. (it had 6 Sqns. On 3 div. I – II – III) the IV Division was in Friaul (garrison) II Div. ObLt. Josef Prohaska – III Div. Major Franz Graf Latour (Major Albert Graf Unverzagt missing after a battle)	

Feldbrigade Generalmajor (provisional) Oberst Marquis Hannibal Sommariva	4942
K.k. IR 18 Rifle Line Inf. Rgt. Graf Patrick Stuart	1741
Cmdr. Obst Franz Weber von Treuenfels - I and II Btns	
II Btn K.k. IR 40 hungarian Rifle Line Inf. Rgt. FZM Graf Joseph Mittrowsky	639
K.k. IR 19 hungarian Rifle Line Inf. Rgt. Freiherr Jozsef Alvinczy de Berberek	1722
I and II Btns. + 2 Coys III Btn. - Cdr.: Barone Lelio Spannocchi.	
K.k. 10th Light Dragoons Regiment Joseph Fürst Lobkowitz	840
(had 6 sqns. on 3 divisions I II and III) Cdr.: Oberst Marquis Hannibal Sommariva – Second Oberst and Commander Max Joseph Fürst Thurn und Taxis. II Div. ObstLt. Alois Graf Harrach – III Div. Major Ignatz Molitor	

Feldbrigade Generalmajor Christoph Freiherr von Lattermann	4105
K.k. IR 43 Rifle Line Inf. Rgt. Graf Anton Thurn-Val Sassina	1948
(IV, I and II Btns.) The III Btn. was at Zara (dalmatia) in garrison duty. Cdr.: Freiherr Ignaz von Loen	
K.k. IR 13 Rifle Line Inf. Rgt. Freiherr Franz Wenzel Reisky von Dubnitz	1911
(I, II and III Btns.) Cdr.: Oberst Freiherr Carl von Brigido	
K.k. 5th Hussar regiment– 2 Sqns – III Div. Major Ferdinand Steingruber	246

Left Wing Gruppe Generalmajor Konrad Valentin Kaim	4501
K.k. IR 24 Rifle Rgt (former Preiss)	1500
(btns I – II – III) - Cmdr Oberst Carl Philipp von Weidenfeld	
K.k. IR 28 Rifle Line Inf. Rgt. (future Freiherr Michael von Fröhlich)	2376
(the former Rgt Wartensleben – on 3 btns.) Cdr.:Oberst Paul Candiani de Ragaini	
K.k. 4th Light Dragoons Rgt. GM Andreas Frh. von Karacsaj de Vale-Sakam 4 Sqns.	625
Had 6 sqns. Cdr.: Oberst Joseph Graf Nimptsch. It will be originally detached as link unit with the Russian Corps Rozenberg. II Div. ObstLt. Carl von Provencheres – III Div. Major Leopold Freiherr Ludwigsdorf (see Russians)	

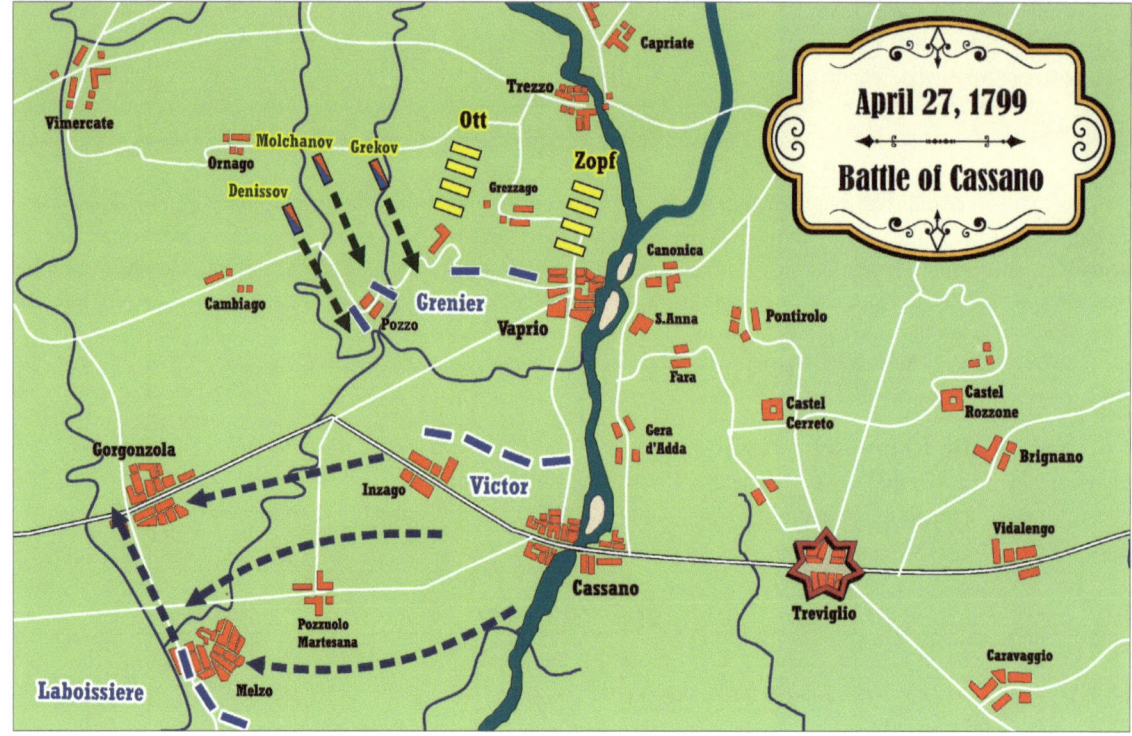

THE AUSTRIAN FLANKING UNITS

LODI was a Celtic village that Romans called, in Latin, "Laus Pompeia" (probably in honour of consul Gnaeus Pompeius Strabo) and was also known because its position allowed many Gauls of Gallia Cisalpina to obtain Roman citizenship. A free Municipality around 1000, it fiercely resisted the Milanese, who destroyed it in April 24, 1158. Emperor Frederick the Barbarossa re-built it on its current location.

Lodi was ruled by the Visconti family, who built a castle. In 1454 representatives from all the regional states of Italy met in Lodi to sign the treaty known as the peace of Lodi, by which they intended to work in the direction of Italian unification, but this peace lasted only 40 years. The town was then ruled by the Sforza family, France, Spain, Austria. In 1786 it became the eponymous capital of a province that included Crema. On May 10, 1796 the young Corsican general Buonaparte won on the river Adda his first important battle, defeating the Austrians and later entering Milan. After that battle the most important Adda's bridge became the Lodi's bridge. Memoir can be found in many French towns as in Paris, 6th arrondissement, Rue du Pont de Lodi.

Feldgruppe Generalmajor Friedrich Freiherr von Seckendorff

Feldbrigade Seckendorff	at Lodi	2 btns	2 sqns	1453
VII Combined Btn Grenzregiment Warasdiner of Varazdin (Croatia)				627
K.k. 5th Hussar Regiment 4 Sqn.				826
It had 6sqns. On 3 Div.s I, II and III in reserve. The IV div. was in Croatia as garrison. Cdr.: Obst Anton Freiherr von Révay – II Div. ObstLt. Freiherr Andreas Szörenyi – 2nd Major Wilhelm Fulda present at the battle.				

Feldgruppe Generalmajor Friedrich Xavier Fürst Hohenzollern-Hechingen

Gruppe Hohenzollern	at Pizzighettone	5 btns	6 sqns	5073

Feldbrigade Generalmajor Freiherr Anton von Mittrowsky

K.k. IR 32 Rifle Rgt. Graf Samuel Gyulai	1482
Cmdr. Oberst Franz Posztrehowsky von Millenburg - (I-II-Btns) III btn to Mantua	
K.k. IR 36 Rifle Rgt. Fürst Carl Fürstenberg	2576
(I-II-III Btn) Cmdr. Oberst Conrad von Thelen	
K.k. 1st Light Dragoons Regiment "Emperor" Kaiser Franz II	1015
They had 6 sqns. on three divisions. Cdr.: Oberst Franz Freiherr von Pilati. II Div. ObstLt. Baron Karl Kölbel – III Div. Major Bernard Kees	

THE VERDERIO AFFAIR

The bad news about the battle reached Milan in the evening of April 27. Therefore almost the whole Cisalpine governement left Milan, taking the national treasure over. The city was abandoned by four of the five Directeurs (Marescalchi, Sopransi, Vertomati and Franchi) along with the French Minister Rivaud and the shocked general Schérer. On April 28, Moreau entered Milano leaving the Grenier division free to continue its march. Géneral Hatry was left at the Sforzesco Castle (the Citadel) in order to organize the 1800 men of the garrison (3 btns.). 8000 men with 22 guns, 1000 cavalrymen in three columns passed quickly through the city during that morning. The day after Moreau reached Novara in Piedmont and there he got the knowledge of the "Verderio affair".

The Sérurier division, as said, was split in two large groups. While Soyez rescued his demi-brigade cruising through the Como lake and Guillet saved his units marching back to Como, the main group had tried to rally

south of Brivio in order to link the right flank with Grenier. The rallying attempt continued through all the day (April 27), while the battle enraged at the Adda bank.

Sérurier's arrest at Verderio was an inexplicable thing. It was a well established custom, among the revolutionary Generals, to march wherever they heard the "son du cannon" (sound of the guns), even if waiting superior orders. Sérurier knew the Brivio crossing and the fire noises told him that a battle was in act at Vaprio. Standing to wait orders was the last thing to do. This conduct, at Verderio, is a reminder of Bonaparte's opinion of him (1796): " *Sérurier se bat en soldat – ne prend rien sur lui – ferme- n'a pas assez bonne opinion de ses troupes – est malade.* " The behaviour of his subordinate, Soyez, which, being cut off blew up the fortifications at Lecco, embarked on the lake and landed in safety, is an evident contrast to the Chief's indecision.

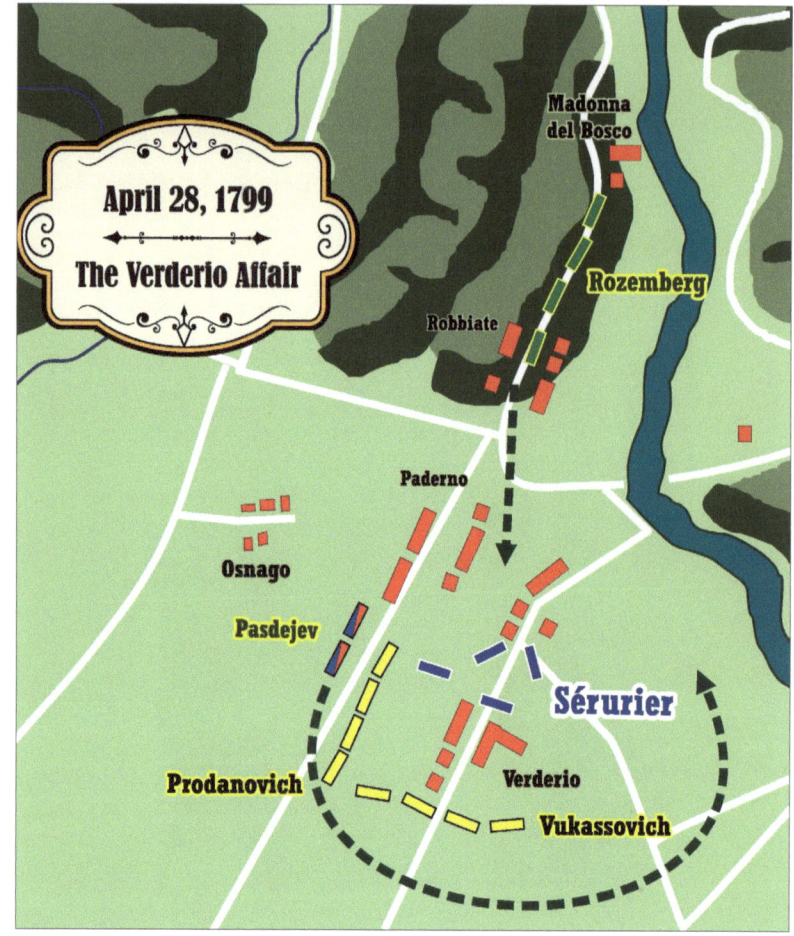

It is strange for a General, who had won a major battle (Pastrengo) performing always in a resolute and military correct way, to seal himself into a Castle (villa), only a month after, undecided on what to do. However Sérurier had been roughly apostrophated after the rout of Parona (March 30) for having left the attack to go too much in depth, an excess of bravery which had costed many losses. So is possible that, in a circumstance in which he had to operate again by own initiative, the decision was opposite: too much movement at Parona, so no actions at Verderio.

The next morning (28) Sérurier was already surrounded into a nearly quiet battlefield. The French division, rapidly, entrenched into the Villa Confalonieri (today Villa Gnecchi-Ruscone), into the Castle and the cemetery. At Verderio the first Austrian squadron which made a reconnoissance near the town was led by Rittmeister Adam Albert Graf von Neipperg (the future general), GeneralStabsOffizier by Vukassovich. Followed a direct, frontal, attack by the Austrian Avant-guard while the Russians of Rozemberg marched around Sérurier flanks. The old, tired, general so reported to the War Minister:

"*Around 3.00 PM of 9 Floréal (of April 28) I realized that enemies were marching against me. Around 4.00 PM the fire combat was engaged with my outposts. Around 4.30 PM I was attacked by all sides, especially by the enemy cavalry which caused us a lot of troubles. We resited with bravery taking masses of prisoners and killing a lot of enemies. They were, however, 17000 around us, of which 8000 engaged in the combats. When we had no more ammunitions the surrender was the only thing to do. Piedmontese cavalry of Fresia made wonders of bravery, more than 200 Dragons were wounded or died on the battlefield, the remaining troops (2400) were made prisoners by capitulation.*"

Christopher Duffy reported other numbers: "*When Vukassovich enumerated his prisoners he found that they amounted to two divisional generals (Sérurier and his cavalry commander Fresia), 241 other officers, 3,487 NCOs and men and 151 non-combatants, along with five cannon. The Austrians agreed to allow Sérurier and his officers to return to France under parole: 'This latter condition was a mark of respect shown to the bravery of old Genera1 Sérurier, ...*"

Ending notes

Why Moreau lost that battle? Knowing that the Austro-Russian did not have any numerical superiority (Melas gruppe was not engaged) we can only suppose a cause in the too difficult (and bad) army deployment. It was a Schérer mistake to suppose a defence widening from the Po to the Como lake, but there were few alternatives. Probably Moreau came too late to take command with efficiency, so he did what he well knew: saving an army in difficulties. An initial withdrawal until the Ticino river could had designed a less wide front to guard, but would have sacrificed the important Piacenza Citadel, on the right Po bank unless they would have ordered Montrichard to leave Ferrara and Bologna and to defend Piacenza (this would have left open the gate to the Armée de Naples, coming to help). The Adda battle was a decisive one. It was the second, consecutive, defeat for the French main army and definitively lowered the troops morale, cleared the ranks (replenished with conscripts or Piedmontese soldiers) and added muscles to the weak and scattered Italian Insurgency.

Duffy wrote: *"The victory on the Adda broke the French forces in northern Italy, doomed their puppet Cisalpine Republic and opened the way to the liberation of Piedmont. As regards the management of the battle on the French side, it is difficult to dissent from the judgement of Moreau in his report to the Directory, in which he pointed out that Schérer had teased out the army along an immense length, and that he himself had taken command 'without knowing how the army was placed, and at a time when the line was already broken – a fact which was not known at headquarters.'"*

Chasteler reported, about the losses

The battle engaged on the five bridges (Brivio – Sérurier forgotten pontoon; Trezzo – Austrian Poneers pontoon; Cassano, the bridgehead; Lodi and Pizzighettone) had costed:

	Officers	Men	Total
DEAD	17	744	761
WOUNDED	122	2791	2913
PRISONERS	57	1155	1212

¾ of the losses were suffered at Vaprio = 2750 men

From other source *"Campagne des Austro-Russes en Italie"*

At VAPRIO	Men	Horses	Total Men lost
DEAD	245	105	1320
WOUNDED	768	150	
MISSING	307	28	

The Archduke Joseph Hussars regiment, on its own, lost 170 horses. from Gachot Edouard "Suvorow en Italie"

From a letter of the Sindaco (1st Citizen) at Vaprio

At VAPRIO	Men	Cavalrymen	Total Men lost
Austro-Russians dead	246	105	1447
Austro-Russians wounded	768	283	

Archiv of Senate Palace, Milan, Reg. N. 466. from Gachot Edouard "Suvorow en Italie"

On May 1st, Suvorov gave these numbers about the losses:

Coalized Army	Lecco Apr 26	Vaprio Apr 27	Verderio Apr 28
	136 dead – 91 wounded	26 Cossacks dead. Austrian 1000 dead or wounded. (Cassano losses known)	(not known)
French Army	2000 dead and wounded 100 prisoners	3000 dead and wounded 2071 prisoners	

French Forces situation after the Adda battles

Piedmont garrisons	9000
Ligurian and Genoan Riviera garrison	5000
Division general Montrichard	2600
Division general Gauthier de Kerweguen	6400
Armée de Naples general Macdonald	20000
Total	43000
Main Army general Moreau	20000
Grand Total	63000

NOTES

1 Officially Moreau had the Directory letter from a Courier (a letter similar to that of Schérer) on April 26, evening when the French front line was already pierced. He, coming from Lodi, didn't know the exact deployment of the Armée.

2 Included the Guards of Light demi-brigade now under Fresia command.

3 **Prince Petr Ivanovich Bagration** (1765 - 24 September 1812, Simy) joined as private the Astrakhan Infantry Regiment in 1782 and participated in a number of campaigns on the Northern Caucasus in 1783-1787. He served under Alexander Suvorov in Crimea and distinguished himself at Ochakov in 1788 and was promoted to captain skipping the rank of sub lieutenant. Bagration was promoted to ensign [*praporshik*] on 9 July 1787, to captain on 18 December 1788 and nominally given rank of sub lieutenant [*podporuchik*] on 9 July 1789. In 1789-1790, Bagration served in Gregory Potemkin's staff and participated in negotiations with representatives of Ali Mahmud Khan of Persia. He also served as adjutant to various generals, including Count Ivan Saltykov and Johann Hermann, who commanded Russian troops in the Caucasus. In 1790, he participated in the campaign against Chechens. By early 1792, Bagration was transferred to the Kiev Horse Jager Regiment and promoted to second major (9 July 1792) and then to premier major (8 December 1793). On 15 May 1794, he was transferred to the Sofia Carabineer Regiment and served in Poland in 1794. In late October, he led his squadron in a surprise attack against a thousand Polish troops camped in woods with a cannon. Bagration's squadron captured 250 men and the gun, while the fleeing Poles lost up to 300 killed and wounded. For this success, Bagration was promoted to lieutenant colonel on 27 October 1794. In November, he followed the main army to Praga, the suburb of Polish capital, but he did not participate in the assault because his regiment was assigned to cover the artillery. Bagration was given command of the 1st Battalion of the Lifland Jagers at Volkovysk in the Grodno *gubernia* in June 1795. After the military reorganization in 1796, Bagration was appointed commander of the 7th Independent Jager Battalion on 28 May 1797. However, his battalion was soon transformed into the 7th Jager Regiment. On 24 February 1798, Bagration was promoted to colonel and, on 28 January 1799, appointed chef of his regiment, now renamed to Prince Bagration's Jager Regiment. He took part in Suvorov's campaign in Italy and Switzerland in 1799. Commanding the advance and rearguards of the Russian army, he distinguished himself at the battles at Brescia, Lecco, Tortona, Alexandria, Marengo, Turin, Tidone, Trebbia and Novi in Italy as well as during the crossing of the St. Gotthard Pass, storming of the Devil's Bridge, actions in Muothatal Valley, Nafels, Netstal, Glarus and the Panixer Pass. For his actions, he was awarded Orders of St. Anna (1st Class), of St. Alexander of Neva, of St. John of Jerusalem, Order of Saints Maurice and Lazarus, Austrian Order of Maria Theresa in late 1799. In 1800, his regiment was transformed into the 6th Jagers (10 April) and Bagration was appointed chef of the Life Guard Jager Battalion on 21 June 1800. Source: Alexander Mikaberidze 2003.

4 **General of Infantry Mihail Andrejevich Miloradovich** began his military service under the command of Suvorov. He was one of the young associates of the great Russian general, such as Bagration and Gorchakov. He took part in the Italian and Swiss campaigns of Suvorov in 1799. In the Italian campaign he was a General of the day and distinguished himself in the battle at Novy on August, 4 (19), 1799. In the Swis campaign he, by his brave actions at the lake Oberaln safeguarded the Russian Army the approaches to the Saint-Gotard pass. Miloradovich took part in the Austerlitz battle in 1805. In the campaign of 1805 he fought very successfully in co-operation with General Bagration against the cavalry of Marshal Murat and the Grenadier Coprs of Marshal Oudinot during the retreating manoeuvre of the Russian Army. In the Russian-Turkish war of 1806-1812 Miloradovich commanded the Corps that on December,13,1806 liberated Bucharest from the Turks. In March of 1807 he defeated Turks at Turbat and on July,2, 1807 after the battle at Obelishty made to retreat the Turkish army of Ali-Pasha of 12 thousands. After this war he was appointed the Governor of Kiev in 1809. In the war of 1812 year he arrived to the Army with 15 thousands of reinforcement on August,15,1812. In the Borodino battle he commanded the right wing of the Russian Army that covered the road to Moscow and then the centre of the Russian Army. After this battle he commanded the rear-guard of the Russian Army. When the Russian Army retreated from Moscow he offered Marshal Murat to conclude a truce to give the Russian troops an opportunity to leave Moscow in order, otherwise he promised to fight to the last soldier. The truce was concluded. During the offensive of the Russian Army he commanded the van-guard of the main army. The Russian troops under his command won the battles at Vyazma and Krasnoe. Miloradovich took part in the campaigns of 1813-1814 years. In the battle of Leipzig in 1813 he commanded The Russian and Prussian Guards. After the war he was the Governor of St.Petersburg from 1818. In December of 1825 some officers with their regiments rose in rebellion against new Emperor Nickolay the I-st. It was the revolt of Decembrists. They with their regiments stood on the Senatskaya Square near the Winter Palace. Nickolay sent Miloradovich to the rebellious soldiers to induce them to go away. He came to them unarmed, but was mortally wounded by one of the rebels Kahovsky by name.

5 **Generalmajor Nikolaj Andrejevic Chubarov** – lieutenant colonel (from 01.10.1797 colonel, c 20.08.1798 general-major). From 17.05.1797 to 17.01.1799 – commander 8th Rgt. Jäger. From 17.01.1799 to 13.05.1799 Chef (Owner) 8th Rgt. Jäger.

6 The Count of Mons was taken prisoner by Austrians at Magnano. Other sources tell he was wounded, other he led a brigade.

7 **Chef de Brigade Pierre Martilliere** - Wounded at Vaprio. Born: 23 March 1759. Chef de Brigade: 20 January 1796 (3e demi-brigade d'Infanterie), General de Brigade: 28 April 1799. Commander of the Legion d'Honneur: 14 June 1804. Died: 20 November 1807 (as a result of wounds suffered at Vaprio)

Chef de Brigade Georges Mouton - Born: 21 February 1770 à Phalsbourg - Chef de Brigade: 26 May 1798 (99e demi-brigade d'Infanterie)- Chef de Brigade: 14 July 1799 (3e demi-brigade d'Infanterie) - Colonel: 24 September 1803 (3e Regiment d'Infanterie). General de Brigade: 1 February 1805. General de Division: 5 October 1807. Count of the Empire: 19 September 1810. Died: 27 November 1838 à Paris.

8 **Pierre Garnier de Laboissière** (1755-1809) Grand Officier de la Legion d'Honneur - 14.06.1804. Reformed in 1776, he was recalled on duty, as second-Lieutenant, on June 15, 1777 ; on June 3, 1779 he was Captain, engaged for the replacements organization in the Montmorency-Dragons. When the regiment took the name of 2e régiment de chasseurs à cheval, on September 17, 1791, he followed the unit, as Captain, in the armée du Rhin. At the combat of Spire, September 30, 1792, with twelve chasseurs, he made prisoners 300 Austrians. On the following 1st of December, he was awarded for that action and named chef de brigade. He was a provisional général de brigade in the armée du Rhin, after May 8, 1793, when, after an unlucky charge, where he fell down with his horse killed, he was prisoners of the Prussians. After the exchange, he was definitevely named général de brigade, then serving under the armies of Rhin-et-Moselle and Allemagne. In 1794 he commanded a Cavalry brigade under the 2nd division - Armée du Rhin. In 1796 he was in the armée d'Angleterre, and then at the Mayence army. On February 23, 1799 he was promoted General-de-division, serving in Italy and Switzerland (years VII, VIII and IX). In 1800 he obtained a command in the Reserve Army, which he mantained until 1801, in the Grisons. Reformed in 1802, he was named "inspecteur général d'infanterie" and entered the French Senate with the direct help of Bonaparte. In 1807 the Emperor gave him the command (March 20) of the 4e légion de réserve de l'intérieur (X Corps) sending him to the Charente. In 1808 he was named Count of the Empire and member of the Supreme Command at Strasbourg. However he did not reach that city because, on March 1809, he died at Paris.

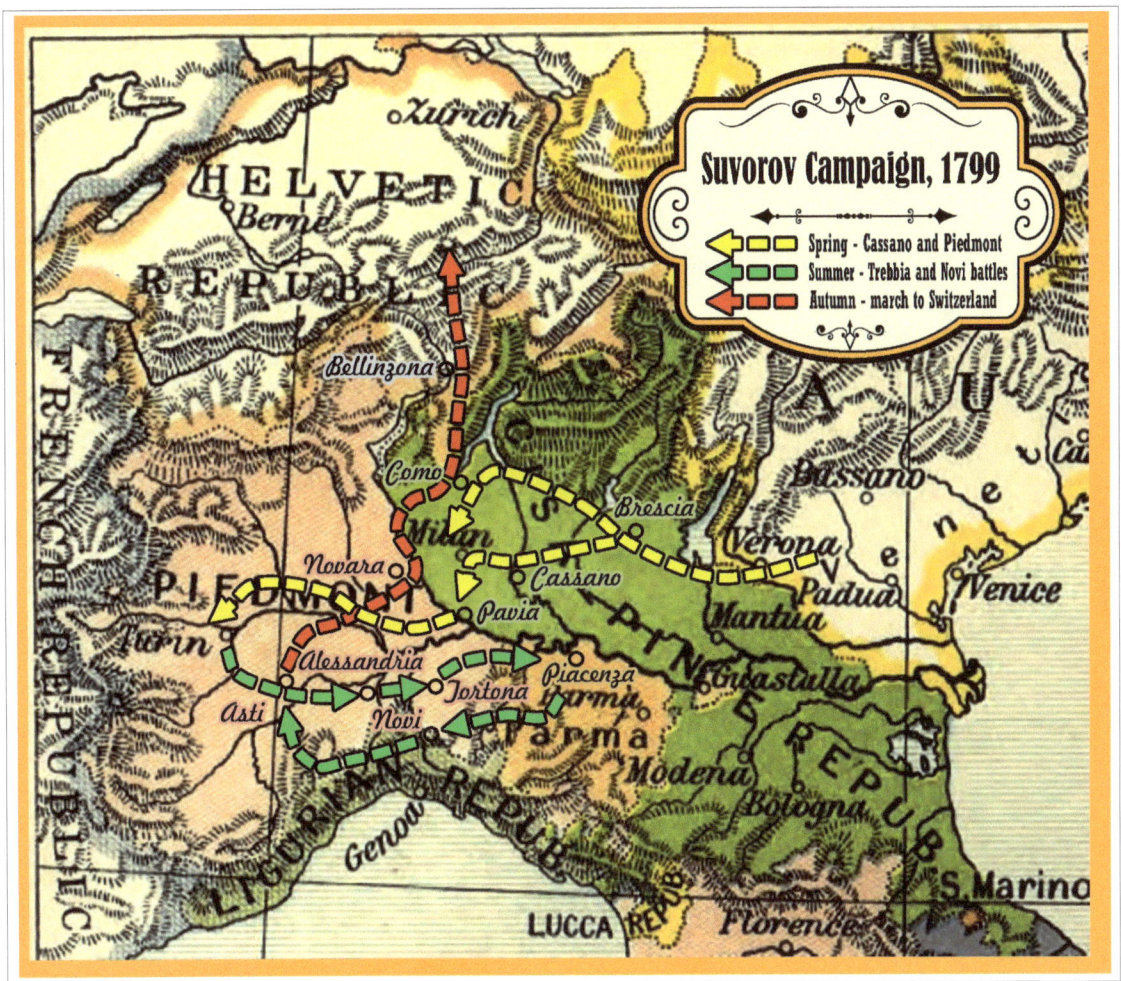

▲ Russian Troops under Suvorov Crossing the Alps in 1799

FROM MILAN TO THE PO RIVER
... and beyond... The New Deployment of the Austro-Russians

PIEDMONT'S INVASION BEGAN MAY 1799

Milano (Milan) January 1799	1250

Général Gilles-Joseph-Martin Bruneteau vicomte de Sainte Suzanne [1] (1760-1830) from 18/10/95 Général de brigade ; from 02/08/96 Général de division – provisional commander at the armée d'Italie 07/03/99-12/03/99. In 1800 Corps commander at the armée du Rhin.

Milano Garrison January - March 1799
III btn/5th Line Demi-Brigade
III btn /30th Line Demi-Brigade
III btn /33rd Line Demi-Brigade
Chasseurs Corses (2 Coys)
Cavalry

11e Hussards Régiment (moved to the Mincio with 4 Sqns) Chef Pierre Ismert	460

1er Régiment Dragons d'Expedition
Infantry Guides
Detachments (artillery+sappers) 3rd – 5th – 6th Art. Rgt

III/2nd Polish Legion Depot Battalion	It was really a IV battalion (Depot). Its soldiers were the last defenders before the withdrawal in April.

Cisalpine Army central Depot
During the evening of April 27 the Cisalpine Government left Milano. The garrison (Gachot referred about 1800 men) was rallied by general Hatry while Moreau continued his retreat toward the Ticino (Tesin) river. The day after they recovered into the Citadel (Castello Sforzesco) (see images).
Garrison April – May 1799
Milano Citadel (Castello) Cdr. Charles-Theodore Beauvais de Preau (08.11.1772-18.04.1830)

Infantry garrison cdr. Chef-de-bataillon Bechard	2376
Guns	119

Cisalpine Depot Btn.
II btn 10th Line demi-brigade
I btn 56th Line demi-brigade
2nd Polish legion Depot

The Castello Sforzesco, or Castle of Milan, stands in the Parco Nuovo; it was built in 1450 by Francesco Sforza on the site of one erected by Galeazzo II. Visconti (1355-1378) and demolished in 1447 by the populace after the death of Filippo Maria Visconti. After suffering many vicissitudes and being partially destroyed more than once, it was restored - including especially the splendid entrance tower by Antonio Averulino, destroyed by a powder explosion in 1521.

Austrian Siege Group

1st deployment
Mailander Belagerungskorps Generalmajor Christoph Freiherr von Lattermann [2]

K.k. IR 13 Rifle regiment Freiherr Franz Wenzel Reisky von Dubnitz	1851
I – II –III btns. cdr.: Obst Freiherr Carl von Brigido	
KK IR 43 line regiment Graf Anton Thurn-Val Sassina	1973
I – II –III btns. cdr.: Freiherr Ignaz von Loen	
K.k. 5th Hussar Rgt. 2 sqns	246

MILANO. In 1385 Gian Galeazzo Visconti was the first lord of Milano and it was under him that the Milan Dome was begun to buid. His sons Giovanni Maria Visconti, at Milan, and Filippo Maria, at Pavia, were the family successors. In 1412, when Giovanni died, Filippo united the Milan duchy under his own rule, and attempted to carry out a policy of enhancement, but with no successes. Filippo was the last male of the Visconti house and, so, at his death, a Milanese Republic was proclaimed (it lasted only 3 years). In 1450 general Francesco Sforza, husband of Bianca, a Visconti maiden, daughter of Filippo, , became the duke of Milan. Under him was enlarged the Castello (which had the name Sforzesco) and was built the Martesana channel, connecting Milan with Cassano on the Adda. When his nephew, the boy Gian Galeazzo, inherited the Duchy, the power was usurped by his uncle Lodovico the Black (il Moro). Lodovico was taken prisoner in 1500 by King Louis XII of France, and Milan was subdue to the French for twelve years. After a short period of Sforzesque dominion, the French, with François Iér, reconquered the Milanese (Marignano battle). The matter changed again when the Holy Roman Emperor Charles V claimed his rights over the Milanese. In 1522 the Imperials entered Milan and proclaimed duke Francesco Sforza (son of Lodovico). Francesco death in 1535 closed the Sforza house. Then the Duchy become the Milanesado (a spanish word) and was under the Spain crown until the War of the Spanish Succession. At the end of that war the city was ruled by Austria and so remained until the Bonaparte arrival in 1796.

▲ Général Gilles-Joseph-Martin Bruneteau vicomte de Sainte Suzanne (1760-1830)

THE NEW FRENCH FRONT

The French retreat was disciplined by three main Columns: the right Column marched towards Piacenza from Lodi, the center from Milano through Pavia and Voghera in direction of the Genoan Republic, the left column, with Moreau and the HQ, through Vigevano and Novara towards Turin (Torino). The artillery commander General Debelle was the first to cross the Ticino river with 36 guns (May 2). Victor followed Grenier and Moreau but was directed to Alessandria. Laboissiere crossed the Po at Casale and deployed his troops to guard the river Tanaro. The Rear-guard was led by general Gardanne who had the task to defend the artillery park with the cavalry. On May 7 Gardanne was reinforced with a new infantry Chasseurs regiment organized in two demi-brigades sent the first to Verrua, the other to Villanuova.

Therefore the bulk of the Army directed towards Genoa borders while the commander in Chief reached Turin, calmed some riots and organized the evacuation of Depots. The Turin Citadel was left under the command of General Fiorella while the territory around the former Savoy Kingdom capital city was guarded by small garrisons. On May 7 Moreau left Turin and tranferred his HQ at Alessandria. In Genoa Perignon took the command of the Right Wing of the army of Italy guarding the territory between the sea until fort Serravalle near Novi. He had under his command the general Lapoype with the Genoese (5000) and Laboissiere (2000 infantrymen and 1 squadron). His brigadiers were generals Musnier and Carra St. Cyr. South of the Po, generals Montrichard and Gauthier were prescribed to join the incoming Armée de Naples (Macdonald). The Grouchy division, former Piedmont's garrison, replenished the Armée d'Italie ranks.

Milano garrison sent forwards as Avant-Guard

Austrian Avantgarde Brigade Generalmajor Freiherr Josef Philipp von Vukassovich   4956 men

Avant Garde Generalmajor Sebastian Prodanovich	1959
II Btn Grenzregiment of Banat (or I btn. 13th GrenzRgt)	837
V Btn Banater Grenzregiment	596
K.k. Light Btn. N. 2 Oberst Carl Prince of Rohan (Italian Btn) later sent to Aosta	526
Hauptkolonne von Vukassovich	2997
KK IR 52 Rifle Hungarian Rgt. Erzherzog Palatin Anton Viktor	1292
I – II btns. cdr.: Graf Johann Nepomuk Khuen de Belasi	
III Btn Grenzregiment of Banat (or II btn. 12th Deutschbanater GrenzRgt) Major Zedzwitz	682
K.k. 9th Hussar Rgt. FML Johann Nepomuk Graf Erdödy de Monyorókerek	310
(Erdödy Husaren) 2 Sqns.	
K.k. 7th Hussar Rgt. 5 – ½ sqns	713
Cdr. : Oberst Carl Freiherr von Schauroth - (it had 6 Sqns. On 3 div. I – II - III) the IV Division was in Slavonia (garrison)	

Capitulation of Milano and redistribution of Austrian forces

Articles de capitulation proposés par le citoyen Bechaud Chef titulaire du second bataillon de la 40-me demibrigade d'infanterie de bataille à Mr. le Comte de Hohenzollern général-major, commandant des troupes Autrichiennes cernant de Chateau de Mitan.	
1. Toute la garnison sortira du chateau le 5 prairial an 7 de la république française, correspondant au 24 Mai 1799, à 9 h. du matin, tambour battant, avec les honneurs de la guerre. Tous les militaires qui la composent seront conduits aux postes françois et remis à la disposition du général en chef de l'armée en Italie.	- La garnison ne servira pas contre les troupes de S. M. l'Empereur pendant un an et un jour, à moins que son échange général ou partiel soit opéré pendant ce temps. Les officiers conservent leurs armes. La garnison sortira demain matin à 9 h. avec les honneurs de la guerre et tambour battant; elle remettra ses armes sur le glacis.
2. Tous les ouvriers, les non-combattants de tout genre et les enfants seront également conduits aux avantpostes françois	Accordé.
3. Dix petits fourgons ou charriots, qui se trouvent dans la place, attelés de leurs chevaux, pourront sortir à la suite des officiers, sans que les objets qu'ils contiennent soyent fouillés ou visités.	Accordé.
4. Il sera fourni les voitures nécessaires au transport des infirmes, des femmes, des enfants et des équipages, qui ne seront pas contenus dans les fourgons ou charriots prédits.	Accordé.
5. Les officiers ayant des chevaux, les sortiront librement. Toute la troupe conservera ses équipages.	Accordé.
6. Tous les soins qu'exige l'humanité seront donnés à tous les malades de la garnison, le nombre des officiers de santé nécessaire à leur traitement pourra rester à Milan ad hoc.	Accordé.
7. Les militaires se rendant aux postes françois seront pendant leur marche sous la sauve-garde de la troupe Autrichienne. L'officier commandant cette dernière sera responsable des mauvais traitements ou des insultes, qui pourroient être faits a la garnison par les habitans.	On le promet, et l'on en aura soin d'après la loyauté connue dans les armées Impériales et Royales
8. Les troupes alliées de toutes les nations qui font parti de la garnison, seront traitées avec les mêmes égards et de la même manière que celles françoises.	Accordé.
	9. Le lieutenant Zoukovich sera rançonné contre un autre officier de la garnison tellement qu'ils peuvent servir tous les deux sur le champ
	10. Un commissaire des guerres restera dans la place pour remettre les magasins d'armes, de munition et de subsistances, plans, lettres et tout ce qui appartient a la république.
Fait double au chateau de Milan le 4 prairial an VII de la république françoise (ce 28 may 1799)	
Le chef de bataillon Béchaud	Baron de Latterman, général de Sa Majesté l'Empereur et Roy
	Le comte de Hohenzollern général-major, commandant le siége

Mailander Belagerungskorps

Generalmajor Christoph Freiherr von Lattermann

GeneralMajor Friedrich Xavier Fürst Hohenzollern-Hechingen	
K.k. IR 24 Rifle Line Rgt (former Preiss)	All battalions to Mantua Siege
(btns I – II- III) - Cmdr Oberst Carl Philipp von Weidenfeld	
K.k. IR 43 Rifle Line Rgt Graf Anton Thurn-Val Sassina	I and II battalions to Mantua Siege
III Btn. K.k. IR 43 Rifle Line Rgt Graf Anton Thurn-Val Sassina	To Prince Rohan Bde. (future Milano garrison)
I – II –III btns. cdr.: Freiherr Ignaz von Loen	
K.k. IR 13 Rifle regiment Freiherr Franz Wenzel Reisky von Dubnitz	I and II battalions to Mantua Siege
III btn, K.k. IR 13 Rifle Rgt. Frh. Franz Wenzel Reisky von Dubnitz	To Prince Rohan Bde. (future Milano garrison)
I – II –III btns. cdr.: Obst Freiherr Carl von Brigido	
VII Combined Btn Grenzregiment Warasdiner of Varazdin	to Mantua Siege
K.k. 5th Hussar Rgt. 1 sqn	To Seckendorff Corps

March towards the Po

The general Chasteler orders, while leaving Milano, were the following:
On May 1st, the Austro-Russian army had to leave Milano advancing towards the Po, the Avant-Guard marching on Pavia. There they had to repair the bridge over the Ticino river and to build a bridgehead at Gravellona. Zoph, Fröhlich and Kaim (Melas) had to reach Lodi, the two Russians divisions (Bagration and Förster in the rear) marched through San Donato, Melegnano and Sant'Angelo, camping in the latter location. Bagration had the task to reach the Po (at Parpanese) and, eventually, to build a boat-bridge in front of Piacenza, after having seized the city from the right Po bank. Finally Klenau had to advance towards Piacenza in order to reach the Appennines passes on the road to Genoa. On the May 1st day the bulk of the Coalition's troops left Milano walls. They marched south, along the Melegnano road, in two large columns: the right one formed by Russians and directed towards Sant'Angelo, the left one formed by Austrians directed to Lodi. The Austrian Kolonne reached Casalpusterlengo, on May 2, and was preceded by an Avantgarde unit led by Oberst Knesevich, also him returned from the Tirol's front, who, in the same day, reached the important fortress of Piacenza. The "true" Avantgarde of the Austrian Corps was led, otherwise, by General Ott who had orders to enter Pavia on the Ticino river (colonel Knezevich was after attached to this unit as their Avantagarde).

▲ The entry of Suvorov in Milan 29 april 1799. Artwork by Adolf Iosifovich Charlemagne

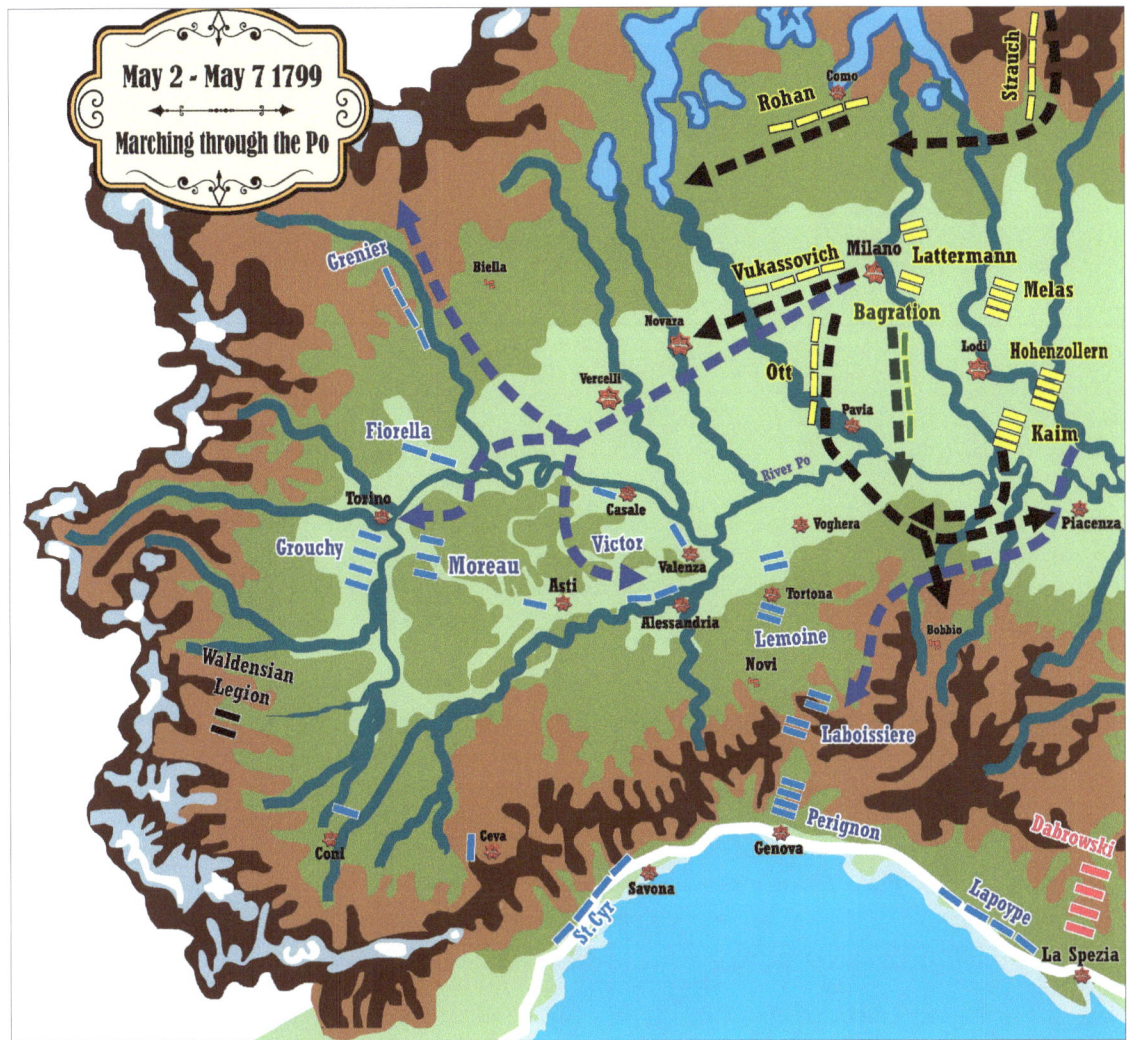

THE PO RIVER

The Po is known to every Italian as the country's longest river, is 652 kilometers (405 miles) long. The Po's waters, fed by 141 tributaries, created the Val Padana, the plain that stretches across northern Italy from the French border on the west to the Adriatic Sea on the east. *Il grande fiume*, the great river, ranges from Turin to some of the country's most beautiful and historic towns: Piacenza, Pavia, Cremona, Mantova, and Ferrara.

At that time, its width was very variable: 487 mt at Turin, 379 mt at Valenza (Valence), 303 mt before the Ticino (Tessin) tributary confluence and 455-530 mt after that confluence, 910 mt at Cremona, 1516 mt near the Taro confluence, only 474 mt at Casalmaggiore, 1396 at Guastalla, 384 mt at Borgoforte, 303 mt at Ostiglia, 484 mt at Occhiobello, 947 mt at Ponte Lagoscuro and only 240 mt at Polesella where it divided its course in several branches near the Adriatic sea. Its depth was usually from 3 mt to 4,50 mt, however, during the autumn-winter flood, it could have had a 18-19 meters depth. It had some permanent fords in its superior course and between the confluence of rivers Ticino and Lambro. After those, one could have found other fords between the Adda confluence and Cicognara, because of the presence of permanent sand banks. Generally Po river had rare and uncertain fords. The most important passages, over the Po, was very few. It did not have permanent bridges after Turin; at Casale Monferrato had a boat-bridge and other similar bridges were at Valenza, Mezzana-Corte (south of Pavia), Piacenza (Plaisance). Some ferry-boats or rafts, driven with ropes, were at Parpanese, Casalmaggiore, Viadana, Borgoforte, San Benedetto, Ostiglia, Occhiobello and Ponte Lagoscuro. As for its tributaries, the Ticino had only two bridges (Pavia and Boffalora).

Österreichische Italienische-Armée
Commander: Feld Marshal Leut. Michael Friedrich Benedikt Mélas
Generalquartiermeister: GM. Johann Gabriel Chasteler Marquis de Courcelles - HQ at Lodi

Avantguard Division Generalmajor Carl Peter Ott de Batorkéz	7507
Avantgarde Generalmajor Ferdinand Johann Morzin	
Jäger Korps Freiherr Constantin d'Aspre 6 coys	713
K.k. Light Btn. Nr. 15 Oberst Bonaventura Mihanovic (croat-slavonian)	795
VI Btn. of Banater Grenzregiment	546
Brigade Generalmajor Friedrich Freiherr Gottesheim	
K.k. IR 39 Rifle Line hungarian Inf. Rgt. Graf Thomas (Támas) Nádasdy	2106
(on 3 Btns.) – Cdr.: Freiherr Johann Nepomuk Abfaltern	
K.k. 7th Hussar Régiment 2 sqns.	188

PAVIA Had about 20.000 inh., on the Ticino river, which is passed by an 87 mt bridge, and on a channel called Naviglio di Pavia. It had only weak fortifications, one Citadel, eight barracks, some hospitals and renown schools (with University).

« Pour entrer dans la ville du côte du sud, il y a un superbe pont de pierre, dont la longueur de 518 pieds ; c'est un pont couvert, sous lequel passe le Tessin. A un quart de lieue, du même côte, coule un autre rivière, sur laquelle est un pont de bateaux (the Gravellone branch of Ticino. NdT) . Elle sert de limite aux Cisalpins et aux Piémontais. »

« A une lieue de Pavie, la route de Voghera traverse le Po sur un pont de bateaux long de 1204 pieds. » (bridge at Mezzana-Corti. NdT). Alexandre Botrouë, chef a la 68ᵉ demi-brigade.

Boffalora, on the Grande-Naviglio at its mouth into Ticino, which had a 515 mt bridge, build on 21 arcs and was managed by Sardinian and Austrian Administrations together.

LODI The seat of the Austrian HQs, was anciently a Celtic village that Romans called, in Latin, "Laus Pompeia" (probably in honour of consul Gnaeus Pompeius Strabo) and was also known because its position allowed many Gauls of Gallia Cisalpina to obtain Roman citizenship. A free Municipality around 1000, it fiercely resisted the Milanese, who destroyed it in April 24, 1158. Emperor Frederick the Barbarossa re-built it on its current location. Lodi was ruled by the Visconti family, who built a castle. In 1454 representatives from all the regional states of Italy met in Lodi to sign the treaty known as the peace of Lodi, by which they intended to work in the direction of Italian unification, but this peace lasted only 40 years. The town was then ruled by the Sforza family, France, Spain, Austria. In 1786 it became the eponymous capital of a province that included Crema. On May 10, 1796 the young Corsican general Buonaparte won on the river Adda his first important battle, defeating the Austrians and later entering Milan. After that battle the most important Adda's bridge became the Lodi's bridge. Memoir can be found in many French towns as in Paris, 6th arrondissement, Rue du Pont de Lodi.

Casalpusterlengo: All the territory between the two rivers Po and Ticino, had always been very important as military strategic central position since the Roman times. It had also a Roman ancient name: Casalis Pistorum. Around the XIV Century this locality became a feudal ownership of the Pusterla family (which name originated the town name). Allied of the Visconti, the Pusterla build a small castle (Castelletum) surrounded by a water ditch. In 1796 Bonaparte crossed the Po near Piacenza and organized his HQs at Casalpusterlengo before the Lodi battle. The town had always been commonly called Casale (and its inhabitants - Casalesi), even if the most famous Casale was that of Monferrato in Piedmont, on the Po.

The Austrian Main Column left Milano on May 1 and reached Lodi at 3.00 AM of the next day, passing through Melegnano. The head of the column was led by General Zoph, who detached 1 battalion Esterházy and 4 Hussars squadron, (as said under the command of Oberst Knesevich) towards Casale (Casalpusterlengo) where the French had weak outpost. Zoph was followed by Generals Kaim and Fröhlich with their divisions. During the same day, Knezevich passed through the Po on ferry-boats and reached Piacenza aklong the right Po bank.

Zoph's Avantgarde Detachment Oberst Vincenz Knesevich Freiherr von Saint-Helena	
At Casale Pusterlengo	
K.k. 2nd Hussar Régiment Erzherzog Joseph Anton - 4 sqns	576
II Btn. K.k. IR 34 hungarian Rifle Line Inf. Rgt. (the former Rgt Esterházy)	537

1st hungarian Division FML Johann Zoph	3748
At Lodi	
K.k. IR 34 hungarian Rifle Line Inf. Rgt. (the former Rgt Esterházy)	537
(no Inhaber. The future IR Frh. Kraj de Kraiova) (had the I and II Btn). Cdr.: Oberst Johann Hillinger	
K.k. IR 40 hungarian Rifle Line Inf. Rgt. FZM Graf Joseph Mittrowsky	1279
I and II btns. Cdr.: Oberst Franz Kreyssern.	
K.k. hungarian Grenadier Btn Oberleutnant Ferdinand Pers	199
K.k. Grenadier battalion Freiherr Georg von Stentsch Graf Anton Schiaffinati	620

Division Generalmajor Konrad Valentin Kaim	4644
Detached to Pizzighettone to siege the fortress	
K.k. IR 24 Rifle Rgt (former Preiss)	1424
(btns I – II – III) - Cmdr Oberst Carl Philipp von Weidenfeld	
K.k. IR 28 Rifle Rgt. Freiherr Michael von Fröhlich	2370
(the former Rgt Wartensleben – on 3 btns.) Cdr.:Oberst Paul Candiani de Ragaini	
K.k. 14th Light Dragoons Rgt. Franz Freiherr von Levenehr	850
Cdr.: Oberst Joseph Zinn. (it had 6 Sqns. On 3 div. I – II – III) II Div. ObLt. Josef Prohaska – III Div. Major Franz Graf Latour	

Division Generalmajor Freiherr Michael von Fröhlich Under provisional command of Generalmajor Franz Joseph Marquis de Lusignan	6409

at Lodi

Feldbrigade Generalmajor Franz Joseph Marquis de Lusignan	
K.k. IR 18 Rifle Line Inf. Rgt. Graf Patrick Stuart	1741
Cmdr. Obst Franz Weber von Treuenfels - I and II Btns	
K.k. IR 19 hungarian Rifle Line Inf. Rgt. Freiherr Jozsef Alvinczy de Berberek	1655
I and II Btns. + 2 Coys III Btn. - Cdr.: Barone Lelio Spannocchi	
K.k. 10th Light Dragoons Regiment Joseph Fürst Lobkowitz	836
(had 6 sqns. on 3 divisions I II and III) Cdr.: Oberst Marquis Hannibal Sommariva – Second Oberst and Commander Max Joseph Fürst Thurn und Taxis. II Div. ObstLt. Alois Graf Harrach – III Div. Major Ignatz Molitor	

Grenadiers Feldbrigade	
K.k. hungarian Grenadier battalion Major Joseph Korherr OberstLeutnant Johann Pértussy	618
K.k. Grenadier battalion Oblt Franz Xavier Weber von Treuenfeld (called Weber Btn.)	457
K.k. Grenadier battalion Graf Joseph Fiquelmont Count Johann Morzin	582
K.k. Grenadier battalion FML Karl Graf von Mercandin Graf Carl Paar	520

Austrian Cavalry detached to the Russians

K.k. 1st Light Dragoons Regiment "Emperor" Kaiser Franz II	1015
They had 6 sqns. on three divisions. Cdr.: Oberst Franz Freiherr von Pilati. II Div. ObstLt. Baron Karl Kölbel – III Div. Major Bernard Kees	
K.k. 4th Light Dragoons Rgt. GM Andreas Frh. von Karacsaj de Vale-Sakam	934
Had 6 sqns. Cdr.: Oberst Joseph Graf Nimptsch. It will be detached as link unit with the Russian Corps Rozenberg.	
K.k. 2nd Hussar Régiment Erzherzog Joseph Anton (4 sqn.)	575

Coalition's Army – Russian Main Army – (Glavnaja Armija)
Commander in chief: Field Marshal Aleksandr Vassiljevic Suvorov Graf Rimniksky

Infantry-general Andrej Grigorjevich Rozenberg Corps

The Russian Avantgarde was deployed along the Po bank, in the territory of the Parpanese village, where was a ferry boat, in front of San Giovanni. On May 2, it was reinforced by a Grenadier battalion in order to pass on the opposite bank the Po river, with the task to approach Piacenza from the right bank.

PIACENZA (Plaisance) not far from the confluence of river Trebbia into the Po. The large river had to be passed through a boat-bridge. It had a strong Citadel (it will be powered on 1832 by Austrians which kept the right to maintain there a garrison also after 1815. On the Trebbia river, there was a stone-wooden bridge built by the Austrians Archdukess Mary-Louise (Piacenza was part of the little Duchy of Parma-Piacenza and Guastalla). The town had some superior schools and a large palace, residence of the Dukes (Palazzo Ducale). It was renowned for the French passage during the Bonaparte's 1796 campaign. Near it, along the Trebbia, Hannibal defeated Romans and the Austrians bote the French on 1746 (an underextimated history sign!!).

Russian Avantgarde Brigade General Prince Petr Ivanovich Bagration	
Imperial Russian 7th Jäger (Jeghersky) Rgt. GM Bagration – 2 Btns	652
cmdr.: Gen. Petr Ivanovic Bagration	
5th Don Cossacks Rgt. Denissov	439
8th Don Cossacks Rgt. Grekov.	489
Imperial Russian Grenadier Btn (GB) Lomonosov	557

Division Lieut. General Ivan Ivanovich Förster (in Russian Ferster)	
Avantgarde Brigade general-major Nikolaj Andrejevic Chubarov [3] (or Shubarov)	
Imperial Russian 8th Jäger (Jegherski) Rgt. Major General Chubarov	708
Chief from May 13: GM Ivan Ivanovich Miller	
Don Cossacks Rgt. Semernikov (Semjornikov)	438
2nd Don Cossacks Rgt. Sujchev	454

Brigade general-major Mihail Mihailovich Veletskji	
Imperial Russian Musketeers rgt. Young-Baden or molodo-Badensky – 2 Btns	1395
Alias Butyrskowo (Butyrsk) - after may 18 renamed as GM Mihail Mihailovich Veletskji Rgt. its former commander	
Imperial Russian Musketeers rgt. GM Baron Ivan Ivanovich Dalheim – I and II btn	1438
or Archangelogorodsky (Archangelsk). Cmdr: Colonel Stepan Nikolajevich Castelli– 2 btns	
had as Chief, from June 26th, General Major Nikolay Mihailovic Kamensky 2nd	
Imperial Russian Grenadier Btn (GB) Sanajev Butyrsk and Archangelgorod Coys	599

Brigade general-major Jacob Ivanovich Tyrtov	
Imperial Russian Musketeers rgt. GM Tuyrtov or Tug'lsky (Tula) – I and II btn	1436
Cmdr.: Major Ivan Fjodorovich Golovin	
Imperial Russian Musketeers rgt. LG Povalo-Shveikovsky or Smolensky (Smolensk) – I and II Btn	1385
cmd: Colonel Grigoriy Dimitrjevich Kazakhovsky	
Imperial Russian Grenadier Btn (GB) Kalemin Tula and Tambow Coys	590

Division Lieut. General Jacob Ivanovich Povalo-Shvejkovsky 1st	
Brigade general-major Mihail Andrejevich Miloradovich 1st	
Imperial Russian Musketeers rgt. GM Mihail Andrejevich Miloradovich or Apsheronsky (Apsheron)	1459
Cmdr. : Lieut. Colonel Stepan Timofejevich Karlov – 2 Btns	
Imperial Russian Musketeers rgt. Lieut. General Förster (Tambov) - I Btn	755
Cmdr.: Lieut. Colonel Zaltser – II Btn detached to Prince Rohan	
Imperial Russian Grenadier Btn (GB) Dendrjugyn	544

Brigade general-major Mihail Semionovich Baranovsky 2nd	
Imperial Russian Musketeers rgt. GM Baranowsky II –	1388
or Nizowski Musk. Rgt. – I and II Btns. cmdr Colonel Mihail Aleksejevic Chitrowo	
Imperial Russian Grenadier Rgt. GdI Rozenberg or Moskowsky (Moskow) – I – II Btns.	1343
cmdr. (until June 10) Colonel Petr Petrovic Passek.	
Don Cossacks Rgt. Molchanov	495
6th Don Cossacks Rgt. Pasdejev (written Posdeev)	420

OTHER COALITION TROOPS – MAY 1st

Milano Siege Group Generalmajor Christoph Freiherr von Lattermann

K.k. IR 43 Rifle Line Inf. Rgt. Graf Anton Thurn-Val Sassina	1973
(IV, I and II Btns.) The III Btn. was at Zara (dalmatia) in garrison duty. Cdr.: Freiherr Ignaz von Loen	
K.k. IR 13 Rifle Line Inf. Rgt. Freiherr Franz Wenzel Reisky von Dubnitz	1851
(I, II and III Btns.) Cdr.: Oberst Freiherr Carl von Brigido	
K.k. 5th Hussar regiment– 2 Sqns – III Div. Major Ferdinand Steingruber	246

Pizzighettone Siege Group

Generalmajore Friedrich Freiherr von Seckendorff and Friedrich Xavier Fürst Hohenzollern-Hechingen

K.k. IR 32 Hungarian Rifle Rgt. Graf Samuel Gyulai	1482
Cmdr. Oberst Franz Posztrehowsky von Millenburg - (I-II-Btns) III btn to Mantua	

K.k. IR 36 Rifle Rgt. Fürst Carl Fürstenberg	2576
(I-II-III Btn) Cmdr. Oberst Conrad von Thelen	
VII Combined Btn Grenzregiment Warasdiner of Varazdin	627
K.k. 5th Hussar Regiment 6 Sqn. Cdr. Freiherr Andreas Szörenyi	826
It had 6sqns. On 3 Div.s I, II and III in reserve. The IV div. was in Croatia as garrison. Cdr.: Obst Anton Freiherr von Révay – II Div. ObstLt. Freiherr Andreas Szörenyi – 2nd Major Wilhelm Fulda present at the battle.	

Slow pontoons teams, a "Lawrence of Arabia" in Piedmont and a strange countermarch

After the Milano fall, the most important thing to do, for Suvorov, was to secure the Coalition's Army left flank. With Mantua besieged, "a thorn in the eye" as the Commander in Chief used to tell, and with General Klenau too weak to have a good control of the right Po banks from the sea to the new front, Suvorov requested the immediate construction of three boat-bridges over the Po, using materials captured at Cremona: two near Piacenza and one at Parpanese. The slow approaching march of the Coalized pontonniers allowed only the construction of the Piacenza facilities, the Parpanese one remaining only a project, with Staff Captain Fürstenberg waiting on the Po bank for nothing. General Vukassovich, who had seized the important Buffalora's bridge (the official Customs between Sardinia and Lombardy), was met by General Ott, come from Pavia to decide where the Avantgardes would have to advance. The two leaders decided also to send into Piedmont an old Hussar officer, previously serving in the Piedmontese army, with the task of organizing and arming partisans against the French: Major Branda de' Lucioni. [4] Vukassovich detached a formation of 25 Hussars from the 7th regiment calling it the "Streifskorps" (Patrol Corps) and sent them towards Novara. Lucioni and his partisans was absolutely prominent in the events which ended in the fall of Turin, the former capital of the Piedmontese Sardinian Kingdom; so an historical correlation with the job of Sir Lawrence, in Arabia during the Great War 1914-1918, doesn't seem so risky. From these men and from the countrymen, the two Avant-Guard Generals learned that the French had organized a line behind the river Sesia, joining the center of their army on the Po, at Valenza. This changed the Suvorov's mind. Suddenly General Ott was ordered to leave Pavia, to cross the Po on boats and to seize Piacenza, continuing the march until Parma and Modena, where he had to link with Klenau Corps. The "countermarch" of the Ott division was an apparently strange order, which many historians had difficulties to clarify. Why Suvorov ordered General Ott to invert his march towards Piedmont? The fact can be explained with the premise that:

a) – General Suvorov, at that time, was very concerned about the possible irruption of the Macdonalds Armée de Naples, against his weak left flank;

b) – in his mind the Right Wing, led by Austrians, would have to be put under General Bellegarde, coming from Switzerland, enclosing the strong Vukassovich vanguard brigade. The Left Wing, instead, had to be immediately reinforced, being Kray Corps blocked in front of Mantua.

It was necessary to send a "rapid deployment force", an Avantgarde, in Emilia, in order to secure the Po flank. The whole deployment along the Po river, in addition, had to be reformed. So Vukassovich was sent into Piedmont, in Avantgarde task and the central Avantgarde (Prince Bagration) was reinforced and sent westwards.

Reorganization of the Coalized Army

The "third" boat-bridge was decided to be constructed at Mezzana-Corte, south of Pavia. The reinforced Russian Avantguard of Prince Bagration was ordered to cross the Po by boats and, then, to reach Voghera and Tortona. The main Army was put in march to-

▲ The Boffalora bridge

wards Tortona, a very important town, which fortress had good probabilities of a long siege resistance and which controlled the road to Genova. On May 5, the first Russian engaged the French at Voghera. It was a short skirmish-combat with strange losses numbers reported: one Russian Grenadier dead, 2 Cossacks and one other Grenadier wounded, while 140 (14?) French were reported as dead with 10 French (one Officer prisoners).
By May 6 to 7, General Bagration strong brigade camped at Voghera.

VOGHERA the ancient named Viqueria in X Century was a walled town often involved in local wars for its strategic position In 1743 (Concordat of Worms) was given to the King of Savoy and five years later it became also a province capital. Its territories extended from Bobbio (higher Trebbia valley) to large parts of the Ligurians Appennines and comprised the Oltrepò Pavese land (the right Po bank part of Pavia province). The town was also the Bonaparte HQ in 1800 (Dattili Palace) before the Montebello battle (called Casteggio by the Austrians).

Russian Avantgarde Brigade General Prince Petr Ivanovich Bagration	
Imperial Russian 7th Jäger (Jeghersky) Rgt. GM Bagration – 2 Btns	652
cmdr.: Gen. Petr Ivanovic Bagration	
Imperial Russian Musketeers rgt. GM Baranowsky II – I Btn. cmdr Colonel Mihail Aleksejevic Chitrov	694
Imperial Russian Grenadier Rgt. GdI Rozenberg II Btn.	672
Imperial Russian Grenadier Btn (GB) Lomonosov	557
Imperial Russian Grenadier Btn (GB) Dendrjugyn	544
Don Cossacks Rgt. Molchanov	495
8th Don Cossacks Rgt. Grekov	489
(May 6-7) It was reinforced by	
Imperial Russian Grenadier Btn (GB) Kalemin Tula and Tambow Coys	590
5th Don Cossacks Rgt. Denissov	439
6th Don Cossacks Rgt. Pasdejev	420
K.k. 4th Light Dragoons Rgt. GM Andreas Frh. von Karacsaj de Vale-Sakam 2 Sqns.	310

The redeployment orders were distributed to the unit from May 5, at Corte d'Olona. In that village, near Pavia, General Rozemberg was ordered to substitute Bagration on the right Ticino bank. Here the Russians formed a second Avantgarde brigade, advancing until Lomello, in front of the powerful "river triangle" French position (were rivers Tanaro and Sesia got into the Po, a difficult and muddy terrain, full of swamps). By nature this land of earth-springs had been, for centuries, an impraticabile swamp, but the monks in the Middle Ages, and the feudal colonization of 1200's years, gradually introduced the rice cultivation. Particularly the Sforza family improved the territory, organizing a complex system of streams and channels wich made the land Lomellina a mosaic of cereals fields. The only structures, which had there some defensive value, were the Cascine (large farms with walled and closed yards).

LOMELLO had an old castle and was partially encircled by ditches and partially walled with two town-doors. The walls, in proximity of the Castle, had a small tower, directly raised from the bastion, called "Torrino (little tower) or Colombaia (building to keep the pigeons). Westwards of the castle flew a large stream, which gave water to the fields and, in part, filled up the castle ditch. The castle itself was very small, more similar to a large square fortified house. At Lomello was sent the:

Avantgarde Brigade general-major Nikolaj Andrejevic Chubarov	3075
Imperial Russian 8th Jäger (Jegherski) Rgt. Major General Chubarov	708
Chief from May 13: GM Ivan Ivanovich Miller	
Imperial Russian Grenadier Btn (GB) Sanajev Butyrsk and Archangelgorod Coys	599
Imperial Russian Musketeers rgt. GM Baron Ivan Ivanovich Dalheim – I btn	719
or Archangelogorodsky (Archangelsk). Cmdr: Colonel Stjepan Nikolajevich Castelli	
Don Cossacks Rgt. Semernikov (Semjornikov)	438
2nd Don Cossacks Rgt. Sujchev	454
K.k. 4th Light Dragoons Rgt. GM Andreas Frh. von Karacsaj de Vale-Sakam 1 Sqn.	157

Fieldmarshal Suvorov reached Bagration at Voghera (he was there on May 7) while Rozenberg deployed his two divisions in front of Pavia, at Dorno. It was an old village, given to Sardinia in 1707 by Austria. Life in the camp was very troubled. Troops of General Rozenberg used such violent behaviours to provoke riots among the peasants. That was a period of high crisis for the great mortality due to "Pellagra" [5], a carential disease which hit the starving populations; so, to the thefts of the Russian troops, were added those of local bands of hungry marauders. It was the prelude to the severe pestilence epidemy, which plagued the Sardinian provinces in 1799,

▲ Russian cossacks cavalry in 1799

worsening the soldiers conditions at the extreme point. The camp, otherwise, did not last for a long time. On May 8, Suvorov gave the order to advance against Valenza and Tortona, deceived by a false new of a French disengagement from the Po fortress Valenza.

At that time, in Italy travelled the son of the Czar, Prince Konstantin (Generalmajor Konstantin Pavlovich Romanov Grand Duke of Russia [6]), coming from Russia through Vienna. His Highness reached the Suvorov's Staff in Voghera (May 7) and the Commander in Chief, when he was announced, loudly screamed "Oh my Dear God! The Son of my Emperor!". The Imperial Prince was there with his own Staff, Cavalry General Derfelden [7], Aides Oferov, Safonov, Komarowsky and Lang.

The presence of a Romanov in the Coalized Army General Staff was very important. Since Suvorov was the Commander in Chief, he, otherwise, had the highest Austrian rank (Feldzeugmeister and after Generalissimus), he wore the white Imperial Austrian uniform and had to be politically very close to the Viennese aims. Having the Grand Duke in the HQ, allowed him to be more free in his political decisions (Suvorov's aims were to act in the name of the Sardinia's King in exile, while the Austrian target was to create a satellite Piedmont at the French borders). Suvorov wanted to re-establish "God and King" in Piedmont, so he got early in some diplomatic troubles with Hofkriegsrat and, mainly, with Austrian Minister Thugut.

Rozenberg Corps camp (at Dorno)	
Brigade general-major Mihail Mihailovich Veletskji	
Imperial Russian Musketeers rgt. Young-Baden or molodo-Badensky – 2 Btns	1395
Alias Butyrskowo (Butyrsk) - after may 18 renamed as GM Mihail Mihailovich Veletskji Rgt. its former commander	
Imperial Russian Musketeers rgt. GM Baron Ivan Ivanovich Dalheim –II btn	719
Brigade general-major Jacob Ivanovich Tyrtov	
Imperial Russian Musketeers rgt. GM Tuyrtov or Tug'lsky (Tula) – I and II btn	1436
Cmdr.: Major Ivan Fjodorovich Golovin	
Imperial Russian Musketeers rgt. LG Povalo-Shveikovsky or Smolensky (Smolensk) – I and II Btn	1385
cmd: Colonel Grigoriy Dimitrjevich Kazakhovsky	
Brigade general-major Mihail Andrejevich Miloradovich 1st	
Imperial Russian Musketeers rgt. GM Mihail Andrejevich Miloradovich or Apsheronsky (Apsheron)	1459
Cmdr. : Lieut. Colonel Stepan Timofejevich Karlov – 2 Btns	
Imperial Russian Musketeers rgt. Lieut. General Förster (Tambov) - I Btn	755
Cmdr.: Lieut. Colonel Zaltser – II Btn detached to Prince Rohan	
Brigade general-major Mihail Semionovich Baranovsky 2nd	
Imperial Russian Musketeers rgt. GM Baranowsky II – II Btn	694
Imperial Russian Grenadier Rgt. GdI Rozenberg or Moskowsky (Moskow) – I Btn.	671
cmdr. (until June 10) Colonel Petr Petrovic Passek.	

Austrian Cavalry detached to the Russians

K.k. 1st Light Dragoons Regiment "Emperor" Kaiser Franz II	1015
They had 6 sqns. on three divisions. Cdr.: Oberst Franz Freiherr von Pilati.	
I Div. ObstLt. Baron Karl Kölbel – III Div. Major Bernard Kees	
K.k. 4th Light Dragoons Rgt. GM Andreas Frh. von Karacsaj de Vale-Sakam 3 Sqns.	467
Cdr.: Oberst Joseph Graf Nimptsch.	
K.k. 2nd Hussar Régiment Erzherzog Joseph Anton (4 sqns.)	575
The «Light Blue Hussars» had 8 sqns. and four divisions. Cdr.: Oberst Vincenz Freiherr Knesevich (at Piacenza) II Div. ObstLt. Gabriel von Hertellendy – III Div. 1st Major Emmerich Dobay – IV Div. 2nd Major Ignaz baron Splenyi	

The Orders for the Austrian Army were the following:
1 – General Ott had to march through Piacenza to Parma, along the Emilia way, and finally had to reach Modena, where he had to meet General Klenau Korps. General Morzin had to be detached in Val di Trebbia to control the Appennines' pass near Bobbio and to secure the right Ott's flank.
From Venice, the Chief General de Montfrault had to commit a task-force, formed by 500 Dalmatians (former Venice Republic soldiers, called Oltramarini), embarked on the Venetian flotilla of Chioggia, which had to disembark between Comacchio, Mesola in order to take Ravenna, near the sea.

Avantguard Division Generalmajor Carl Peter Ott de Batorkéz	6356
Avantgarde Generalmajor Ferdinand Johann Morzin at Bobbio	2008
K.k. IR 40 Rifle Rgt. FZM Graf Joseph Mittrowsky I and II btns Cmdr. Oberst Franz Kreyssern	1279
III Btn K.k. IR 28 Rifle Rgt. Freiherr Michael von Fröhlich	729
End May: the III Btn. was detached. 4 coys recovered into Piacenza Citadel together with 2 coys of the 6th Banater Btn. 2 Coys detached at Bobbio in higher Trebbia valley.	
Brigade Generalmajor Friedrich Freiherr Gottesheim	4348
Jäger Korps Freiherr Constantin d'Aspre 6 coys	713
K.k. Light Btn. Nr. 15 Oberst Bonaventura Mihanovic (croat-slavonian)	795
VI Btn. of Banater Grenzregiment	546

K.k. IR 39 Rifle Line hungarian Inf. Rgt. Graf Thomas (Támas) Nádasdy	2106
(on 3 Btns.) – Cdr.: Freiherr Johann Nepomuk Abfaltern	
K.k. 7th Hussar Régiment 2 sqns.	188
Detachment Oberst Vincenz Knesevich Freiherr von Saint-Helena at Piacenza (attached to Ott Division)	
K.k. IR 28 Rifle Rgt. Freiherr Michael von Fröhlich I and II Btns.	1641
(the former Rgt Wartensleben) Cdr.:Oberst Paul Candiani de Ragaini	
K.k. 14th Light Dragoons Rgt. Franz Freiherr von Levenehr 2 Sqns.	283

General Kaim was sent to Pizzighettone in order to end that siege (with part of Hohenzollern and Seckendorff units), with the orders to return as soon as possible, marching towards Tortona.

Division Generalmajor Konrad Valentin Kaim	7134
Detached to Pizzighettone to siege the fortress	
K.k. IR 24 Rifle Rgt (former Preiss)	1424
(btns I – II – III) - Cmdr Oberst Carl Philipp von Weidenfeld	
K.k. IR 32 Hungarian Rifle Rgt. Graf Samuel Gyulai	1482
Cmdr. Oberst Franz Posztrehowsky von Millenburg - (I-II-Btns) III btn to Mantua	
K.k. IR 36 Rifle Rgt. Fürst Carl Fürstenberg	2576
(I-II-III Btn) Cmdr. Oberst Conrad von Thelen	
VII Combined Btn Grenzregiment Warasdiner of Varazdin	627
K.k. hungarian Grenadier Btn Oberleutnant Ferdinand Pers	199
K.k. 5th Hussar Regiment 6 Sqn. Cdr. Freiherr Andreas Szörenyi	826
It had 6sqns. On 3 Div.s I, II and III in reserve. The IV div. was in Croatia as garrison. Cdr.: Obst Anton Freiherr von Révay – II Div. ObstLt. Freiherr Andreas Szörenyi – 2nd Major Wilhelm Fulda present at the battle.	

Group Generalmajor Friedrich Xavier Fürst Hohenzollern-Hechingen

Detached to Milano, in order to take the command of the Capital and to deploy the Heavy Siege Park taken from Pizzighettone (4 guns – 28 pdrs., 4 mortars and 8 guns 12 pdrs.)
Imperial Russian artillery battery Lieut. Ivanov (from Pizzighettone). Had to join the main Russian Corps with its 6 guns – 12 pdrs. and 2 Unicorn ½ pood-guns.

Siege Group Generalmajor Johann (Giovanni) Graf Alcaini

After the Orzinuovi fortress fall had to march towards the Boffalora bridge in order to join the Right Wing (Vukassovich – Rohan – Strauch).

Milano Siege Group Generalmajor Christoph Freiherr von Lattermann

Had to wait Hohenzollern and to give him the command. Had to send 500 bread-rations to Como

The main Austrian Army had to wait Cambio's bridge finished (in front of Piacenza). Then hado to pass through the Po marching towards Voghera in order to reach Tortona, Torre Garofoli (near Alessandria) and Novi, to defend the roads to Genova.

Field Marshal Leut Michael Friedrich Benedikt Mélas	13865

Generalquartiermeister: GM. Johann Gabriel Chasteler Marquis de Courcelles

Division FML Johann Zoph	
Had to leave IR 28 at Piacenza with 2 Levenehr Sqns. (to Ott) and had to continue the march towards Voghera.	
K.k. IR 34 hungarian Rifle Line Inf. Rgt. (the former Rgt Esterházy)	1074
(no Inhaber. The future IR Frh. Kraj de Kraiova) (had the I and II Btn). Cdr.: Oberst Johann Hillinger	
K.k. 14th Light Dragoons Rgt. Franz Freiherr von Levenehr 4 sqns.	567
Cdr.: Oberst Joseph Zinn. (it had 6 Sqns. On 3 div. I – II - III)	
II Div. ObLt. Josef Prohaska – III Div. Major Franz Graf Latour	
Division Generalmajor Freiherr Michael von Fröhlich	

Had originally to march towards Pavia, pass over the Ticino, through Albignola and Sannazzaro de' Burgondi, along the left Po bank to reach a projected new bridgehead in a locations near Valenza. However its units waited at Casalpusterlengo and marched across the Po with Zoph.

Avantgarde Feldbrigade Generalmajor Graf Joseph Mittrowsky	
K.k. IR 8 Rifle Rgt. (former Huff Rgt)	2695
Cmdr. Obst Johann Schröckinger von Heidenburg (I-II III Btns)	
K.k. 2nd Hussar Régiment Erzherzog Joseph Anton - 4 sqns	576

Feldbrigade Generalmajor Franz Joseph Marquis de Lusignan	
K.k. IR 18 Rifle Line Inf. Rgt. Graf Patrick Stuart	1741
Cmdr. Obst Franz Weber von Treuenfels - I and II Btns	

K.k. IR 19 hungarian Rifle Line Inf. Rgt. Freiherr Jozsef Alvinczy de Berberek	1655
I and II Btns. + 2 Coys III Btn. - Cdr.: Barone Lelio Spannocchi	
K.k. 10th Light Dragoons Regiment Joseph Fürst Lobkowitz	836
(had 6 sqns. on 3 divisions I II and III) Cdr.: Oberst Marquis Hannibal Sommariva – Second Oberst and Commander Max Joseph Fürst Thurn und Taxis. II Div. ObstLt. Alois Graf Harrach – III Div. Major Ignatz Molitor	

Grenadiers Feldbrigade	
K.k. hungarian Grenadier battalion Major Joseph Korherr OberstLeutnant Johann Pértussy	618
K.k. Grenadier battalion Oblt Franz Xavier Weber von Treuenfeld (called Weber Btn.)	457
K.k. Grenadier battalion Graf Joseph Fiquelmont Count Johann Morzin	582
K.k. Grenadier battalion FML Karl Graf von Mercandin Graf Carl Paar	520
K.k. Grenadier battalion Freiherr Georg von Stentsch Graf Anton Schiaffinati	620

NOTES

1 Gilles Joseph Martin Bruneteau, Viscount de Sainte-Suzanne, count of Empire, was born in Mothé near Poivre (Aube), March 7, 1760. First Lieutenant with regiment of Anjou in 1779; when the Revolution outbroke, he adopted its principles, fought with distinction in the defence of Mainz. He quickly arrived at the rank of brigade general, in the armée de Rhine-and-Moselle. When Desaix carried out the passage of the Rhine, Sainte-Suzanne engaged the Austrians, who arrived from higher Rhine, was at Simmern, Urlafen and Windschliegen, where he captured many prisoners. In 1796 he was charged with the command of 5th military division (Strasbourg). He was at Kehl fortress and then he was called at the War Office, where he was pointed out by his knowledge. In 1799, the Government having offered to him a provisional command as an army Chief, at the armée d'Italie, generale Sainte-Suzanne refused it, agreeing to manage the Cisalpine capital city, Milan. In the following year he was at the army of the Danube, under Moreau, leading the left wing, 16.000 men strong.
He moved on Ulm, as ordered by Moreau, and was attacked by the Austrian, leaving the left Danube bank. Then Sainte-Suzanne aws charged to organize the Reserve Corps formed at Mainz. With these tropps he advanced, crossed again the Danube and defeated the Austrians at Neu Wissembourg and Hanau. He was named Grand Officier of the Order de la Légion d'Honneur and Senateur directly from Napoleon. On May 19, 1806, he received the Senate district of Pau, and, in 1807, the command of the 2nd Reserve Legion. Named Inspector of the Boulogne camp, in 1809, he made all the provisions useful to put the camp in a substantial safety. For these merits he was created count of the Empire. In 1814, he agreed with the acts of the provisional Government, become Pair of France, knight of Saint-Louis, "commandant d'armes" at Landau in 1815, and, on August 31, he obtained the patent letter from Louis XVIII which confirmed the title of Count.

2 Feldmarschall Freiherr Christoph von Lattermann (born at Olmütz – Olomouc on July 14th 1753 – died in Vienna on 5.10.1835). Son of a famous commander, baron Franz Lattermann, the Owner of KK IR 45 in 1792.

3 Generalmajor Nikolaj Andrejevic Chubarov – lieutenant colonel (from 01.10.1797 colonel, c 20.08.1798 general-major). From 17.05.1797 to 17.01.1799 – commander 8th Rgt. Jäger. From 17.01.1799 to 13.05.1799 Chef (Owner) 8th Rgt. Jäger.

4 Major Branda Lucioni, 8th Hussar Rgt. (detached to the 7th), was born in 1740 in Winterberg (today Vimperk) in Bohemia, where his father, an italian Officer from Abbiate Guazzone, near Tradate, was in garrison duty. In 1799 he was 59 years old, having had a slow military career. On April, 28th 1799, leading an austrian hussars patrol, he entered Milano, still occupied by French. People were very enthusiast with that early patrol so, Austrian commanders, gave him a wild-card to organize italian catholic insurgents against French. On 1st of May he passed the Ticino to organized sabotages along the river banks (blocking the French fording) and then began the recruitment (reclutamento a massa) of the lombard "paysans". The signal of the Insurgent Mass call to arms was a rythmic bells sound, similar to a fast hammer beating (campane a martello). The Lucioni Corps (variable from 6000 to 10000 bad armed landfellows and catholic farmers) was called Christ's Mass (Ordinata Massa Cristiana) and its Mission was a deep hate against the French, "cursed by the Lord". On May 13th he did a "Proclama" to the people requesting to avoid pillages and personal vengeances and, fighting, he approached Turin. His men, called "brandaluccioni or branda", achieved the result to blockade the city, with the Turin National Guard inactive and uncertain on what to do. General Fiorella, the Turin commander in the Citadel, became very angry with allied Piedmontese troops, calling the Brandas "brigands, son of a slave ..."
Two French expeditions (17 and 19 may) failed the task to sweep away Insurgents. On may 24th finally the Austrians arrived

in Turin (general Vukassovic), together with the Russian avantgarde of general Bagration, and the city fell. On June, 9th Fiorella capitulated leaving the Citadel and going to prisony. Major Branda Lucioni, retired during the same year, died in Vicenza on August 22, 1803.

5 **Pellagra** is a vitamin deficiency disease caused by dietary lack of niacin (vitamin B3) and proteins, especially proteins containing the essential amino acid tryptophan. Pellagra was first described in Spain in 1735. It was an endemic disease in northern Italy, where it was named "pelle agra" (pelle, skin; agra, sour); probably caused by a poor diet based only on corn (Polenta) or where the maize was the dominant food crop. The symptoms usually appeared during spring, increase in the summer due to greater sun exposure. The main results of pellagra can easily be remembered as "the four D's": diarrhea, dermatitis, dementia, and death.

5 **Generalmajor Konstantin Pavlovic Romanov Grand-duke of Russia** Constantine was born at Tsarskoye Selo on 27 April 1779. Of the sons born to the tsar Paul Petrovich and his wife Maria Feodorovna, the princess of Württemberg, none more closely resembled his father in bodily and mental characteristics than did the second, Constantine Pavlovich. The direction of the boy's upbringing was entirely in the hands of his grandmother, the empress Catherine II. As in the case of her eldest grandson (afterwards the emperor Alexander I), she regulated every detail of his physical and mental education; but in accordance with her usual custom she left the carrying out of her views to the men who were in her confidence. Count Nicolai Ivanovich Saltykov was supposed to be the actual tutor, but he too in his turn transferred the burden to another, only interfering personally on quite exceptional occasions, and exercised neither a positive nor a negative influence upon the character of the exceedingly passionate, restless and headstrong boy. The only person who really took him in hand was Cesar La Harpe, who was tutor-in-chief from 1783 to May 1795 and educated both the empress's grandsons. Like Alexander, Constantine was married by Catherine when he was not yet seventeen years of age (26 February 1796), a raw and immature boy, and he made his wife, Juliane of Saxe-Coburg-Saalfeld (Queen Victoria's aunt), intensely miserable. After the first separation in the year 1799, she went back permanently to her German home in 1801, the victim of a frivolous intrigue, in the guilt of which she was herself involved. An attempt made by Constantine in 1814 to win her back to his hearth and home broke down on her firm opposition.

7 **Cavalry General Otto Wilhelm Hristoforovich Derfelden** - (1735 - 1819). In 1757 he began his service as Corporal in the Horseguards. He bote the Turks at Maksimen and Galatz, during the second Turkish War (1789); promoted by Suvorov after the Turks defeats at Focsani and Rymnik. During military actions against Poles he took part in the assault at Prague (1794) obtaining the St. George 2nd Class Cross. In 1795 he was promoted to the rank of General in Chief. In 1797 he retired. In 1799 Derfelden was early recalled as general Cavalry Inspector of the Finland and St. Petersburg divisions; then he was again appointed to service, with the assignment to escort grand duke Konstantin Pavlovich to Italy. Suvorov immediately entrusted to him a Corps command.

▲ Russian Don cossacks cavalry in 1799

Division Lecourbe in Switzerland May, 1799

36th Line Infantry Half-brigade

44th Line Infantry Half-brigade

109th Line Infantry Half-brigade

I Bn. 38th Line Infantry Half-brigade

12th Dragoons one Sq.

12th Light Infantry Half-brigade

76th Line Infantry Half-brigade

6th Line Infantry Half-brigade Detachment

II Bn. 38th Line Infantry Half-brigade

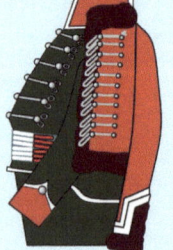
Cisalpine Hussars and Guides

THE SWITZERLAND BORDER COMBATS MAY-JUNE 1799

THE NORTHERN FLANK THE ADVANCE OF THE K.K. TIROLER ARMÉE

Threats from the North

During the few days, in which Suvorov had a rest in Milano, couriers reported French movements from the Switzerland against Canton Ticino and, therefore, against the lakes situated north of Milano (Maggiore and Como). The Como garrison was alerted and general Strauch was sent there to secure the Lake Maggiore banks. General Vukassovich was sent towards Novara to engage the French rearguard. The Northern flank of the two armies was initially in Valtelline, where operated the link units between Italy anf Grisons (Graubünden fronts).

Valtelline

(Ger. Veitlin; the name comes from the former capital, Teglio, near Tresenda), properly the name of the upper valley of Adda, in north Italy. Historically and officially, it also comprises the Italian Liro or San Giacomo valley, which extends from the Splugen Pass past Chiavenna (where the Liro is absorbed by the Mera, flowing from the Swiss Val Bregaglia) to the Lake of Como, the Mera entering this lake slightly to the north of the Adda. In 1797 Bormio and Valtellina were annexed to the Cisalpine republic, in 1805 to the kingdom of Italy (of which Napoleon was king), and in 1815 (despite the remonstrances of the Raetian leagues) to the kingdom of Lombardo-Venetia, held by the emperor of Austria. In 1859 they became, like the rest of Lombardy, part of the kingdom of united Italy. Poschiavo followed the fortunes of the "Gotteshausbund." It became (after 1798) part of the canton Raetia of the Helvetic republic, and in 1803 of the canton of the Graubunden or Grisons, which was then first received a full member of the Swiss Confederation.

The French deployment at the Swiss borders was initially offensive in order to try the southern link with the Schérer's army. When the 1799 Campaign outbroke (Masséna was the first to move troops forward), the French border's unit, operating on Valtelline Alps, was the General Dessolle brigade. It was a mix of French and Cisalpine troops, having this formation during the early phase of 1799 campaign and before Magnano battle.

Division General Jean-Joseph-Paul-Augustin Dessolle (called Dessolles) [1]	
in Valtellina	5091
ADC: Adjudant général Fressinet : Brigadiers : Antoine-Louis-Popon Maucune	
Artillery (2nd Piedmontese artillery brigade Colonel Cappello) and Sappers	343
Cisalpine Expeditionary Detachment btns I and II	700
12th Light Demi Brigade Chef Guy Louis Henry Valory [2]	2000
39th Line Demi Brigade Chef Antoine-Louis-Popon Maucune [3]	2000
12th Rgt. Chasseurs	48

** Clausewitz gives a total of 6500 men with Lechi – In campaign they were no more than 3500

Brigade General Conte Giuseppe Lechi	1771
ADC: Adjudant général Andrea Miloshevich	
Cisalpine 3rd Line Demibrigade Chef de Brigade Andrea Miloshevic, Dalmatian Italian	1328
(the DB had 3 Battalions - I/3 Chef Morosini and after Guidoni, then Cappi, II/3 Scotti, III/3 Martincourt)	
I Btn 1st Cisalpine Light Demi-Brigade (btn Girard)	443
Detached	
Cisalpine Volunteers Troops at Lecco (National Guard)	700

After Magnano, Dessolle was ordered to join the Armée d'Italie leaving the Border's control to Lecourbe division. On April 4, after the Taufers combat, the tired general Dessolle brigade reached Tirano, in Valtelline, where he left the command of the garrison to general Loison and from where he began his travel to the south, to join Moreau army, on April 20. In the mean time an Austrian Avantgarde Group was detached, by Bellegarde, from the K.k. Tiroler Armée to substitute the already engaged Vukassovich Gruppe. At the time when Dessolle left the valley, in Val Camonica, north of Bergamo, was deployed the Oberst Strauch's brigade.

May 27-28, 1799 — Battle of St. Gotthard

Tyroler Armée general Bellegarde Avant-guards	
Avantgarde Feldbrigade Oberst Gottfried von Strauch 4 (IR 11 commander)	7181
Strauch, with the Engadin front moving forward, entered the val Camonica. He decided to place his outposts roughly from Edolo to the Incudine, because of the enemy dislocation on mountain Mortirolo, and, in the night before April 29, along with 4 battalions, 7 companies and an half squadron began the advance march to link with the armies in Italy, while, on Tonale pass (4 btns and half squadron in Val Camonica with outposts at Tonale pass), was left Colonel count Carneville with 4 battalions, a half schwadron and an unit of Tyroler Landesschützen. Count Bellegarde sent themselves the instruction to immediately advance against Tirano, securing the right over Puschiavo, and the left over Morbegno, with Colonel Strauch always in taut connection with him in order to receive real time news about the enemy.	
K.k. IR 11 Rifle regiment (former Graf Michael Wallis)	1923
I – II Btns. (III btn. left behind as garrison - IV btn at Prag - Bohemia) – Cdr.: Oberst Gottfried von Strauch	
K.k. Grenadier bataillon Graf Nikolaus Weissenwolf	772
I Btn K.k. IR 30 Rifle Inf. Rgt. Fürst Carl Joseph de Ligne Cdr. Oberst August Husmanns – 3 Coys	300
K.k. 10th Light Infantry Btn. Oberlieutenant Franz von Siegenfeld (italian-venetian)	892
Jäger Freikorps Major Johann Le Loup (dutch Btn. - 1 coy)	112
K.k. 9th Hussar Rgt. FML Johann Nepomuk Graf Erdödy de Monyorókerek (Erdödy Husaren)	65
Reaching the Italian plain the Erdödy squadron was re-united under Strauch (115 men) and half 7th Hussars squadron was attached to Rohan's brigade	
And, following Strauch's brigade, part of the same command, and with the task to link right with the Tiroler Army at Poschiavo, left with Strauch Group, leading towards Tirano, was the:	
Detachment Oberst Graf Georg Simon de Carneville	
Tiroler Schützen Botzen, Sterzing, Neumarkt, Passeier Freiherr von Cazan 4 coys	320
K.k. 11th Light Infantry Btn. Oberst Graf Georg Simon de Carneville (istrian)	434
III Btn. K.k. IR 11 Rifle regiment (former Graf Michael Wallis)	950
I Btn Banal Grenzregiment or I Btn - 11th Banal Rgt. of Petrinja - Major Boichetta	781
III btn Grenzregiment of Banat (or II/12 GR Deutschbanater - Major Anton Zedtwitz)	682
K.k. 9th Hussar Rgt. FML Johann Nepomuk Graf Erdödy de Monyorókerek (Erdödy Husaren)	50

Carneville detachment was followed and supported by another Tyroler Armée's unit, sent to support the Advance towards the lower Adda. The books called its commander La Marcel, Lamarselle a.s.o. but the unit was the:

Feldbrigade Generalmajor Oberst Ludwig Wolff de la Marseille [5]	3137
I btn 5th Grenzregiment Warasdiner-Kreuzer of Varazdin	693
I btn K.k. IR 9 Rifle Rgt. (former Clerfayt) Cdr.: Obst Ludwig Wolff de la Marseille	606
K.k. IR 33 Rifle Rgt. Graf Anton Sztaray	1838
I – II - III btns. Cdr.: Oberst Johann Kalnássy de Kalnáss	

It remained for some time as Valtelline garrison. Then he reached the Bellegarde army in Piedmont.
After the Adda battles it was necessary to garrison the access to the Swiss canton Ticino. So the Austrians sent a brigade to Como and to the homonym lake, north of Milano.

Como April 30 - May 7, 1799

COMO. In 1127 Como lost the Ten years war against the nearby town of Milan. A few decades later, with the help of Federico the Barbarossa, German Emperor, its citizens, the "Comaschi", had the revenge when Milan was destroyed in 1162. The city had walls and Federico promoted the construction of several defensive towers around the city borders, of which only one remains, the Baradello tower.

From that time Como followed the events of the Duchy of Milan, through the French invasion, then the Spanish domination until 1714, when the territory was taken by the Austrians. Napoleon descended into Lombardy in 1796 and French again ruled it until 1815, when the Austrian Government was resumed.

Feldbrigade Oberst Prinz Victor von Rohan [6]	2609
Jäger Freikorps Major Johann Le Loup (dutch Btn. - 3 coys)	359
III btn. K.k. IR 52 Hungarian Rifle Rgt. Erzherzog Palatin Anton Viktor	764
K.k. Light Btn. N. 14 Oberst Prince Ludwig (Louis) Rohan (italian Btn.)	590
K.k. 7th Hussar Rgt. Half sqn.	60
Pioneers Detachment	81
Imperial Russian Musketeers rgt. LG Förster (Ferster) or Tambowski (Tambov) – II Btn (attached after May 6)	755

Valtelline Garrison
Armée d'Helvetie – Right Wing (May 4, 1799)

2nd Right Wing Division General Claude-Jacques Lecourbe

* numbers from "Mémoires de Masséna"	10483
Brigade generals : Loison and Demont	
Artillery and sappers	184
36th Line Demi-brigade– I and II btn – Chef Pierre Bellon Lapisse	1569
44th Line Demi brigade – I and II btn - Chef Jean Bertholet	1976
109th Line Demi-brigade – I and II btn - Chef Jean-François Clerc [7]	1843
38th Line Demi-brigade Chef Marie-Guillaume Daumas	1586
12th Rgt. Chasseurs Chef général François-Joseph Offenstein	115
12th Light Demi brigade Chef Guy Louis Henry Valory	1247
76th Line Demi-brigade Chef-de-brigade Goré – I and II btn	1955

The Division was divided in two groups:

Armée d'Helvetie – Right Wing

2nd Right Wing Division General Claude-Jacques Lecourbe [8]

* numbers extimated	4234
Artillery and sappers	134
36th Line Demi-brigade– I and II btn – Chef Pierre Bellon Lapisse	1065
44th Line Demi brigade – I and II btn - Chef Jean Bertholet	1175
109th Line Demi-brigade – I and II btn - Chef Jean-François Clerc	1245
I Btn 38th Line Demi-brigade Chef Marie-Guillaume Daumas	590
12th Rgt. Chasseurs chef général François-Joseph Offenstein [9]	115

This were the French units in the Italian-Swiss borders on May 4, 1799. Above is the former General Demont (taken prisoner) brigade of Lecourbe division.

General Lecourbe, having lost the flanking left right link brigade Dessolle, which had joined the main army in Piedmont, sent one of his brigades (Loison) to secure the right flank. After the Adda battle Loison was forced to withdraw along the Misoccersthal (Mesolcina, from Chiavenna through Splügen pass) by general Strauch ad-

▲ The Suvorov troops passage of St. Gotthard Pass in 1799 .

vance. On May Lecourbe left Lenz (reached on 4th), passed the St. Gotthard and joined Loison (May 10) at San Giacomo. Both reached Bellinzona on May 11, with a force of about 8000 men (Clausewitz).
The Austrian entered Chiavenna (May 8-9) and found 26 bronze guns with other 10 iron pieces abandoned from Loison's sudden retreat.

Brigade General Louis-Henri Loison[10] from Tonale-Valtelline to Canton Ticino – Airolo - * numbers extimated	3707
Artillery and sappers	50
12th Light Demi brigade Chef Guy Louis Henry Valory	1247
76th Line Demi-brigade Chef-de-brigade Goré – I and II btn	1055
6th Line Demi brigade detachment	240
II Btn 38th Line Demi-brigade	600
Expeditionnary forces I and II btns.	400
Cisalpine Hussars and Guides	115

May 10 – the Austrian Advance
General Carneville was ordered to join Strauch at Tirano (Valtelline). The K.k. Tyroler Armée advanced into Grisons and its Avantagarde brigade St. Julien reached Süs with 3 battalions, having 10 coys deployed to secure the mountain-flanks. General Loison kept occupied the Splügen Pass (the road from Chiavenna to the Canton Ticino) with 900 men. Lecourbe and 8000 French passed over San Bernardino Pass and entered Bellinzona meeting Loison at San Giacomo. General Rohan advanced from Como to Lugano and Bironico. He was too weak to resist to an eventual Lecourbe's attack.

Feldbrigade Oberst Gottfried von Strauch (IR 11 commander)	4914
Jäger Freikorps Major Johann Le Loup (dutch Btn. - 1 coy)	112
K.k. Grenadier bataillon Graf Nikolaus Weissenwolf	772
K.k. IR 11 Rifle regiment (former Graf Michael Wallis)	1923
I – II Btns. (III btn. left behind as garrison - IV btn at Prag - Bohemia) – Cdr.: Oberst Gottfried von Strauch	
K.k. 11th Light Infantry Btn. Oberst Graf Georg Simon de Carneville (istrian)	434
K.k. 10th Light Infantry Btn. Oberleutenant Franz von Siegenfeld (italian-venetian)	892
I Btn Banal Grenzregiment or I Btn - 11th Banal Rgt. of Petrinja - Major Boichetta	781

This Corps remained in Valtelline

Feldbrigade Generalmajor Oberst Ludwig Wolff de la Marseille	4437
I btn 5th Grenzregiment Warasdiner-Kreuzer of Varazdin	693
I btn K.k. IR 9 Rifle Rgt. (former Clerfayt) Cdr.: Obst Ludwig Wolff de la Marseille	606
I Btn K.k. IR 30 Rifle Inf. Rgt. Fürst Carl Joseph de Ligne Cdr. Oberst August Husmanns – 3 Coys	300
K.k. IR 33 Rifle Rgt. Graf Anton Sztaray	1838
I – II btns. Cdr.: Oberst Johann Kalnássy de Kalnáss	
III Btn. K.k. IR 11 Rifle regiment (former Graf Michael Wallis)	950
K.k. 9th Hussar Rgt. FML Johann Nepomuk Graf Erdödy de Monyorókerek (Erdödy Husaren)	50

Prince Rohan in Canton Ticino
"On May 11, at Lugano, arrived the Austro-Russian force of about 3000 men, before the evening. They were headed by some "fourriers" who ordered to burn out all the Liberty-trees ... The Imperial troops were received from Lugano citizens with pleasure and enjoyment, along with high "hurray" cries ... Those troops stopped a while to eat and rest, then, in the night

darkness, set off towards Monte Ceneri, where the French were camped. At dawn it began a strong fire fight, which lasted all the day; however it was not decisive because the French remained in their position. Incoming the evening, the Austro-Russians camped along the Agno bank until the Bironiche...

Many of those villages, where Imperial troops and particularly the Prince Rohan Companies marched through or camped, were damaged. They looted all what they could steal, money, furnitures and all sorts of transportable things. Also the Russian stole a lot, but in a more polite way: they gave compliments and hugs to whom they met along the road, then, chuckling, took their watches, belts (if men), rings, jewellery, earrings, gold or silver (if women), what they could find. The Russian had the tradition to make their religious Christian Orthodox sign of the Cross sign before every thieving act. "

Source Rinaldo Caddeo, *I primi anni del Risorgimento Ticinese nella Cronaca inedita di Antonio Maria Lagh"*, Modena 1938, pp. 65.

Canton Ticino

(or Tessin*)*, a canton of Switzerland, situated on the southern gradient of the Helvetic Alps and inhabited by a population of which the majority speaks Italian. It takes its name from the Ticino river, which have its upper part within the canton, until the Lago Maggiore, in which he ends its Switzerland course.

The canton had many different conquests performed by different members of the Swiss Confederation. Historically the Italian Switzerland had three territories: (1) the Val Leventina conquered by canton Uri in 1440; (2) Bellinzona; the Riviera and the Val Blenio, all conquered in 1500 from the duchy of Milan by cantons Uri, Schwyz and Nidwalden; (3) Locarno, Val Maggia, Lugano and Mendrisio, seized in 1512 by the Swiss Confederates coalized in a Holy League against France. These districts were led, until the last 1700's years, by local chiefs called "bailiffs".

In 1798 the people were divided among the conservative Swiss and the progressist republican "Cisalpine " parties, but remained with the Swiss. Having rejected their historical chiefs, they organized two new cantons of the Helvetic republic - Bellinzona and Lugano. In 1803 officially born the Canton Ticino, becaming a full component of the Swiss Confederation. From 1810 to 1813 it was occupied by the French troops of the Emperor. The carriage road over the St Gotthard (1820-1830) was begun to be projected (and built) in 1814, while before that year only mountain tracks passed over the Alps. Bellinzona (or Bellenz) was the real political capital of Canton Ticino. The town is 105 Km far from Lucerne, 19 Km. from Lugano and 14 Km. from Locarno aside of Lake Maggiore, these two towns having been also former canton capitals. Bellinzona, in 1500, was occupied by Uri and, three years after, the French King allowed its management to cantons Uri, Schwyz and Unterwalden, which ruled it very unkindly, through their bailiffs, until 1798. In that year it became the capital of the canton Bellinzona while in 1803 it was united to the newly-formed canton Ticino.

▲ St. Gotthard Pass occupied by Suvorov troops in 1799 . Paint of A. Kotsebu (1815-1889)

May 12. First combat at Monte Cenere (today Monte Ceneri)
General Strauch left Chiavenna in order to support Prince Rohan. The latter boldly attacked the Monte Ceneri's French outposts, surprising them and claiming 300 prisoners. The Prince took position into the former French defences.

May 13. Second combat at Monte Cenere
Prince Rohan had deployed his outpost on Monte Ceneri to watch the St. Gotthard road. On May 13 he was attacked by Lecourbe vanguard and repulsed behind the "Lakes line", the middle point of which was at Ponte Tresa. After this combat, Lecourbe, having had news of an Austrian advance in Grisons returned to St. Gotthard pass leaving the lone Loison to front Rohan. However other Austrian units were coming (Strauch from the Splügen pass and Hohenzollern from Milan).

Milano May 12, 1799

Feldbrigade GeneralMajor Friedrich Xavier Fürst Hohenzollern-Hechingen	
K.k. IR 24 Rifle Line Rgt (former Preiss)	1424
(btns I – II – III) - Cmdr Oberst Carl Philipp von Weidenfeld	
VII Combined Btn Grenzregiment Warasdiner of Varazdin	627

May 14-16. Another Prince arrived
The K.k. Tiroler Armée concentrated its troops (division Hadik - brigades De Briey and Nobili) in the valley of Albula, brigade Friedrich Bellegarde at Fillisur. General Lamarseille was at Castasegna (he occupied Chiavenna and the Splügen Pass, left by Strauch, during the next day 17). General Bellegrade received new orders from Vienna (Hofkriegsrat): he had to leave Switzerland reaching Suvorov in Italy for the widening of the new Italian front. General Strauch was near Bellinzona but, above all, Prince Hohenzollern reached Como (Ponte Tresa on may 17) with 5 battalions and a Russian artillery battery.

Como May 16

Feldbrigade GeneralMajor Friedrich Xavier Fürst Hohenzollern-Hechingen	
Imperial Russian Artillery Reserve battery – 4 guns	
K.k. IR 24 Rifle Line Rgt (former Preiss)	950
(btns I – II) - Cmdr Oberst Carl Philipp von Weidenfeld	
III Btn K.k. IR 43 Rifle Line Rgt Graf Anton Thurn-Val Sassina	659
K.k. IR 13 Rifle regiment Freiherr Franz Wenzel Reisky von Dubnitz	1234
I – II –btns. cdr.: Obst Freiherr Carl von Brigido	
K.k. 5th Hussar Rgt. 1 sqn	123

May 18. The Taverne (Taverna) battle
The Hohenzollern "rescue" Group reached Ponte Tresa at midnight of May 17-18. Oberst Brigido with his battalions, the Russian battery and the Hussars squadron marched from Ponte Stresa to Agno and there Hohenzollern divided his brigade in three small Columns advancing towards Taverna (Taverne). At dawn (18) the demi-brigade at Taverna was driven back. General Lecourbe Rear-guard recovered to Bironico while Austrians began the third attack on Monte Ceneri. The French were pushed back north and had heavy losses (about 400 men out of combat of which around 100 Officers were made prisoners). Loison retreated to Bellinzona where he was forced to abandon the town in a hurry, losing 10 guns. He reached Biasca in the middle Ticino covering the St. Gotthard Pass – Airolo road.

The Austrian losses were: 9 dead and 25 wounded. Before returning to the siege of Milano, Hohenzollern left the front line on new positions: Prince Rohan from Lugano, Ponte Tresa until Luino, after the occupation of Taverna; Strauch camped at Lugano. Rohan kept two battalion of the Hohenzollern group (they will be the future Milano garrison).

III Btn. K.k. IR 43 Rifle Line Rgt Graf Anton Thurn-Val Sassina
III btn, K.k. IR 13 Rifle Rgt. Frh. Franz Wenzel Reisky

General Nobili reached the Splügen Pass through Tufis, followed and supported by St. Julien. On May 20, Bellegarde got a Suvorov's letter with the order to march towards Chiavenna and to enter Lombardy. On May 23 the K.k. Tiroler Armée Left Wing was at Chiavenna with Hadik Division and Loudon's brigade. The Austrian HQs were put there, waiting to continue the march. General Friedrich Bellegarde was sent at Morbegno as garrison and Nobili was advanced towards the Splügen Pass, waiting to understand which the Lecourbe's intentions were. In Ticino Rohan pushed forward two battalions at Biasca, abandoned by the French and camped at Giornico on May 26. General Strauch stood at Bellinzona with 3 battalions and his cavalry. On May 26 he was reached by General Hadik's Staff, which did not stop there continuing the march towards St. Gotthard. He took the command of the Avantguard Prince Rohan detachment. In the morning of May 27 the Austrian column overrun the French outposts at Piotta village, forced them to withdraw in Airolo.

May 27-28 The Sankt Gotthard Pass battle

Fieldmarschal Leut. Hadik began a mountain "guerrilla" combat against the French (around 2000) at Airolo-St. Gotthard. General Lecourbe was forced to strengthen the pass with other 900 infantrymen. The French resisted until the following day. On 28 evening, at 6.00 PM, General Strauch renewed the attack against Airolo, in a more traditional way, with three columns and forced the French garrison to withdraw to Urseren (today Andermatt). The French losses were estimated in about 200 men. At Urseren (May 29) the French were engaged the St. Julien's vanguard (1 Btn. of six) which had cut off their withdrawal way along the Reusstal. Loison tried to open the passage to north boldly fighting onto and nearby a dangerous ancient bridge, which name would have to be renowned in the next future, the Devil's bridge (Teufelsbruck). [11] The task was almost impossible

In the meanwhile, at Riva (on the northern branch of Como lake) brigades De Briey and Bellegarde (Friedrich), partially embarked and partially by road, took the way towards Como. On May 28 brigade Nobili followed the previous units reaching the town of Gera (he will be at Como on may 30).

Right Wing Division

St. Gotthard Pass - * numbers estimated

Brigade General Louis-Henri Loison	3600
Artillery and sappers	110
109th Line Demi-brigade – I – II and III btn - Chef Jean-François Clerc	2210
76th Line Demi-brigade Chef-de-brigade Goré – I and II btn	1155
Cisalpine Guides and Expeditionnary forces Chasseurs a pied	60
12th Light Demi brigade detachment	65
At Altdorf	
General Claude-Jacques Lecourbe	
38th Line Demi-brigade I and II btn – Chef Marie-Guillaume Daumas	1200
Cisalpine Hussars	60
3 Grenadiers Coys	??
At Schwitz	
12th Light Demi brigade I and II btns. - Chef Guy Louis Henry Valory	1180
6th Line Demi brigade detachment	240
II Btn. 36th Line Demi-brigade	580

Division Generalmajor Karl Joseph Graf Hadik von Futak [12]

At Bellinzona - St. Gotthard Pass

Feldbrigade Oberst Gottfried Freiherr von Strauch	5026
K.k. Grenadier bataillon Graf Nikolaus Weissenwolf	772
K.k. IR 11 Rifle regiment (former Graf Michael Wallis)	1923
I – II btns. - Cdr.: Oberst Gottfried von Strauch	
K.k. 10th Light Infantry Btn. Oblt. Franz von Siegenfeld (italian-venetian)	892
K.k. 11th Light Infantry Btn. Oberst Graf Georg Simon de Carneville (istrian)	434
K.k. Jäger Korps Major Johann Le Loup (1coy - Dutch)	109
I Btn Banal Grenzregiment or I Btn - 11th Banal Rgt. of Petrinja	781
K.k. 9th Hussar Rgt. FML Johann Nepomuk Graf Erdödy de Monyorókerek	115
C.te Oberst Franz Freiherr von Stephaics - ¾ sqn.	

in Reusstal

Feldbrigade Oberst Graf Joseph Johann Saint Julien-Wallsee [13]	4292
K.k. IR 47 Rifle Rgt. Graf Franz Kinsky	2222
I - II - btns. Cdr.: Graf Joseph Solaroli	
K.k. IR 46 Rifle Rgt. Freiherr Franz von Neugebauer	887
II – ½ III btn. (I-IV Btns. Innsbruck-Tyrol garrisons) - Cdr.: Major Graf Starhemberg	
III Btn. K.k. IR 37 Rifle Rgt. (former De Vins)	849
½ Btn. K.k. 13th Hungarian Light Infantry Major József de Munkátsy	334

▲ St. Gotthard Pass. Suvorov meeting with the friars. Paint of A. Kotsebu (1815-1889)

May 29 – Garrisons
In Valtelline (as Group Reserve)

Feldbrigade Generalmajor Oberst Ludwig Wolff de la Marseille	3187
I btn 5th Grenzregiment Warasdiner-Kreuzer of Varazdin	693
I btn K.k. IR 9 Rifle Rgt. (former Clerfayt) Cdr.: Obst Ludwig Wolff de la Marseille	606
K.k. IR 33 Rifle Rgt. Graf Anton Sztaray	1838
I – II btns. Cdr.: Oberst Johann Kalnássy de Kalnáss	

Feldbrigade Oberst Prinz Victor von Rohan
At Bellinzona

Jäger Freikorps Major Johann Le Loup (dutch Btn. - 3 coys)	359
III btn. K.k. IR 52 Hungarian Rifle Rgt. Erzherzog Palatin Anton Viktor	764
K.k. Light Btn. N. 14 Oberst Prince Ludwig (Louis) Rohan (italian Btn.)	590
Pioneers Detachment	81

June 1799 - the June – Securing the Border
On June 1 General Loudon entered Como escorting guns, trains and baggages of Hadik's division (while the Bellegarde's Group Park marched in Tirol through the Adige-Verona road). Hadik's cavalry was with him. In the late evening General St. Julien occupied the Devil's Bridge, definitevely securing the St. Gotthard Pass. In order to avoid French attacks from the Canton Valais (Wallis), General Rohan was ordered to reach the Simplon Pass and to extend the control until Domo d'Ossola, in Piedmont, while Strauch marched to Oberwald in Canton Valaise with 4 coys Wallis and 4 coys Siegenfeld to help the Insurgents against French General Xaintrailles (6000 men). On St. Gotthard remained the Siegenfeld Btn. (2 coys) and 1 coy of Le Loup Jägern. Other 2 Wallis Coys marched to the North under Captain Preising, followed by other 2 Banal Coys (the rest of the Banal battalion was sent

to reinforce St. Julien with a Le Loup coy). Carneville and the remaining Wallis Coys seized St. Gotthard while Weissenwolf Grenadiers and the cavalry grouped in the Reserve. De Briey marched North with 5 battalions to support the southern St. Gotthard occupation and to clear Airolo from French (this event was completed only on June 7). General Nobili was sent at Varese from which he had to support either Rohan either Hadik, whenever it would have been necessary.

The French Counterattack

On June 1st, General Lecourbe counterattacked pushing back St. Julien until the Devil's bridge. It followed an hard battle in which the weak and scattered Austrian troops lost 1000 prisoners. The St.Julien annihilation forced Austrians to recall Prince Rohan in order to reinforce Hadik. General Xaintrailles in Valais advanced towards Airolo, having beaten Strauch and the irregulars bands. On June 6 De Briey marched to Airolo to reinforce Hadik Gruppe. Prince Rohan was ordered to resume his march trough Val Toce towards Simplon Pass and, if possible, to give 4 mountain guns (Gebirgsgeschütze) with ammunitions to the Valaise Insurgents. FML Hadik remained at St. Gotthard Pass to secure the Italienische Armée northern flank, while the rest of the K.k. Tiroler Armée marched towards Piedmont to join Suvorov and Melas. So Bellegarde and Loudon left Como on June 6 and the gathering day was fixed at Acqui (Piedmont) for June 10. Bellegarde had now 7403 men, 343 cavalrymen in 11 Btns. and 2 Sqns. Loudon attached the former Nobili cavalry and Lamarseille followed the Bellegarde's vanguard.

The army Wing in Switzerland and the Piedmont Corps

NOTE: There were two Orders of battle about the left wing of Tyroler Armée, which operated from Grisons till Valais. The first was communicated by General Bellegarde himself, while the second was communicated by General Hadik de Futak in his "Standenausweise" of June 9th. With regards of his Gruppe, Hadik referred a total of 12597 men, while Count Bellegarde, on May 29, told about 15388 men. This significative different opinion probably stated the losses in the St. Gotthard battles (see the battered St. Julien brigade, halved).

Bellegarde's 2nd Group HQ at Airolo (Canton Ticino, Switzerland)

Division Generalmajor Karl Joseph Graf Hadik von Futak

At St. Gotthard Pass

Feldbrigade Oberst Gottfried Freiherr von Strauch	4740
K.k. Grenadier bataillon Graf Nikolaus Weissenwolf	772
K.k. IR 11 Rifle regiment (former Graf Michael Wallis)	1793
I – II btns. - Cdr.: Oberst Gottfried von Strauch	
K.k. 10th Light Infantry Btn. Oblt. Franz von Siegenfeld (italian-venetian)	892
K.k. 11th Light Infantry Btn. Oberst Graf Georg Simon de Carneville (istrian)	434
K.k. Jäger Korps Major Johann Le Loup (1coy - Dutch)	109
I Btn Banal Grenzregiment or I Btn - 11th Banal Rgt. of Petrinja	781
K.k. 9th Hussar Rgt. FML Johann Nepomuk Graf Erdödy de Monyorókerek	115
C.te Oberst Franz Freiherr von Stephaics - ¾ sqn.	

Feldbrigade Oberst Victor Prince von Rohan 2530 men

At Simplon Pass

Jäger Freikorps Major Johann Le Loup (dutch Btn. - 3 coys)	359
III btn. K.k. IR 52 Hungarian Rifle Rgt. Erzherzog Palatin Anton Viktor	764
K.k. Light Btn. N. 14 Oberst Prince Ludwig (Louis) Rohan (italian Btn.)	590
II Btn. Imperial Russian Musketeers rgt. LG Förster (Ferster) or Tambowski (Tambov)	757
K.k. 7th Hussar Rgt. ½ sqn	60

The brother to be detached in the Aosta valley to seize the Great St. Bernhard Pass

Feldbrigade Oberst Carl Prince von Rohan 700 men

K.k. Light Btn. N. 14 Oberst Prince Ludwig (Louis) Rohan (italian Btn.)	700

in Reusstal

Feldbrigade Oberst Graf Joseph Johann Saint Julien-Wallsee	4292
K.k. IR 47 Rifle Rgt. Graf Franz Kinsky	2222
I - II - btns. Cdr.: Graf Joseph Solaroli	
K.k. IR 46 Rifle Rgt. Freiherr Franz von Neugebauer	887

II – ½ III btn. (I-IV Btns. Innsbruck-Tyrol garrisons) - Cdr.: Major Graf Starhemberg	
III Btn. K.k. IR 37 Rifle Rgt. (former De Vins)	849
½ Btn. K.k. 13th Hungarian Light Infantry Major József de Munkátsy	334

Division FML Heinrich Joseph Johannes Graf von Bellegarde [14]
At Varese

K.k. Tiroler Armée Total	15283
Artillery, Pioneers and Sappers	1161

At the beginning of the second coalition war, spring 1799, Bellegarde had the command over the k. k. Tiroler army (strength of about 46,600 men or 50 battalions and 14 Squadrons), granting links between the k. k. Hauptarmée in Swabia under Archduke Charles and the k. k. Italienisches-armée under field marshal-lieutenant Kray deployed by the Etsch (Adige) river. On 4 April 1799, Bellegarde struck the French troops under brigade general Dessolle at Taufers and Münsters (Engadin) and, after the triumphant combat of Remüs (April 30, 1799), pushed the Lecourbe's French troops out of the Engadin.

Feldbrigade Generalmajor Graf Johann Nobili [15]	4298
K.k. IR 15 Rifle Rgt. Oranien Prinz Wilhelm	1813
I – II btns. Cdr.: Oberst Anton Retz	
K.k. 9th hungarian Light Infantry Btn. Major Carl Greth	614
½ Btn. K.k. 6th Light Infantry Major Carl Freiherr von Trauttenberg (serbian-croatian)	259
IV Btn 6th Grenzregiment Warasdiner-St.Georger or II btn/6th GR Major Vukassovic ?	927
K.k. Jäger Korps Major Johann Le Loup (2coys - Dutch)	228
Feldbrigade Generalmajor Graf August De Briey [16]	1948
K.k. IR 23 Rifle Rgt. Grossherzog Ferdinand von Toscana	1948
I – II - III btg. Graf Otto Philipp Hohenfeld	
Feldbrigade Generalmajor Friedrich Bellegarde [17] (brother)	2537
III Btn. K.k. IR 34 Hungarian Rifle Rgt. (the old Esterházy regiment	650
K.k. IR 58 Rifle Rgt. Freiherr Peter von Beaulieu	411
Remnants of I - II btns. Cdr.: Freiherr Joseph von Zeegraedt	
III Btn. K.k. IR 33 Rifle Rgt. Graf Anton Sztaray	815
½ I Btn. K.k. IR 38 Rifle Rgt. Herzog Ferdinand von Württemberg	369
½ III Btn. K.k. IR 30 Rifle Infantry Rgt. Fürst Carl Joseph de Ligne	292
Grenadier Bde FML Johann Ludwig Alexander Alformerius Frh. von Loudon [18]	2047
K.k. Grenadier bataillon major Franz Wouwermanns	508
K.k. Grenadier bataillon Graf Otto von Hohenfeld	497
K.k. Grenadier bataillon Freiherr Carl von Görschen	717
K.k. Grenadier Bataillon Oberleutnant Carl Soudain	325
K.k. Cavalry brigade (from Brigade Nobili)	457
K.k. 3rd Light Dragoons Rgt. FM Erzherzog Johann Baptist Chevauxleger division 1 - ½ Sqn.	198
K.k. 9th Hussar Rgt. FML Johann Nepomuk Graf Erdödy de Monyorókerek	259
C.te Oberst Franz Freiherr von Stephaics - 1 – ½ sqns.	

Variant Hadik's Order of battle June 9, 1799

Division Generalmajor Karl Joseph Graf Hadik von Futak	16053
in Reusstal	
Feldbrigade Oberst Graf Joseph Johann di Saint Julien-Wallsee	2095
K.k. IR 47 Rifle Rgt. Graf Franz Kinsky	687
I - II - btns. Cdr.: Graf Joseph Solaroli	
K.k. IR 46 Rifle Rgt. Freiherr Franz von Neugebauer	815
II – ½ III btn. (I-IV Btns. Innsbruck-Tyrol garrisons) - Cdr.: Major Graf Starhemberg	
III Btn. K.k. IR 37 Rifle Rgt. (former De Vins)	423
½ Btn. K.k. 13th Hungarian Light Infantry Major Jozséf de Munkátsy - 3 coys	170

At St. Gotthard Pass

Feldbrigade Oberst Gottfried Freiherr von Strauch	4740
K.k. Grenadier bataillon Graf Nikolaus Weissenwolf	714
K.k. IR 11 Rifle regiment (former Graf Michael Wallis)	1701
I – II btns. (IV btn at Prag - Bohemia) - Cdr.: Oberst Gottfried von Strauch	
K.k. 10th Light Infantry Btn. Oblt. Franz von Siegenfeld (italian-venetian)	683
K.k. 11th Light Inf. Btn. Obst Graf Georg Simon de Carneville (istrian)	392
K.k. Jäger Korps Major Johann Le Loup (1coy - Dutch)	109
I Btn Banal Grenzregiment or I Btn - 11th Banal Rgt. of Petrinja	967
K.k. 9th Hussar Rgt. FML Johann Nepomuk Graf Erdödy 1 sqn.	174

at Simplon Pass

Feldbrigade Oberst Prinz Victor von Rohan	2530
II Btn. Imp. Russian Musketeers rgt. LG Förster (Ferster) or Tambowski (Tambov)	757
Jäger Freikorps Mjr Johann Le Loup (dutch Btn. -3 coys)	359
III btn. K.k. IR 52 Hungarian Rifle Rgt. Erzherzog Palatin Anton Viktor	764
K.k. Light Btn. N. 14 Oberst Prince Ludwig (Louis) Rohan (italian Btn.)	590
K.k. 7th Hussar Rgt. ½ sqn.	60
Feldbrigade Oberst Prinz Carl von Rohan	
K.k. 2nd Light Infantry Btn Oberst Carl Prince of Rohan (Italian btn)	700
Chiavenna garrison	
III Btn. K.k. IR 47 Rifle Rgt. Graf Franz Kinsky	700
Morbegno garrison	
III Btn. K.k. IR 11 Rifle regiment (former Graf Michael Wallis)	700
Feldbrigade Generalmajor Graf Johann Nobili	2937
K.k. IR 15 Rifle Rgt. Oranien Prinz Wilhelm	1706
I – II btns. Cdr.: Oberst Anton Retz	
K.k. 9th hungarian Light Infantry Btn. Major Carl Greth	734
½ Btn. K.k. 6th Light Infantry Major Carl Freiherr von Trauttenberg (serbian-croatian)	281
K.k. Jäger Korps Major Johann Le Loup (2coys - Dutch)	216
Feldbrigade Generalmajor Graf August De Briey	3051
K.k. IR 23 Rifle Rgt. Grossherzog Ferdinand von Toscana	2119
I – II - III btg. Graf Otto Philipp Hohenfeld	
IV Btn 6th Grenzregiment Warasdiner-St.Georger or II btn/6th GR Major Vukassovic ?	932

Sources :
- Clausewitz General Carl von, "*Hinterlassenes Werk des Generals Carl von Clausewitz – erster Theil – Die Feldzüge von 1799 in Italien und der Schweiz*", Ferdinand Dümmler, Berlin 1833.
- Günther Reinhold, "*Le Alpi a ferro e fuoco*" ed. by Giulio Ribi, Dadò Ed. Locarno 2002. A Swiss Italian translation of the book "*Der Feldzug der Division Lecourbe im Schweizerischen Hochgebirge 1799*", Schweizerischen Offiziers-Gesellschaft Basel, 1895 and J. Huber. 1896.
- Smola Karl Freiherrn von, darg.v. "*Das Leben des Feldmarschalls Heinrich Grafen von Bellegarde*" Heubner Verlag, Wien 1847.
- Smola, Karl Freiherrn von, Major im kais. Österr. Generalquartiermeister-Stabe, dargeßtellt von, "*Das Leben des Feldmarschalls Prinzen Friedrich Franz Xavier z u Hohenzollern-Hechingen*", Wien, Schaumburg & Compagnie. 1845 .ioneers

NOTES

1   **General Jean-Joseph-Paul-1 1 1 Augustin Dessolle** Born in Auch (Gers), on July 3, 1767, well erudite by his uncle, the future bishop of Digne and Chambery, took the military Service at the First Coalition time. Was Captian in the légion *des Montagnes*, unit of the armée des Pyrénées-Occidentales, where his skills, with an indefatigable aptitude, made him aide-de-camp provisoire of general Reynier. He was after attached to the adjudants-généraux group. He had some troubles for the Nobility Exclusion Act but soon he was recalled under the army flags and definitively named adjudant-général in 1794. He was at First Italian Campaign with Bonaparte, who choose him to bring the provisional documents of Leoben treaty at Paris. When in Paris he met général Moreau, who ordered him to report to the Directory the facts on the Rhine passage. On May 31, 1797 he was named général de brigade and in 1798, Moreau, gave him the command of a Reserve Corps for a mission in the Canton Grisons, East Switzerland. During the Second Coalition War, he occuppied the Valtelline after some hard combats and, on Mars 16, 1799, only with 4500 men, passed the Wormser-Joch attacking 7000 Austrians at Glurns and Taufers (he took there 400 prisoners and 20 guns). After the successive combat at Santa Maria, he was named général de division.

Recalled from Moreau, who wanted him as his Chief of Staff, he left the Valtelline command to general Loison, reaching the armée d'Italie in the plains. In effect he had all the skills of a good Chief of Staff being aware of all the branches of the Art of war, passionate, active and accurate in his proposals. He ended the year as Commander of the Ligurian troops.

2 Chef-de-brigade Guy Louis Henri Valory (1757-1817) - baron of the Empire, général-de-brigade – infantry. Commander of the Légion d'Honneur - 14.06.1804. 1794 - Chef-de-brigade - 45e demi-brigade provisoire. 1796 - Chef-de-brigade - 12e Light infantry demi-brigade. 1803 - général-de-brigade (29.08.). 1805 – brigade commander – 3e division of infantry – Armée d'Italie. 1808 - baron of the Empire (02.07.). 1809 - brigade commander of infantry - II Corps - Armée d'Allemagne. 1810 - commander of military Department (13e military District). 1813 - commander 1e brigade - 6e division of infantry - II Corps.

3 Chef-dbrigade Antoine-Louis-Popon Maucune, baron. Born on February 21, 1772 at Brives (Corrèze), was second Lieutenant in the Pioneers on February 1, 1786, first Lieutenant and was reformed in 1789. With the outbreak of the Revolution he enrolled as Grenadier in the 4th Paris Volunteers battalion (1791) ; the authorities gave him bach his rank (First Lieutenant in the 23e régiment d'infanterie) in 1792. He was in campaign in the armée du Nord during the same year, where he was wounded by a shot in the left thig, at the seize of Melun. In 1793 he was transferred to the Armée des Alpes fighting in Piedmont as a Partisan Chief; was wounded again by a bayonet cut in the right arm at Bardenèche in August. In 1794, promoted as Captain, he was in all campaigns of the armée d'Italie, until 1801, obtaining the rank of
chef de bataillon from Bonaparte at the Arcole battle (1796). In 1799, during the first Taufers assault, he received two fire wounds (right thig and left shoulder), being promoted as Chef-de-brigade of the 39e demi-brigade de ligne on the battlefield. In August, at Novi, he distinguished himself for bravery and was shot in the right foot. His rank was confirmed by a First Consul Act in 1801 when, after the peace, returned to Paris garrison before being sent to the Montreuil camp. He was there until 1805, member and Officer of the Légion-d'Honneur from 1804, attached to the Corrèze electoral District. With the 2nd division of the VI Corps (Grande Armée) he was in the 1806-1807 campaigns. On March 10, 1807, he was promoted to Général de brigade. After the Tilsit treaty he returned in France becoming baron of the Empire in 1808. From that year until 1813 he was in the Peninsular War and in Portugal. He captured a bridge at Alba de Torres, was wounded at Bussaco, and wounded again at Fuentes de Onoro. On October 18, 1812, the armée de Portugal Avantgarde, under his orders, captured Castilho de Peones, Quintanavides and Santa Olalla. During that month he advanced, fighting, from Monasterio, through Burgos, until Valladolid. Fought at Tamamès and Villa-Muriel and was mentioned by general Souham. Transferred to the armée d'Italie he spent there last Service years retiring before the Bourbons return. After the 100s Days (charged with the command of the Lille Nationa Guards division, but never arrived there) he definitevely retired on October 21, 1818. He died on February 18, 1824.

4 Oberst (provisional Generalmajor) Gottfried von Strauch. From April 1799 provisional brigade commander, led his IR 11 (former Wallis) in Valtelline occupying the Aprica pass and the Mortirolo where was attacked by the French Dessolle's rearguard. He had heavy losses and was forced to defend on a frozen snowy terrain with the bayonets. Then passed forward to guard the Splügen pass remaining in Switzerland (Canton Valaise) to link the right Coalition flank with the Hadik's Corps. In november he captured the mount St. Gotthard. His behaviour during the campaign was awarded with the definitive promotion to Generalmajor. In 1808 he became the Owner of the K.k. IR 24, the old Preiss and then Fürst Carl Auersperg, as Field Marshal and gave his name to that regiment along 28 years. He was also named baron (Freiherr) retiring from the military career as Feldzeugmeister on January 1836. Wurzbach Constantin, *Biographisches Lexikon des Kaisertums Österreich*, 39th Tome, K u. K Hofdruckerei, Wien 1879 available at http://www.literature.at/webinterface/library/ALO-BOOK_V01?objid=11805&zoom=6.

5 Oberst Ludwig Wolff de Lamarseille Born at Mons (Belgium) 1746 (dead on October 11, 1804 at Mons). At the age of 14 he was cadet in the Wied Infanterie, where he became a very young Officer and Captain, 22 years old (38th Infantry Regiment l'Aisne). In 1788 he was promoted Major of the Gemmingen infantry regiment (during the Turkish wars) and then returned to his former regiment to participate (1790) in the campaign against the Dutch Insurgents. Having distinguished in that campaign, he was named Lieutenant-Colonel in the Clerfayt infantry regiment n. 9. In 1794 he took command of a vacant Grenadiers battalion (former Rousseau) attaching it to the divisions Murray, Clerfayt and De Ligne. He was with Wurmser (Higher Rhine) in 1795 distinguishing himself at Mannheim and in the attacks against Schwetzingen and Heidelberg. On April 1796 he was promoted Colonel of the regiment n. 9 following the Archduke Charles in campaign. During the 1799 campaign he was attached to the Tiroler Armée of General Bellegarde. There he led an Avantgarde brigade fighting on 26-27 March and entering Süs town in Engadin. Then he was committed to the near Valtelline to support General Strauch Advance. On June 20 he fought at Bosco (Marengo) and Cassina Grossa. He led there the General Alcaini Detachment in their march from Marengo to Spinetta, taking prisoner a whole French battalion. On September 1799 he was promoted Generalmajor (he obtained also the military Cross of Maria Theresia for the 1796 combat at Kirchheim, but only in 1801). After the Luneville Treaty (1801), on May, he finally retired after a 44 years long Service in the army. He died at the age of 58 in Mons, his family town.

6 Prince Victor-Louis-Meriadec de Rohan-Guemené, Duke of Montbazon, future Austrian Field Marshal born in Paris on July 20, 1766 (emigré) and dead at Sechrowen (Sichrow, Bohemia) on December 10, 1846. His brother Jules-Armand-Louis de Rohan-Guemené (Paris Oct. 20, 1768 – Sechrowen Jan. 13, 1836), who will become a generalmajor, commanded a Light battalion. The other brother, Charles-Alain-Gabriel de Rohan-Guemené (Paris Jan.18,. 1764 – Paris Apr. 28, 1836) who will become a Field Marshal, led another Light battalion. In 1794 he passed from the British Army (he was also in the French Service for 13 years) to his brother's battalion as a Colonel. In 1801 was Generalmajor receiving from the Emperor the command of k.k. IR 21. In 1809 led a Reserve Corps of 12 Grenadiers battalions. The year after he retired in his estates in Bohemia. For his brave campaign in Italy (1805) he received the Maria Theresia award. Wurzbach Constantin, *Biographisches Lexikon des Kaisertums Österreich*, 26th Tome, K u. K Hofdruckerei, Wien 1879.

7   Reinhold Günther told that the 109e (900 men) arrived on May 7 substituting the 44e Line demi-brigade attached to Soult's division. In "*Le Alpi a ferro e fuoco*" ed. By Ribi Giulio, Dadò, Locarno 2002.

8   **Général de Division Claude-Jacques Lecourbe** Born February 22, 1758 at Ruffey near Lons-le-Saunier in Jura (not Besançon),had a sudden death on October 23,1815 at Belfort. Son of Claude Guillaume, cavalry officer of an ancient family of the Franche-Comte, and Marie Valette, he was volunteer in the Aquitaine 35e infantry regiment (1777). In 1785 he left the service as a simple Corporal. Became the commander of the National Guard at Ruffey-sur-Seille (Jura, August 1789). In 1791 he was named Captain of the 8th coy (August) and Commander (November) of the 7th battalion of Jura Volunteers. On September 8, 1793, under general Houchard, he engaged the British at Hondschoote, near Dunkerque. At Wattignies (October 16) he was noted by division general Moreau, who said: "Lecourbe ira loin!". In 1794, after a trial for some false accusations from which he was totally discharged, he was named Général de brigade a titre provisoire (June 12), distinguishing him self at Sprimont and at the siege of the castle Liechtenstein (1795). In August 1796 he was Général de division provisoire under Moreau. He became renowned for his charges under the fortress Kehl walls. Officially he had the rank of Général de division only on February 5, 1799, taking command of the right wing of the Helvetian army under Masséna. In August and September 1799 he delayed the advance of Suvorov at St. Gotthard, allowing the French to win at Zürich. In 1800 he was general-lieutenant in the Rhine and Danube armies. Being very close to Moreau, a friend of him, he went into troubles with Bonaparte (1804), retired and reached his home at Ruffey where he lived (for a period he was also at Bourges) from 1813. The return of the King awarded him with the Legion d'Honneur and the rank of general infantry Inspector of the 6th territorial division. During the 100s days, however, he served the Emperor, leading the Corps of Belfort, which had the task to block the Austrians. After Waterloo, on August 31, the King forced him to the definitive retirement and, while he was waiting for the Royal trial he suddenly died at Belfort.

9   He was the former Chef of the 44th Line demi-brigade.

10   **General Louis Henri Loison.** Born at Damvilliers (Lorraine - May 16, 1771), dead on December 30, 1816, near Liege. In 1791 he was second Lieutenant, then quickly became Captain of the Hussars and, in the Rhin and Moselle army he was Chef and after provisional general-de-brigade. In 1796 had some political troubles and he was put under general Bonaparte. After having served in the Interior army, in 1798, he was sent in Italie and reformed. Recalled with the new war, he distinguished himself fighting on St. Gotthard passes and, for that, he was promoted to general-de-division (September 1799) replacing general Lecourbe in the command of the 2nd division of the Armée d'Helvetie. After the promotion he returned at the St.Gotthard beating Suvorov's Russians. Returned at Paris, he received the personal compliments of Bonaparte, who called him in the Reserve Army. Deployed in the Avant-Guard, he organized the artillery movements on the San Bernardo pass and led his troops in the attack of Fort Bard (Aosta valley). After having reached Brescia, he disordered and routed the Austrian brigade Loudon. During the 1800 campaign he distinguished also at Pozzolo, Parona and at the Brenta river. He rapidly reached the fame of a strong "warrior" participating at Austerlitz. Then he was in Portugal at Almeida and Guarda and, in 1808, he was created Count. Operated under Massena and in 1812 was in Russia, organizing a Reserve Corps of about 10000 men. At Vilna he was not employed. After the defeat he returned in Paris, where he retired from Service (also if he made some services during the 100s days).

11   The legend tells that the Devil made a agreement with the people who want a bridge over the gorge called Schöllenenschlucht (over Reuss stream). It was very hard to build and so the Master carpenter said "this bridge only the Devil could build out!". So the Devil came and said: "I'll build it, but the first living soul who'll pass through will have to come with forever!". A smart farmer had a brilliant idea. He bound his male-goat loosely and threw it on the other side. The furious Devil seized a large rock block and threatened therewith to destroy its work. On that an old little woman came and scratched a cross into the stone. When the devil saw this, left the stone which landed in the vicinity of Göschenen (the Teufelsstein). Since the bridge was built in the 13th Century, unfortunately we have no document to verify the lore, even pacts signed by Devil himself. The bridge was buil over the Schöllenen gorge between Andermatt and Göschenen on the northern side of the St. Gotthard road.

12   **Feldmarschall-Leutnant Karl Joseph Graf von Hadik-Futak.** Was born in 1756 at Leutschau (today: Levoca/Slovakia). He was the second son of a famous Hussars commander and hungarian leader, Andreas Reichsgraf von Hadik-Futak (1710-1790). When 17 years old the young Hadik enrolled in the kaiserlich-österreichische Armee (1733), being attached to this father's regiment Husaren-Regiment Nr. 3. On March 1st, 1776 he was promoted to Chieftain (Rittmeister) and fought in the Bavarian Succession War against Prussians (1778/79) becoming a Major on May, 29 1779. On May, 1st 1784 was Oberstleutnant and in July 1789 – when 33 y.o.- Oberst and Commander of the famous Husaren-Regiments Nr. 16 „Graf von Blankenstein". Volunteer during the Turkey Wars (1787-1792) Hadik distinguished himself at Belgrad. In 1790 was commanded to the Netherlands. With the beginning of the first Coalition War, in April 1792, he was at Brussels. At Maubege he obtained the command of the Avantgarde trying to pass the Sambre river. After he fought under Albert Herzog von Sachsen-Teschen in the unlucky battle at Jemappes (6 November 1792).
With his regiment he was (spring 1793) under the command of the Oberbefehlshaber Feldmarschall Prinz von Sachsen-

Coburg-Saalfeld fighting at Aldenhoven (1 March 1793) and Neerwinden (18 March 1793). From 15th to 16th October 1793 Hadik and his Hussars Blankenstein was at Wattignies under Feldzeugmeister Graf von Clerfayt; there he was so brave to be noted, commanding the left wing of the Austrian Observationskorps, formed by three Squadrons of his regiment and four of the Coburg-Dragoons. On October 16th he was newly attacked at Beaumont. His counterattack led to the French defeat in which Hadik took 5 guns and baggages. This granted him the 34th Promotion of 7th July 1794 with the Cross of Maria-Theresien-Orden.

From 1795 he was a Brigade commander in the k.k. main Army of Lower Rhine under Feldmarschall Graf von Clerfayt, and battled at Steinbach. During the 1796 campaign Hadik was very active. So he was noted by the Archduke Charles in the battles of Wetzlar (15 June 1796), Uckerath (19 June 1796) and Amberg (24 August 1796) as in the great battle of Würzburg (2 September 1796). For his bravery at Würzburg, Hadik had the 51st Promotion on 29 April 1797 with the Commander Cross of the Maria-Theresien-Orden. In spring 1797 he was promoted Feldmarschall-Leutnant and had a division, with which in April 1797 he was in northern Italy against Napoleon Bonaparte.

During the Second Coalition War, spring 1799, he was a division commander in the k.k. Italienisches-Tyroler-Armee, first fighting in Tirol and after taking a part in the battle of Novi (15 August 1799) where he commanded the right wing attack Kolonne. During the 1800 campaign Hadik fought at Cadibona (6 April 1800) and was with his division at (26 May 1800) Romano against the Napoleon Reserve-Armee. At Marengo on 14 June 1800 he commanded the first main Kolonne of the Centre (6 Btns. And 9 Sqns., together 5.000 men). Near the Fontanone creek, against the French brigade Rivaud, the Graf Hadik was mortally wounded. He was carried into Alessandria by his soldiers and there (24 July 1800 – when 44 y.o.) he died. Feldmarschall-Leutnant Karl Graf von Hadik-Futak was a true, old, austrian nobleman. He had a good military talent, as cavalry leader overall, but also as avant.garde organizer.

13 **Johann Joseph St. Julien Wallsee**, Not to be confused with the other Generalmajor, Johann Franz, sent early to Verona to support the right wing of Kray.

14 **Heinrich Joseph Johannes count of Bellegarde** was born on 29 August 1756 in the Court Saxon capital Dresden. His father was the Saxon, at that time, war minister Johann Franz of Bellegarde. Originally the family Bellegarde originated out of an old Savoy nobility. The young Bellegarde entered, 20 years old - 1776, as a Fähnrich into the Court Saxon army, however changing in the year 1781 into the imperial-Austrian army. In 1785 was Colonel and commander of the Dragoons regiment n.1 "Archduke Joseph Anton of Tuscany" (renamed in 1795 as dragoon-regiment no. 26 "Archduke Johann), which he leaded until 1793. In the following war against the Turkish empire (1787-1792), the young Bellegarde was repeatedly able to distinguish himself as a cavalry leader. With his regiment Bellegarde fought in the successful siege of the fort Schabatz on the Save (today: Sabac/Serbia), and in the combat at Semlin (Zemun), as well as in the successful siege of Belgrade (autumn 1789).

By the outbreak of the first coalition war (1792) count Bellegarde, with his regiment in the Corps of the FZM Prince of Hohenlohe-Kirchberg, stood by the Rhine and the Moselle rivers. In spring 1793, Bellegarde took service in the Austrian main army as a general staff officer under field marshal prince of Saxon-Coburg-Saalfeld, and was at the sieges of the French fort Valenciennes (25. May until 27 July 1793) and Maubeuge (30. September until 16 October 1793). In 1794 was promoted to general major and was awarded with the knight cross of the Maria-Theresien-order, in the 33rd promotion, for his bravery on the battlefield (the 25 May 1794).

On 12 March 1796 was promoted field marshal-lieutenant, and attached as an Aide of the Archduke Charles, with whom he remained since 10 February 1796 as Reichsgeneralfeldmarschall and Supreme Commander (Oberbefehlshaber) of the k.k. Niederrhein-Armee. With Archduke Charles, Bellegarde took part in the main battles of the 1796 campaign, Wetzlar (15. June 1796), Malsch (9. July 1796), Neresheim (11. August 1796) and finally Würzburg (2. September 1796). The Count Bellegarde, in the following year, accompanied the Archduke to north Italy. On this war theatre, where also the winning Archduke was able to do nothing, count Bellegarde was ordered, with general major count Merveldt, to negotiate an armistice (7 April 1797) with Napoleon Bonaparte in Judenburg. Later he took part at the negotiations of Leoben as well as at those of Campo Formio. During the army-reforms of 1798, count Bellegarde was a member of the Militär-Hof-Kommission under FML Alvinczy, and studied the possibility to introduce in the imperial-Austrian army of the corps-system, similar to that already available in the French army. At the beginning of the second coalition war, spring 1799, Bellegarde had the command over the k. k. Tiroler army (strength of about 46,600 men or 50 battalions and 14 Squadrons), granting links between the k. k. Hauptarmée in Swabia under Archduke Charles and the k. k. Italienisches-armée under field marshal-lieutenant Kray deployed by the Etsch (Adige) river. On 4 April 1799, Bellegarde struck the French troops under brigade general Dessolle at Taufers and Münsters (Engadin) and, after the triumphant combat of Remüs (April 30, 1799), pushed the Lecourbe's French troops out of the Engadin.

On 16 May 1799, Bellegarde received the imperial Hofkriegsrat order to reach the Italienisches Armée with 15,000 men, marching over the Alps unitil the Piedmont where was the coalized Russian-Austrian army under the command of the famous Russian field marshal Alexander Wassiljewitsch Suworow count Rimniksky (1729-1800). The count of Bellegardes march over the Alps began on 15 May 1799 in Wallenstedt, advanced then over Chur and reached, through the Splügen-pass, Chiavenna on 21 May. From there he went to Como where he embarked his troops on the lake finally reaching Milano. After Milano, he went to Pavia where he united himself with field marshal Suworow army. At the end of Mays 1799 Bellegarde, placed under the command of Suworow, received the order to siege, with his corps, first the citadel of Tortona and after to conquer the fort of Alessandria. On 20 June 1799 at Cassina Grossa (also known as San Giuliano near Marengo) he was attacked by Moreau losing 1,000 fallen and wounded, 1,300 prisoners as well as 3 guns. Then he leaved the siege of Tortona and withdrew behind the Bormida river. From 22 June 1799, count Bellegarde, with his reinforced corps of 21,000 men, began the siege of Alessandria, which finally capitulated on 22 July 1799. In the bloody battle of Novi, on 15 August 1799. count Bellegarde commanded a division under FZM Kray and fought on the right wing of the allied army against the French division Grouchy. Recalled in September 1799 at the imperial Court in Vienna, Bellegarde served there as a counselor of the tricky Foreign Minister Johann Amadeus Francis de Paula baron of Thugut (1736-1818).

After the defeat of cavalry general Melas in the battle at Marengo, on 14 June 1800, count Bellegarde, promoted to General d. Kavallerie rank, received the command of the Italienisches Armée, in autumn. His Italian Army had a Main army with an effective strength of about 55,000 men deployed along the river Mincio. On 25th and 26 December Bellegardes troops fought against the French Italian army under general Brune (66,000 men and 160 guns) in a stubborn fight for the river bridges at Pozzolo, Borghetto, Valeggio and Monzambano, episode known as Mincio battle. …. Heinrich Graf von Bellegarde, who took part in 18 campaigns from 1788 to 1815, died in Vienna on 22. July 1845.

15   **Generalmajor Count Johann Nobili.** (italian) Austrian Field marshal; Chevalier of the Maria Theresia Order; born (1760) and died (10 October 1823) at Padua, Italy. Cadet of the Imperial Engineers Military Academy he saw the first battles during the Bavarian Succession War. In 1782 as lieutenant, suddenly become 1st lieutenant, he distinguished himself during the Turkish War (battles of Palanka and Schabacz - 24 april 1788) fightinh with Prince de Ligne. He was also at the Belgrade Siege. He became a Chieftain of the army of Netherlands taking part at the attack against Valenciennes (26 July 1793) where he was awarded with the Minor Cross of the Maria Theresia Order. He was a specialist of the siege warfare and, particularly about the field fortifications (trenches, lunettes, fleches, redoubts etc.). On 7 July 1794 he obtained the Great Cross of the Maria Theresia Order being promoted to Major. In the meanwhile he had brevely fought at Cugnon (18.9.1793) and Arlon (16.4.1794) where he had to lead a detachment in the general Beaulieu group. On 8 October 1796 at Mühlberg, and on 19 at Forchheim he was very efficient and so he was promoted as Lieutenant-Colonel. He spent the most part of his career as Staff Officer for Fortifications. In 1799, he was sent to Mantua to coordinate the siege operations of the Kray's Belagerungs-Armée. There acted as Colonel leading also a brigade approaching from the Tirol. In 1800 became Generalmajor and in the following year was promoted Engineer field marshal. He spent the last days of the military life as Director of the military Ingenieur-Akademie. Finally he was sent to re-organize the Venetian fortresses in Italy and died in Padua at the age of 63 years.

16   **Graf August Briey de Vierset** (Belgian). In 1792 was Grenadier Battalion's commander at Jemappes and in 1793 at Aldenhoven and Famars. He distinguished himself during that Campaigns. In 1797 he was promoted Generalmajor and in 1798 he was employed in the Reserve-Corps of the Ober- Oesterreich. In the 1799 he was attached to the Army in Tirol, fighting at Martinsbruck und Nauders before following the Bellegarde's Advance into Italy.

17   Count Heinrich of Bellegarde had an older brother, **Marquis Friedrich of Bellegarde** (The lesser one (but the elder) Friedrich Joseph Anton Gabriel Noyel Graf v. Bellegarde, (25.3.1752 - 4.1.1830), 23.3.1797 mRv. 16.5.1797 GM, 29.10.1800 prov. FML 9.11.1800 FML, 1809 i.R.), who acted as a general major and brigade commander during the 1799 campaign and at the battle of Marengo - 14 June 1800. He received the command of an attack Kolonne, after the deadly wounding of field marshal-lieutenant Karl count of Hadik-Futak. During the third coalition war of 1805, Friedrich, promoted field marshal-lieutenant by brother Bellegarde, defended successfully Venice against the French-Italian siege troops.

18   **Feldmarschall-Leutnant Johann Ludwig Alexander Freiherr von Laudon (Loudon)** Originary from an old irish family, Johann Ludwig Alexander Freiherr von Laudon, born in 1762 at Riga/Latvia. Until 1789 he had been in the Imperial russian Army as Chieftain, when was called for the K.k. Austrian Army by his famous uncle Feldmarschall Gideon Ernst Freiherr von Laudon (1717-1790). Uncle Gideon kept Laudon as personal Aide-de-camp. As nephew-of-art his military career was very plain reaching early the rank of (1792) Oberst and Commander of the Infanterie-Regiment Nr. 29 „Olivier Remigius Graf von Wallis" (once called „Laudon"). With that regimant he was (1793) on the Rhine front with Graf Wurmser distinguishing himself during the assault against the lines of Weissenburg (13. October 1793 - in the fourth Angriffskolonne under Generalmajor Mészáros). After the 1795 campaign he was promoted (May 1796) to Generalmajor. Laudon followed Feldmarschall Graf von Wurmser on his way to northern Italy and had a Brigadekommando in Tirol under Feldmarschall-Leutnant Davidovich.

Entrusted to the security of lower Tirol and Garda lake roads and acting as second commander in Davidovich corp, he took active part during the november 1796 offensive in Titol against the french division Vaubois, covering the Army flanks. During the days of the battle of Rivoli (14.-15. January 1797) he was ordered to make a diversionary attack against Brescia. During the remaining period of 1797 campaign Loudon acted as Rearguard commander beating Serviez on 27. March 1797 at Glanig, taking Botzen, Lavis and Trient (Trento), and failing only to occupy Roveredo and the main Adige's road. For that actions he was awarded with the Ritterkreuz des Maria-Theresien-Ordens (8. July 1797 – 53rd Promotion). Beginning the 1799 campaign he had a new command in Tirol, but his behaviour was not resolute losing some positions on the Swiss border. For this he was called at Vienna by the Hofkriegsrat and had a military trial; however his noble origins again saved the career. Recalled in Italy Generalmajor von Laudon had a command at the battle by Novi (15 August 1799), leading a Grenadier brigade with some successes. In 1800 he was finally promoted Feldmarschall-Leutnant and sent to Galicia to serve there …After the Peace of Schönbrunn (14. Oktober 1809) he retired reanching the family estate at Hadersdorf near Vienna. There he died, on 22. September 1822.

▲ The new French commandant in Italy Jean Victor Marie Moreau (Galerie des Batailles, Palace of Versailles)

THE PIEDMONT'S INVASION
THE FALL OF THE SARDINIAN FORTRESSES

THE FRENCH MILITARY OCCUPATION OF PIEDMONT

Général de division Emanuel Grouchy HQ at Torino (Turin) [19]

The military control of Piedmont was under general Emanuel Grouchy. At the Eve of the Adda battle, the concerned Commander in Chief, Schérer, sent urgent orders to Grouchy, imposing him to control that exposed land:

"Vous resterez dans le Piémont, ou votre présence peut être du plus grand poids pour le maintien de le tranquillité dans le pays. C'est surtout dans ces circonstances que le talent dans les chefs doit suppléer au nombre, et, à ce double titre, votre présence dans le Piémont est indispensable."

... and about the Piedmontese garrison troops:

"Je vous engage en même temps à employer toutes les mesures qui vous paraîtront convencibles pour l'engagement de ces corps piémontais. Ne négligez rien, mon cher général, pour mettre les bataillons de garnison de tous ces corps on mesure de tenir, autant que possible, le bataillon de campagne au complet."

In April the alarm was high into the Piedmont. Grouchy, ordered by Schérer to envoy as many possible regular troops reinforcements to the Adda front, sent his "right arm", general Bertrand Clauzel, to Grenoble, in order to beg general François Müller to give him one more demi-brigade, for the control of a land which was ready to explode in riots.

After that vopygae, the brigadier general Clauzel was attached to the Schérer army on April 17. He reached Piacenza with a battalion (I Btn 68th demibrigade) and two squadrons of 12th Dragoons. With the Clauzel departure, Grouchy wrote to Schérer: *"Le Piémont est extrémement dégarni; la fermentation y est grande surtout dans la partie qui avoisine la Ligurie; et malheureusement les moyens de contenir le pays sont insuffisants. Comptez toutefois sur mes efforts et sur mon zéle ..."*

On April 25, Grouchy sent to Paris a convoy full of precious art objects, gathered in Piedmont, under the escort of his aide de camp, Captain Dupuy.

The Country (former Kingdom of Sardinia) had been divided into four military departments. They were so organized in April 1799:

1- Sesia Department (HQ at Vercelli): under adjudant général Mossard

Division de l'Ouest – (Novara and Vercelli) Général de brigade baron Robert Motte [20]	??
Mainly formed by milice and Piedmontese provincial troops	
Cisalpine gunners coy at fort Bard and in Aosta valley	??

2 -Stura Department (HQ at Mondovì): under adjudant général Jean-Mathieu Seras [21](Piedmontese from Osasco)

107th Line infantry demi-brigade II and III btns at Coni (Cuneo)	??
I Swiss or Security Foreign Btn "Alemanno" or German Btn (Switzerland) – Major Kornfeld	400 *
II Swiss or Security Foreign Btn "Grigioni" or Grison Btn (Switzerland) – Major Christ	400 *
Legione Valdese (Milice) [22] chef-de-brigade Giacomo Marauda	1500
Cisalpine gunners coy at Coni (Cuneo)	??
Cisalpine gunners coy at fort Fenestrelle	??

* Estimated numbers.

3 -Tanaro Department (HQ at Alessandria): under adjudant général Jacques Louis Delabrosse called « Flavigny ».

Division de l'Est (Alba and Asti) - Adjudant-général Jacques Louis Delabrosse dit « Flavigny »	??
Mainly formed by milice and Piedmontese provincial troops	
24th Line Demi Brigade Chef de Brigade Vital – III Btn.	800
II Btn 1st Cisalpine infantry demi-brigade (former regiment Aosta infantry)	800
II Btn 3rd Cisalpine infantry demi-brigade (former regiment Regina infantry – the Queen's own)	800
Cisalpine gunners coys	2

The Department had also the command over the fortresses of Tortona, Alessandria (see after), Valenza and Casale (this latter poorly walled). However the "true" commander of the territory was the Chief of Alessandria Fortress, general Clauzel, who took the command from the Chef de brigade Vital.

4- Eridan [23] Department (HQ at Turin): under adjudant général Francesco Federico Campana, Chief of the Turin National Guard. Before the April crisis, Turin had a garrison of 3438 men.

Piedmontese National Guard of Turin Adj-Général Francesco Federico Campana	??
Torino Place commander : Chef de Brigade Jules-Alexandre Léger Boutrouë	
68th Line infantry demi-brigade II and III btns Chef de Brigade Jules-Alexandre Leger Boutrouë	??
I Btn 107th Line infantry demi-brigade	??
II Cisalpine Light infantry demi-brigade	300
Cisalpine gunners coy chef-de-bataillon Antonio Bonfanti – sent to Genua before Turin blockade	??
7th Dragoons Rgt. chef d'escadron Jean-Jacques Laveran	??

All the above units were heavily involved in every day "police" actions since the winter months of 1799, against rebels and insurgents, often organized by former royal Piedmontese officers. They entered the Campaign when the Coalition army invaded Piedmont. As said, the anti-French feelings were more and more growing up in the minds of the Piedmontese citizens. The anti-French uprising spreaded in the mountain districts and in the Monregalese (Mondovì), so the Grouchy "call to arms", of April 30, for the callback of the Piedmontese provincial battalions, had an insufficient outcome indeed. Grouchy could only count (apart few hundred French) on 2 Piedmontese line battalions at Alessandria (II/1st Aosta, II/3rd Regina), 2 foreign battalions between Cuneo (the Kornfeld "alemanno") and Oneglia (the Christ "grigione"), 2 patriot-battalions in Turin (II light demi-brigade in formation), 6 companies of artillery (Alexandria, Turin, Cuneo and Fenestrelle) and 17 invalids companies. All troops which had remained in Piedmont for garrison tasks.

On May 3, Moreau reached Turin in order to save the baggages and, above all, concentrating a new republican government in the Valdese mountain territory (which had to connect Cuneo and Turin and to maintain open one withdrawal way until the Dauphinée). The Commander in Chief, after Schérer, had to reach, later, Alessandria returning eastwards (the sole stone bridge at Turin allowed to pass the Po from left to right bank, where were the eastern fortresses and Alessandria).

TURIN SET UP THE RESISTANCE

The short Moreau's visit, combined with the cold welcome of Turin civil administration, made the French very concerned about the situation. The army, however, needed soldiers and generals at the Po, and so Grouchy was attached to the Moreau convoy, leaving behind a stubborn Italian (corsican) Officer to rule Turin.

Géneral de division Pascal Antoine Fiorella	2838 (of 3438)
Adjutant-général Philibert Fressinet	
I Btn 107th Line infantry demi-brigade	??
Cisalpine gunners of the Citadel	
2 Piedmontese artillery coys	
Pieces (184 mortars, 30 howitzers, 30 guns howitzers, the rest of medium – small calibre, 40000 rifles)	374
National Guard of Turin	??
2 patriots Btns or 2nd Piedmontese demi-brigade légère Chef Carlo Trombetta di San Benigno	300

Turin (Torino), on the confluence of the Dora-Riparia river into the Po, each be passable on solid stone bridges; around 100,000 inhabitants. Former Capital of Kingdom of Sardinia and royal Siege. Its Citadel (a regular pentagon with bastions) was the main fortress of the place with about 14 km of tunnels underground linking the castle with the city. Turin had an artillery-foundry, an artillery workplace, a great arsenal, a weapons factory, une manufacture d'armes, a pulver-factory and a salpetre refinery. It had also an explosives workshop, a military academy, university, two large hospitals and fine barracks. The city, one of the nicest in Italy, had large straight roads.

Many important roads started from Turin, to Genoa, to Alessandria, to the Col di Cadibona and La Bocchetta. These were the roads which passed the Alps:

1° The causeway (mountain road) from Turin to Nice through Coni (Cuneo), the Col de Tende and the Col de Brou, elongating through southern France. On that road, at Savigliano, inserted itself the Mondovi to Ceva road; from Ceva, that road elongated, by a fork, to Savona or to Albenga and Oneille (Oneglia), through the Corniche way to Garessio and Tanaro valley. To the Ceva road, at Savona, jointed, at Carrara, the pathway coming from Alessandria (through Acqui and the Bormida valley).

2° The road from Turin to Barcelonette and Gap, through Coni (Cuneo), Demonte in the Stura valley, and through the Col d'Argentière, where met that of Mont-Dauphin to Tournoux and Col du Vars.

3° The road from Turin to Briançon, through Pinerolo, Pragelato valley, Cesanne and Mont-Genevre. At Briançon this road went forward until either Gap, through the Durance valley, either till Grenoble through Monestier valley, La Grave and Bourg-d'Oyssans.

4° The causeway from Turin to Chambéry, through Rivoli, the Susa pass, the Mount Cenis and the Arc valley. Along that road, near Susa, began a rural road leading, through the Exilles valley, until Cesanne reaching the previous road.

5° The road from Turin to Aosta, through Ivrea, in the Dora-Baltea valley. In the Aosta valley this road changed into a very difficult path, going up until the Grand Saint-Bernard and leading to Martigny, in the Rhone valley; where it passes through the Petit Saint-Bernard, ending at Chambery, into the Isere valley in France.

6° The road from Turin to Brieg, in the Rhone valley, through Vercelli, Novara, north to the Maggiore lake, and up to Domo d'Ossola till the Simplon pass.

All other carriage-roads or bridle paths, which led to Savoy, to Switzerland or France, across the Alps, were passable only in summer. All Piedmontese roads depended heavily on the weather. In the plains, cut by channels and streams, from the Po until the Ticino, it was almost impossible to march in rainy days.

▲ Général de division Emanuel Grouchy

THE VUKASSOVICH PURSUIT

Moreau was forced to send his Chief of Staff, Dessole, to Genoa to enlighten the dark situation of rear communications, continually cut by Insurgents, brigands and "barbets" (mountain marauders from the Nice county). Grouchy became the provisional Chief of Staff. On May 10, all nothern part of Piedmont could be considered lost, while the French had in front the Coalition army and a force of 20000 fanatic peasants on their rear. Incredible was the Grouchy "gaffe" (otherwise ordered by Directory) when he ordered the expulsion, from the army, for all troopers and officer born in Savoy or in the Nice County, treating them as Sardinians "emigré". The Act, very unpopular among who had distinguished himself fighting for France at Verona and on the Adda, caused the birth of new enemies, who were the most dangerous having the knowledge of the French situation and that of their native lands roads and tracks. Half of the French troop were employed in itinerant columns charged to secure the roads and camps in Piedmont. The Insurgence outbroke everywhere. Branda Lucioni (see part 2C) on May 6 entered Chivasso, very close to the capital city. After having raised other insurgents he avoided the engagement with the French "arriere garde" at Settimo

▲ Map of the Turin's fortifications

and reached Ivrea, occupying it. North of the town, the Bard fortress was already in the insurgents hands, who had cut many roads, to Aosta and, by May 8, those of Asti, Acqui, Tortona, Casale and Valenza.

Chivasso was provided with a superb castle, strengthened town's walls and the so – called "Cerche", i.e. two wide and deep moats starting from the Po as far as stream Orco, thus surrounding the town itself at the East and North boundaries through artificial canals called "rogge" (irrigation channels), designed to reclaim and irrigate neighbouring fields. In 1705 the town, without losing its strategic and commercial importance, heroically withstood French troops' siege, thus enabling Turin, the State capital, to get ready for the self – defence against the invaders and avoiding its taking by storm. During Napoleonic period, the ancient fortifications began to be demolished.

Ivrée (lvrea), on the Dora-Baltea, 8,000 inhab. A town encircled by walls and defended by a weak fortress and a Citadel. The Fort de Bard, on Dora-Baltea, fell by treason in 1799 but was hardly defended by Austrians in 1800. Later it was demolished by explosives. Controlled the single causeway of the Aosta valley, to Grand and Petit St. Bernard.

In the middle of that mass of rioters, general Vukassovich was advancing, cautiously, towards Turin. Left the Boffalora bridge on May 5, the Austrian general reached Novara the day after and, after a pause to make some reconnaissance, was in Vercelli on May 8 capturing 30 French guns. Having, the French, burnt out the bridge over the river Sesia, Vukassovich stopped his Advance.

The column was splitten in two branches; on May 10: the first reached Arona on the Maggiore lake, capturing the French garrison with some guns (17); the second crossed the repaired bridge driving to Biella and reaching, the day after, Ivrea where they met Branda Lucioni and his Christ Mass.

It was the time to try the capture of Turin and to surround the French left wing. Branda Lucioni was sent ahead to investigate and to took secret contacts with the administrator and with the National Guard in Turin. The first approach to the city happened on May 15 with secret contacts between Lucioni and the National Guard of Turin. The insurgents had the camp, outside Turin near Settimo while Vukassovich vanguard passed the Po on boats capturing the weak garrison of Casale Monferrato castle..

First Coalition approach: May 15, 1799	
7th Hussar Rgt. Detachment Major (of Reserve) Branda Lucioni	25
the Ordered Christ's Mass (Insurgents)	3000

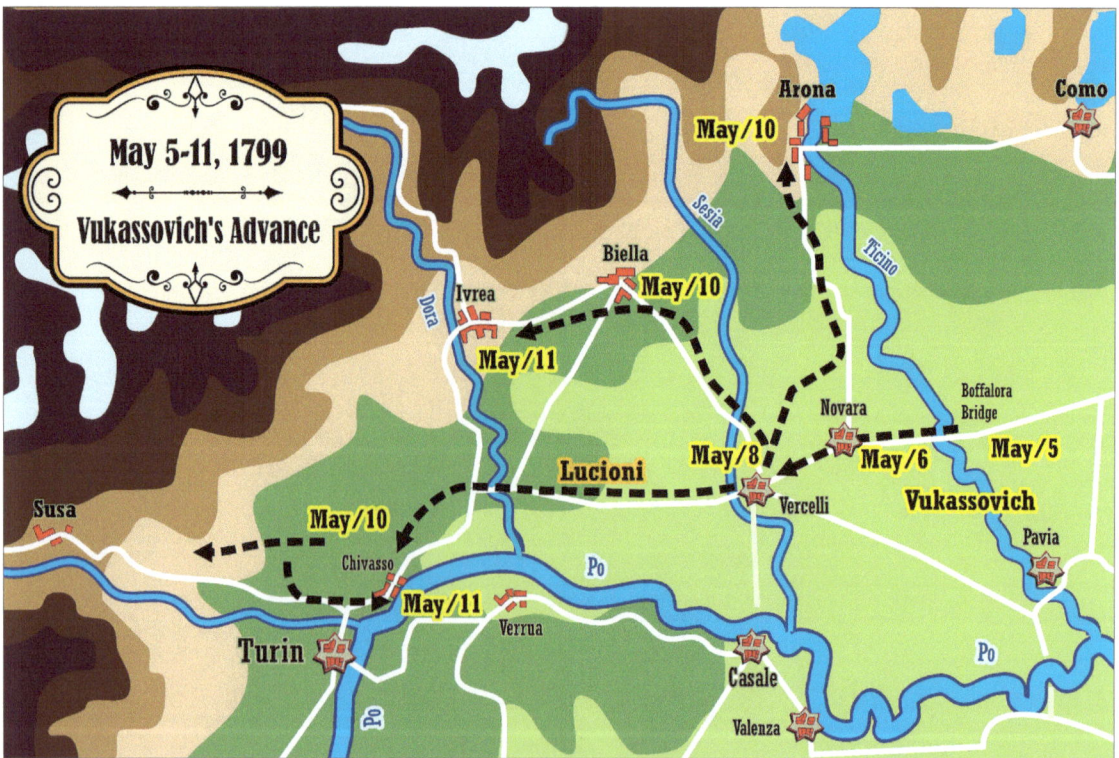

Rear threats for the French

On May 15, after the Bassignana engagement, the division Grenier was alerted by a serious menace in its rear. Moreau sent a "mobile" column against Asti, blocked by rioters.

Mobile Column Adjutant-général Philibert Fressinet to Asti

Artillery	1 gun
63rd Line infantry demi-brigade Chef-de-Brigade Villaret [26]	6 coys
20th Light infantry demi-brigade	1 btn
18th Regiment de Cavalerie Chef-de-Brigade Denis Terreyre [27]	2 Sqns.

Whenever Asti would have been cleared, Grenier had to commit an other "mobile" column to secure other rebel towns as Alba, Casale and Carmagnola.

Mobile Column Général de Brigade Louis François Félix Musnier de la Conserverie [28]

Grenadiers Coy (107th Line demi-brigade)	
33rd Line infantry demi-brigade Chef-de-brigade François Roguet	
12th Dragoons regiment 2 sqns.	

The Fate of Tortona

Tortona (Tortone), on Scrivia river; about 10,000 inhabitants. It was surrounded by walls and had a castle, on a hill, which overlooked the town and the Piacenza's road (to Alessandria). Known in ancient times as Derthona, the city was probably the oldest colony under Roman rule in the westernmost section of the Valley of the Po, on the road leading from Genua (Genoa) to Placentia (Piacenza). The city was founded circa 118 BC - 123 BC at the junction of the great roads; the Via Postumia and the Via Aemilia Scauri which merged to become the Via Julia Augusta. The site made Dertona an important military station under the Romans. The Castle: set on the Savo hill had seen many changes. The original Ligurian castle complex was firstly transformed into a Roman stronghold, then into a Medieval castle, which came under siege several times and was also destroyed on several occasions, it was re-built and re-fortified so that by 1773, thanks to the design feat of the military engineer Bernardino Pinto, commissioned by Vittorio Amedeo III, it became a magnificent fortress. Following the destruction of the same on the orders of Napoleon in 1801, certain remains of the walled town structure are still visible as well as the bell-tower of the fortress church, truly symbolic of the town. The castle, not the walled town, was the last "French" fortress to surrender, Genoa apart.

Garrison

II Btn. 68th Line infantry demi-brigade Chef de Brigade Jules-Alexandre Leger Boutrouë (not in town)
It will be substituted by
III Btn. 63rd Line infantry demi-brigade – Chef Villaret

45ᵉ demi-brigade de ligne detachment

Fanteria provinciale or Piedmontese Milice

On May 9, the IR 19 Alvinczy, vanguard of the Fröhlich division, approached the walls, shot 20 explosive cannonballs and forced the weak French garrison to enter the castle. The town was occupied by general Zoph with 4 battalions and 3 squadrons in order to secure the road to Alessandria and the Scrivia's bridge.

On May 13, after the Bassignana battle, when the Coalized Army moved forward against Alessandria, General Zoph remained behind to watch the siege.

Siege Group FML Johann Zoph	
K.k. IR 19 Hungarian Rifle Rgt. Freiherr Jozsef Alvinczy de Berberek	1654
I – II btns and 2 coys of IV btn Cdr.: Freiherr Carl Adorjan [29] instead of Barone Lelio Spannocchi	
Imperial Russian Musketeers Rgt GM Baron Ivan Ivanovic Dalheim - II btn	734
K.k. 14th Light Dragoons Rgt. Franz Freiherr von Levenehr 1 sqn	135

On May 17, the control of Tortona was left to general Seckendorff and reinforced by the Russian detachment Castelli.

Brigade Generalmajor Friedrich Freiherr von Seckendorff	
K.k. IR 19 Hungarian Rifle Rgt. Freiherr Jozsef Alvinczy de Berberek	1654
K.k. IR 34 Hungarian Rifle Rgt. (future Freiherr Kraj de Kraiova)	1074
(former Esterházy) (I-II Btns) Cmdr. Oberst Johann Hillinger	
K.k. 5th Hussar Rgt. 4 sqns	500
Russian Cmdr. Ad interim: Colonel Stepan Nikolajevich Castelli	
Imperial Russian Musketeers Rgt GM Baron Ivan Ivanovic Dalheim - II btn	734
5th Don Cossacks Rgt. Denissov	432
2nd Don Cossacks Rgt. Sujchev.	465

The Cossacks were sent in patrols to control the road to Genoa, through Novi and Serravalle. Tortona was theater of an hard siege combat in the following months, also after the French defeats at the Trebbia and at Novi. The two utter siege Coalition's groups were formed in the following orders of battle:

Tortona June, 1799	
Austrian Cmdr. Generalmajor Johann Graf Alcaini	
K.k. IR 19 Hungarian Rifle Rgt. Freiherr Jozsef Alvinczy de Berberek	1036
I – II btns and 2 coys of IV btn - Cdr.: Freiherr Carl Adorjan	
K.k. 5th Hussar Rgt - 1 sqn	125
KK Light Dragoons Rgt. Nr. 8 Friedrich Wilhelm Carl Herzog Württemberg	710
Cmdr. Oberst Johann Festenberg Freiherr von Hassenwein, (1 - 2 - 3 div. - 6 sqn.)	

Russian Cmdr. Ad interim: Colonel Stepan Nikolajevich Castelli	
Quartiermeister Oberst Cherwenko	
Imperial Russian Musketeers Rgt GM Baron Ivan Ivanovic Dalheim - II btn	734
8th Jäger (Jegherski) Rgt. Major General Chubarov now Miller– I and II btns	555
chief from 13 May: GM Ivan Ivanovic Miller	

Blockades of Tortona and Gavi ³⁰ - July, 23rd – August 6th 1799

Austrian Cmdr. Generalmajor Johann Graf Alcaini	
K.k. IR 19 Hungarian Rifle Rgt. Freiherr Jozsef Alvinczy de Berberek	1344
I – II – III btns - Cdr.: Freiherr Carl Adorjan	
VII Combined Btn Grenzregiment Warasdiner of Varazdin	523
K.k. IR 34 Hungarian Rifle Rgt.	1242
(the old Esterházy regiment) I - II – III Btns – Cdr.: Cmdr. Oberst Johann Hillinger	
K.k IR 28 Rifle Rgt. Freiherr Michael von Fröhlich	1946
(former Rgt Wartensleben – I-II-III Btns) Cmdr. Oberst Franz Eder von Hartenstein	
Cavalry Reserve	
K.k. 1st Light Dragoons Rgt. Kaiser Franz II	888
Cmdr. Oberst Franz Freiherr von Pilati (8 sqn.)	
K.k. 5th Hussar Rgt - 8 sqns	953
KK Light Dragoons Rgt. Nr. 8 Friedrich Wilhelm Carl Herzog Württemberg	900
Cmdr. Oberst Johann Festenberg Freiherr von Hassenwein, (1 - 2 – 3 div. - 6 sqn.)	

The Fall of Turin

As told, Lucioni, as soon as crossed the Ticino river, had immediately begun to raise the peasants of the Novarese and the Vercellese territories. He freed the city of Novara, Vercelli and Santhià. Then he went ahead, north, in direction of the Canavese and the Biellese territories heading towards Ivrea, Pontestura and Chivasso.

Branda Lucioni had been chosen by Suvorov, just for his military talent, like his own "trader" with the civilians. We know, in fact, of about a Suvorov proclaim, in which the Russian general exhorted *"the faithful soldiers of the king of Sardinia"* to concur to the liberation of their native land and *"to take arms against the French under the command of Major Branda Lucioni, commander of the Christian Mass"*.

While the Russian headed to Alexandria, in fact, Branda Lucioni remained alone with its men in the environs of Turin, where he had put his headquarters, near the Stura river. From that point he often made raids without stopping in a permanent place, succeeding, in this way, to block the city of Turin from all sides and to control the Po. He had a complete success raising the people at the outcry of *"Viva il Re, viva l'Imperatore, viva Gesù, viva Maria, morte ai francesi, morte ai giacobini"*. [31]

The city of Turin had a double government. The military one was led by general Fiorella while the civil administration was ruled by the Piedmontese Municipality, under which were the republican troops of the National Guard. Formed on December 18, 1798, by the French authorities (only few days after their income in city), the Turinese National Guard replaced the ancient city military troops, with an innovative organization. The city was divided in numbered quarters called "islands", from which every male citizen, in age comprised between eighteen and fortyfive years, had to serve in the Guards.

In this way they had to organize four demi-brigades, each of three battalions. The 72 Officers assembled themselves in order to elect the Chiefs of the demi-brigades. They were assisted from a Chief of general Staff with four Aides; a Cashier and a Surgeon completed the organic of Staff. The demi-brigades did have a formal strength of 2.632, 3.042, 3.125, 3.652 men, with a grand total of 12.451 combatants, of which 288 were Officers and 480 non-commissioned officers. These men were subordinated to a Board of Directors, named among the higher Officers of the Municipality and led by a commander in chief. Grouchy named commander in chief, of the entire Guard, the lawyer, and fervent Jacobin, Francesco Federico Campana, with a rank of Adjudant Général.

An old saying in Italy tells "*Piemontesi voltagabbana*" (Piedmontese! Turncoats.) Probably one of the origins of the saying could be reported in that disgraceful 1799 campaign. By a side, now, it is difficult to attribute the precise moment when the members of the Guard took the decision to turn their flags, however a concrete detail in the matter happened on May 5, 1799. That day, French general Jean Marie Moreau, probably impatient for a too much judicious attitude of Turinese, and disappointed for the evasive answers that the Guard persisted to give, invited to join the own forces to the French troops in the fight against the Coalition's army. But that callback did not have some outcome. "*Almost all the Guard's Officers went in front of the Board of Directors declaring they will not want to take the arms against the Austro-Russians.*". This decided the fate of Turin.

The secret plan, in order to dismiss the French, would have to be played on two directions: part to eliminate the commander Campana and the other to prevent the organization of the patriots in armed battalions. For the first issue, the Board of directors introduced an official question of Campana destitution to the Turinese municipality. The municipal organ, in this phase uncertain and incapable to take position, assented to give the total Guard command to the Board. In order to try definitively to have the approval from the Turin citizens, they began to distribute false news about war, with the aim to weaken the republican minds and to take from their own part all undecided citizens. These deep anti-Jacobin feelings, which the French called "the black League", were also a sign of dissatisfied minds and had strong roots in the country own tradition, heavily influenced by priests and aristocrats.

▲ Austrian soldiers in 1799 by R.Knotel

The Municipality, however, had to combat with the stubbornness of the place commander, general Fiorella. Not even when grenades and "*small gun balls of four and eight pdrs.*" hit the rooms, giving them to flames (one grenade murdered two persons), Fiorella drew back his mind. After this episode, the Municipality determined to send a delegation to the general quarters. This delegation had the task to influence Fiorella in order to surrender the city to Branda Lucioni, who acted in the name of general Chasteler. Fiorella received the delegation laying on a bed, with a bored and sleepy attention, and said that, for his own experience of war, those grenades were barely Branda "bravados", denying, moreover, the existence of Austrians troops at the city doors. He then dismissed the Municipals remembering them he would have defended the place "jusqu'à la mort". The day after this encounter, the Austrians finally arrived. On May 22, on the hills around Turin appeared the first vanguards of the coalized units; they deployed at Sassi and, after having thrown the "Liberty Tree" down, continued to march towards the city until reaching, without particular problems, the Madonna del Pilone.

On May 25, nine days after the conquer of Casale castle, the Hungarian baron Joseph Philipp Vukassovich, commander of the imperial vanguard, came in Borgo di Po, on the right river bank, and deployed two batteries, near Turin, (just on the Superga height): one (four 12 pdrs. pieces) on the blockhouse of the hill and the other (2 howitzers) on the public square of the church.

Second Coalition approach: May 24, 1799

Austrian Avantgarde Brigade Generalmajor Freiherr Josef Philipp von Vukassovich	
Avant Garde Generalmajor Sebastian Prodanovich	
II Btn Banater Grenzregiment (or I btn. 13th GrenzRgt)	837
III (VI?) Btn Grenzregiment of Banat (or II btn. 12th Deutschbanater GrenzRgt) Major Zedzwitz	682
K.k. Light Btn. N. 2 Oberst Carl Prince of Rohan	526
Hauptkolonne von Vukassovich	
KK IR 52 Rifle Hungarian Rgt. Erzherzog Palatin Anton Viktor	1292
I – II btns. cdr.: Graf Johann Nepomuk Khuen de Belasi	
K.k. 9th Hussar Rgt. FML Johann Nepomuk Graf Erdödy de Monyorókerek	466
(Erdödy Husaren) 3 Sqns.	
K.k. 7th Hussar Rgt. 6 sqns	773
Cdr.: Oberst Carl Freiherr von Schauroth. With 4 Sqns. II Div. (see after) Obstlt. Graf Thomas Dessöffy (dead at Parona) then Major Franz Szabo – III Div. 1st Major Szabo then Major Joszef Meszko – IV div. 2nd Major Joszef Meszko then Major Felix Graf Montecuccoli	
Russian Avantgarde Brigade Generalmajor Petr Ivanovich Bagration	
7th Jäger Regiment GM Bagration – I and II Btn	624
cmdr.: Gen. Petr Ivanovich Bagration	
Imperial Russian Grenadier Btn (GB) Lomonosov	501
8th Don Cossacks Rgt. Grekov.	414
2nd Don Cossacks Rgt. Sujchev.	465
Austrian Hauptkolonne Division Generalmajor Conrad Valentin Kaim	
K.k. IR 8 Rifle Rgt. (former Huff Rgt)	2662
Cmdr. Obst Johann Schröckinger von Neidenberg (I-II-III Btns) – I and II btns. will be sent at Alessandria on July	
K.k. IR 32 Hungarian Rifle Rgt. Graf Samuel Gyulai	1392
Cmdr. Oberst Franz Posztrehowsky von Millenburg - (I-II-Btns)	
K.k. IR 36 Rifle Rgt. Fürst Carl Fürstenberg	2276
(I-II-III Btn) Cmdr. Oberst Conrad von Thelen	
K.k. 1st Dragoons Rgt. Kaiser Franz II	914
6 sqns. - Cdr.: Oberst Franz Freiherr von Pilati	

At that time, Vukassovich, become in possession of Turin fortifications designs and been informed from Branda Lucioni about the intentions of the National Guard, yearning to find one pacific solution, around six in the morning, wrote a letter to the Turinese Municipality and to the National Guard. He, premising his pacific intentions, invited (however placing a "pacific" two hours term) them to open the city doors, demanding also to avoid the engagement of the Turinese population in an obstinate and impossible defense. Municipality answered to have some delay in the "ultimatum", preferring to hear Fiorella about the situation. They decided also to offer a significant sum (money) to Fiorella in order to make the request more persuasive. A medical doctor, Bonvicino, was chosen for the "business". Today is impossible to know if Fiorella agreed or if he wanted more money. The Chief, however, decided to resist into the Citadel, but allowed the Municipality to send out a delegation to treat with the Austrians.

During the dark night between 25 and 26 (May) the Turinese delegation went outside the walls and was received by general Chasteler and the Grand Duke Constantin, who had followed the Bagration's vanguard. It returned in Turin with a dead-line of six hours for an other definitive answer to the surrender request. The secret pact was that, with the daylight, the Coalized troops had to shoot some "salvoes" and consequently had to observe if the city doors would have been opened. With doors closed, instead, they would have begun the bombardment. But all went as stated. After the first gunshots, the Hussar patrols of Major Meszko found the city door (Porta Po) open and entered the walls. On June 22, the Chancellor of the republican government, Pico, emigrated to Briançon, wrote these words: *"The betrayal of the iniquitous National Guard is sure. Was it which tossed itself against the French, disarming them."*

General Kaim led the occupation detachment preceded from the (not so) Christian Mass of Branda, guilty of a bloody Jacobin chase. The Austrian general rapidly occupied the Turin arsenal in which were found 100 pieces of 3 and 6 pdr., 6 mountain guns, 20 six pdr. long-pieces, 40 twelve pdr. siege-pieces, 6 ten-inches mortars (or 60 pdrs.), 24 six-inches mortars (10 pdrs.), 50 Coehorn mortars ... a total of 301 pieces, 6000 quintals of powder, 60000 rifles, 400.000 ammunitions.

Aleksander Vasiljevič Suvorov entered Turin, around 3.00 hours in the afternoon of May 26, and his arrival was an event full of political meanings, other than a simple military strategic act.

Upgrading the occupation

When Suvorov entered the city, general Fiorella was taking a cup of coffe in the "Cafè d'Catlina" inn. He ran quickly into the Citadel and prepared his defense. Conrad Valentin Kaim was ordered to siege the Citadel with his 5740 soldiers, 700 Austrian and Piedmontese artillerymen and 100 pieces. During the first June days, Fiorella continued to bombard the city, while the Austrian engineers arranged the trenches with which they could get close to the Citadel walls. Heavy rains delayed the works and so the first approach trench was ready only by June 18. The continuing and harassing bombardment, made by Fiorella guns, got general Suvorov very angry. He was not the kind of man who loved to waste his time. On June 20 he aligned the French prisoners in some ranks, frontally to the Manor, threatening to kill them if the Citadel did not give up.

General Fiorella ceased the fire and asked for the capitulation. He left Turin with his 3400 men (more than 300 French died or were wounded during that siege), many of whom were Swiss or Piedmontese, reaching Coni (Cuneo), the soldiers continuing their retreat until the French border, as stated in the Capitulation Act.

Suvorov quickly organized a new Municipality for Turin, giving the highest charge to Count Carlo Francesco Thaon di Sant'Andrea, the former Tortona's Governor, a French-Piedmontese from Nice. This was a bad move on the frail chessboard of politics; the Austrians did not agree at all. The new Municipality became also the *"Consiglio supremo interinale per S.M. il Re di Sardegna"* (provisional Supreme Council in the name of H.M.S. the King of Sardinia), directly showing what Suvorov had in mind to do. He created also a Sardinian War Minister, a name suggested by the King: Antonio Filippo Maria Asinari di San Marzano, Marquis de Caraglio. The Austrians were very angry till to phisically impede the Was Minister to enter in his new office. The challenge for the supremacy in the occupied Piedmont, between the Russian Commander in Chief and Baron Michael Friedrich Benedikt von Melas, began very unkindly. The final act of that challeng is known. Suvorov tried to force the situation directly calling at Turin the exiled (in Sardinia) King Carlo Emanuele. In the late August, however, he was ordered by Czar Paul (but above all by Kaiser Franz II) to reach the Swiss front, leaving the Piedmont. The King was stopped by Austrian at Livorno (Leghorn) and forced to stay at Florence (an other kind of opulent exile), where he abdicated in 1802. So the Imperials from Vienna mastered Turin.

NOTES

19   **Général de division Emanuel Grouchy** The future Marechal (Paris, 1766 - Saint-Etienne, 1847) in 1792, was promoted maréchal de camp and commanded the cavalry of the Armée des Alpes. Was in Vendée during the Civil war. In 1793 abandoned the army, because of a republican decret which excluded noblemen from ranks. Then he returned in the national Guard as a simple soldier. On 11th june 1795, however, was reintegrated as général de division, a rank obtained frome the national « commissaires » during the precedent year. Was chef d'état major in the Armée de l'Ouest and after he became second commander with Hoche in Vendée. In 1796, the Directory confirmed Grouchy as 2nd commander of that Army and ordered him to develop planes for an expedition to Ireland.However the voyage never occurred. In 1798 he was detached to the Armée d'Italie under Joubert. Before the engagement at the front he was the Governor of Piedmont. Then participated at the Novi battle (15 august 1799) where, suffering 14 wounds , was taken prisoner.

20   **Général de brigade baron Robert Motte** (Born 03/12/1754 at Calvados – l'Oudon - Notre-dame-de-fresnay- died 1829). On 22/04/94 was Général de brigade à titre provisoire then confirmed (13/06/95) Général de brigade.

21   **Adjudant général Jean Mathieu Seras** Born on April 16, 1765, at Osasco (Piedmont), Seras joined the French army in 1791, with the rank of Sous-lieutenant. He was at the Alps War, at the Toulon Siege and in the armée des Pyrénées-Orientales, under Augereau, whom followed, in Italy, in 1795. He was named général de brigade on August 1799, leading a brigade at Novi, then général de division in 1805, being often in campaigns with Masséna in Italy. He participated, with the armée d'Italie (prince Eugène), in the 1809 campaign, was severely wounded on July 5, at Wagram. He was named Count of the Empire for his Valour in November of the same year. He was in Spain in 1810 and 1811, and after had the command of several military places.He died in Grenoble on April 14, 1815.

22   After the fall of Turin and the occupation of the Valdese valleys Marauda brought his Legion at general Duhesme camp in the Corps des Alpes.

23   Eridanus was the ancient name of the river Po.

24   **Chef d'escadron Jean-Jacques Laveran,** led the 7th Dragoons, as the provisory chef de brigade, instead of Jean-Joseph Burgairolles, retired. Laveran was officialy the new chef of the regiment on 17 germinal an VII; confirmed with brevet of 2 floréal an VII.

25   **Général Pascal-Antoine Fiorella**, born 7 February 1752, Ajaccio, died 3 March 1818, Ajaccio. Entered military service as a volunteer with the Royal Corsican regiment, in garrison at Antibes, on 24 June 1770, and in the following month became second lieutenant in the Colonel's Company. He continued to serve with this unit as lieutenant (1774), then as second captain (1781). On 14 May 1788 he transferred with this rank to the Corsican Chasseurs, formed by splitting his former regiment into two. At the time of the formation of the battalions of volunteers, he was elected lieutenant-colonel of the 4th of Isère (18 November 1791). He served with the Army of the Alps, particularly at the affair of the Col de La Madeleine, and, having become chef de brigade of the 46th Line (27 February 1794) he was wounded at the action of Colle Ardente (26-7 April 1794). On 24 December 1795, the Directory confirmed his appointment to the rank of general of brigade, signed by Massena. In Italy, in 1796, he distinguished himself at Mondovì (22 April), at Castiglione (3 and 5 August) and in the actions around Mantua. On 14 November 1797 he became a general of division in the service of the Cisalpine Republic. At the time of the disasters in Italy after the formation of the Second Coalition, his superiors appointed him commander of the fortress of Turin (3 may 1799). The defensive works were in a poor state, and the garrison was insufficient in numbers and quality. It not being possible to defend the town effectively, General Fiorella took measures to reinforce the citadel. From 4 June 1799 the enemy opened his entrenchments and commenced a deadly and destructive bombardment. When all defence seemed impossible, a council of war of the fortress decided for surrender (20 June). The garrison was to made prisoner, but to keep it for the Republic, the general offered himself instead, with his staff, and was taken to Austria as a prisoner. In 1801, he was reintegrated as a general of brigade in the French service, and employed in Italy. On 30 April 1804, he became lieutenant-general in the service of the Italian Republic. During the whole period of the Empire, he exercised commands in Lombardy and Venetia, except for a short campaign in the Tyrol in 1809, at the time of the insurrection of the hotel-keeper Andreas Hofer. On 10 October 1809, he became a senator of the Kingdom of Italy. He had then remarried in the country, to Marie-Félicité Goetti (1805). He left the Po valley in 1814, and, during the Hundred Days, was for a some weeks the commander of the arrondissements of Ajaccio and Sartène. Under the Restoration, he had serious difficulties in having validated his appointment to the rank of lieutenant-general, which had been obtained in the Kingdom of Italy. He succeeded none the less (16 February 1817). The governor of Corsica, the Marquis de Rivière, held him, however, to be somewhat suspect. In his report on the subject of retiring Fiorella, he did not fear to say "the general has the right to the maximum according to his age and the seniority of his service, but he has behaved badly, and will always behave badly towards the King, according to the reports I have had. He only deserves the minimum". A road in Ajaccio is named after him.

26   **Chef-de-Brigade Antoine-Francois Brenier de Montmorand**, previously wounded at Verona (twice: on April 4 and 17, 1799) and named General-de-Brigade on the battlefield on June 15, was repalced by:
Chef-de-Brigade Villaret (confirmed in 1800?) not so known. Villaret was renowned as one among the best officers of the armée d'Italie. He died on April 15, 1800, during the assault of Hermette mountain, being substituted by Captain Blanc.

27   The future 27th Dragoons Regiment (Created in 1674 and named Royal-Normandie in 1762, becoming the 19e Regiment de Cavalerie in 1791 and the 18e Regiment de Cavalerie in 1792. Finally in 1803, the Regiment became the 27e Regiment de Dragons). Chef-de-Brigade Denis Terreyre - Colonel in 1803. Born: 5 October 1756. Chef-de-Brigade: 30 July 1794. Chef-de-Brigade: 30 July 1794-1803 Colonel of the 27th Dragoons 1803-1806. General-de-Brigade: 14 November 1806. Commander of the Legion d'Honneur: 25 December 1805. Baron of the Empire: 29 June 1806. Died: 14 February 1823.

28   **Louis François Félix Musnier de la Conserverie** tborn on January 8, 1766, in Longueville, Pas-de-Calais, and died on November 15, 1837 in Paris. In 1780, entered the Paris Military academy at the age 14 as junior gentleman. In 1782 he was second lieutenant in the Piedmont regiment. In 1792: Captain in the same regiment and sent to the Rhine army, where he was aide-de-camp of general-in-chief Lamarlière (probably Jean Fabre of Martillière). Passed to the West coasts army, he became Major. On September 5, 1795, he was chief of brigade at the 187e battle half-brigade. On June 25, 1796, he was chief of brigade at the 60e half-brigade of infantry and, on July 18, 1796, reached the North army, in Holland, where was named adjudant-General and Colonel chief of the general staff at the 187e half-brigade. Till the end of 1798, employed with the army of Italy, he seized by surprise the Novara fortress in Piedmont, action which will be worth to him the patent of brigadier general. On December 17, 1798, it was named brigadier general. In 1799, he had a brigade command in the reserve army. On June 8, 1799, passed through the Po, close to Piacenza, and entered that city. On June 14, 1800, he fought at Marengo, at the head of the 9th light infantry regiment, the Desaix avant-garde. In 1803, it was named provisional commander of the 15th military division in Rouen. In 1804, he received the award of the Legion d'honneur. On February 1, 1805, he was promoted major general. In 1808, he was transferred to Spain army and on. June 23, 1810, at Margalef, in front of Lérida, he took 6 000 prisoners of O'Donnell corps come to help Lérida, where army of Aragon was sieging. On August 28, 1810 he became Grand Officer de la Legion d'Honneur. On January 20, 1811 he was also Baron of the Empire. At the end of 1813, returned to France he became commander at Besançon. In 1814, he made the France campaign taking part under Augereau in the defense of Lyon. With the first Restoration, he was made knight of Saint-Louis and general infantry inspector for the places of Boulogne, Calais, Saint-Omer, Dunkirk. On December 31, 1814, he was made count. In June 1815, he was the general inspector of 10th and 11th divisions. Retired by royal decree on September 4, 1815.

29   **Baron Carl Adorjan** took over the command of his regiment from the provisional commander **Barone Lelio Spannocchi**. Adorjan will be prototed to Generalmajor and led a brigade at the Genola battle (November) where he died on the battlefield.

30 **Gavi** An imposing fortress on the top of the Gavi rock. From the strategic location, it can be assumed that a castle existed here as long ago as pre-Roman or Roman times. In the middle Ages, the castle was adorned by two trapezoidal towers and by high walls that made it impossible to trespass by weaponry of the time. The first important changes took place in 1625, during the French siege, when the French and Savoy army used artillery for the first time. Vincenzo da Fiorenzuola was charged with the project. He was one of the biggest experts in military buildings, and he cooperated with architect Bartolomeo Bianco. Under the supervision of both of them, within a few years, the castle became the fortress we can see today. The old castle was lowered and turned into the Maschio del Forte (Keep), six impregnable ramparts were erected, and joint by strong barrages with fitted embrasures. In the lower part of the fortress the Cittadella (Citadel) was built, it had dormitories, kitchens, water reservoirs, cells for prisoners and stables. Later, between the end of the sixteen hundreds and the beginning of the seventeen hundreds, also the Monte Moro was fortified. The fortress became then absolutely impregnable, it could also accommodate a garrison of considerable dimensions. The castle was the scene of its last battle during the Napoleonic period. The fortress, in fact, was the last French stronghold to withstand the Austro-Russian army before Napoleon's victory in Marengo, on 14th June 1800.

31 "Hurray for the King and the Emperor, Up with Jesus and Holy Mary, death to the French, death to Jacobins!"

▲ Russian grenadier drummer and infantry officer in 1799 by A.V.Viskovatov

▲ French 8th Cavalry in high dress 1799.

WAITING FOR MACDONALDS ARMY MAY-JUNE 1799

LAST HOPES THE BASSIGNANA AND MARENGO BATTLES

The Road to Genoa

The most important road from Piedmont to Genoa was the Giovi pass causeway. It led from Novi (Ligure) to Ronco, through the Serravalle fortress and along the valley of the Scrivia creek. Its control was essential. Another alternative causeway reached the Fort of Gavi from Alessandria and Novi, passed the Appennini mountains at the Bocchetta pass leading to Campomorone and finally to Genoa. This latter was often preferred by French, because considered less dangerous (the Austrians being around Tortona). In every case the control of the town of Novi was fundamental. On May the 9th the Coalized army was again in motion with Kaim crossing the Scrivia creek. Chasteler blew in the gates of Tortona, and entered it under the fire of the French garrison sheltered in the citadel. Vukassovich advanced on Casale Monferrato and Novello along the keft Po bank. Karacsaj was detached to Novi, Serravalle and Gavi, and insurrections against the French were raised at Mondovì, Ceva. On May 10 the Austrians advanced. The cavalry brigade of Karacsaj with the Cossacks extended the control over the terrain between the Scrivia and the Bormida river. Some patrols approached Alessandria coming from Novi and Pozzolo-Formigaro. On May 11 the Russians moved forward with the Förster division. It occupied Castelnuovo di Scrivia, where they put the HQs, while Karacsaj improved the occupation of Novi. At that time Alessandria was isolated.

The troops which prepared the attack to the fortresses of Alessandria and Valenza were:

Avantgarde Brigade Generalmajor Andreas Freiherr Karacsaj de Vale-Sakam [32]	
K.k. IR 28 Rifle Rgt. Freiherr Michael von Fröhlich I and II Btns.	1641
(former Wartensleben) Cdr.: Oberst Franz Eder von Hartenstein – it had to be attached to Ott's division at Piacenza	
K.k. IR 34 hungarian Rifle Line Inf. Rgt. (the former Rgt Esterházy)	1074
(no Inhaber. The future IR Frh. Kraj de Kraiova) (had the I and II Btn). Cdr.: Oberst Johann Hillinger	
it will be detached to the Seckendorff Gruppe and substituted by imperial regiment nr. 8 (former Huff)	
K.k. 4th Light Dragoons Rgt. GM Andreas Frh. von Karacsaj de Vale-Sakam	934
Had 6 sqns. Cdr.: Oberst Joseph Graf Nimptsch. It will be detached as link unit with the Russian Corps Rozenberg.	

Russian Avantgarde Brigade General Prince Petr Ivanovich Bagration	
Imperial Russian 7th Jäger (Jeghersky) Rgt. GM Bagration – 2 Btns	652
cmdr.: Gen. Petr Ivanovic Bagration	
Imperial Russian Musketeers rgt. GM Baranowsky II – I Btn. cmdr Colonel Mihail Aleksejevic Chitrov	694
Imperial Russian Grenadier Rgt. GdI Rozenberg II Btn.	672
Imperial Russian Grenadier Btn (GB) Lomonosov	557
Imperial Russian Grenadier Btn (GB) Dendrjugyn	544
Imperial Russian Grenadier Btn (GB) Kalemin Tula and Tambow Coys	590
Don Cossacks Rgt. Molchanov	495
8th Don Cossacks Rgt. Grekov	489
5th Don Cossacks Rgt. Denissov	439
6th Don Cossacks Rgt. Pasdejev	420

Suvorov's statement to the Austrian Emperor on May 10 was the following:

" *Our speed made us masters of Tortona. The enemy did not have time to throw 2-3.000 men inside. It left the ammunition for Tortona and Alessandria in Novi.*

Alessandria! We must guard it. The enemy have no opportunity to raise his troops there, whenever by the Genoese, which are very few, probably 5 - 6.000 men, and, realistically, not the best troops. However the enemy can entrench itself, particularly if we leave the necessary time to do so, and this will make our attack very difficult...

Valenza! - can become important: for now is not so. Enough to do some fake attack before it.

12 May - Excellency Rozenberg can come only today. The pontoons however tomorrow. – We try so much as possible to set them soon in march.

1) We must be at one time on all positions. As for Bagration he does not have at all to engage himself – only some observations, not too early, not too late. He can let Novi controlled by a small commando. If he will fall, however, into some [enemy] positions during the incoming night, and if that point is supported by others, then everything must be attacked together.

2) Orba, Bormida, Tanaro. The pontoons were thrown, above or on the water, where it is most comfortable in order of the enemy deployment, and in order of the obstacles expected. With this events' speed, Order and Position! The game of the Guns! After this achievement, we must attack quickly the enemy with cutting and thrusting weapons. Then it is not necessary to stop during the artillery fire. The units cooperate in a similar way, as their want.

3) The most important. As soon as the victory outlines, the enemy must already be cut off. In addition the Cossacks add a good distinctiveness. Excellent is the use by throwing them around hostile Cavalry, particularly the heavy. Our cavalry must support it. This latter strikes also strongly into the hostile cavalry, while being supported by the Cossacks, which annihilate the enemy. The quickness overcomes the batteries without losses if the cavalry good performs. So it also can be supported in particular by the Jägern, whenever they not put in danger themselves."

Clash at Ponte Stura

So ... *"Valenza! - can become important: for now is not so."*. The Suvorov's plans were mainly to fasten the offensive, heading towards Turin. The Austrian mind was more cautious, trying to avoid too many conquest by the Russian Commander. With this premise, it became obvious that the Russian had to open the hostilities. Rozenberg, who had followed Vukassovich's advance, placed his camp at Frascarolo, the May 10-11 night. Here he was informed about the Austrian clash (and defeat) of Ponte Stura. In effect, on May 10 morning, 120 German soldiers and 51 volunteers (insurgents) from Trino Vercellese has passed across the Po by boats. They spreaded among the Ponte Stura roads, overrun a French outpost, (obviously) burnt our the Freedom-Tree putting, at its place, a large Christian Cross, calling the town priest to bless the new symbol. At 3 PM, afternoon, 150 Republicans tried to recuperate the position, but they were repulsed leaving on the ground 6 dead and 5 prisoners. On the following day, at Ponte Stura converged a strong Austrian detachment of about 300 men. However the town was attacked by two battalions of the 106th demi-brigade, come from Casale through the Grana. They deployed themselves in three column starting from San Salvatore and Mirabello and assaulted Ponte Stura from three directions: from the main road to Alessandria, from the "Cascina" of the Po and from the track to Ortiglia. In spite of the strong resistance of the Austrians-peasants detachment, the French seized the Castle entering in its gardens takin over 300 Austrians prisoners. After the insurgents had left the town, Ponte Stura was roughly pillaged.

On that same day, May 11, Rozenberg crossed the Po at Valenza, Suvorov himself overlooked this probe-operation, for the extreme danger of the passage, since the southern (right) bank of the Po commanded the stream, which was cut, there, into several channels forming islands. The Russians got possession of Mugarone, the larger of the Po islands, notwithstanding the opposition of the Adjutant-General Gareau.

The French defence was based on a three fortresses triangle (Casale, Valenza and Alessandria) with an utter, inner, triangle formed by the confluence of three major (at that time) rivers: Tanaro, Bormida and Po.

Valenza The Latin writer *Caius Plinius II The Elder*, described the town in the following terms *"forum fulvi quod valentium"* (fulvi=golden) , including the town of Valenza amongst the most important in this part of Italy. Going back into the ancient history, the tradition says that the birth of this characteristic, which brought the name to the town, all over the world, was done by the golden sands of the river Po. Sure is that the big river, on which settled Ligurian in the 10th Century B.C., had for the town considerable importance and influence. "High town on the water" was called by military engineers in the 17th Century, noticing the natural terracing, in the point where Sesia and Tanaro merge into the Po. It was connected with two good roads with Alessandria and Casale and, with an eastwards trail, to the village of Bassignana.

Casale on the Po or Monferrato is a town in the Piedmont, part of the province of Alessandria. It is situated about 60 km east of Turin on the right bank of the Po, where the river runs at the foot of the Monferrato hills. It was sacked by the anti-imperial troops of Vercelli, Alessandria and Milan in 1215, but rebuilt and fortified in 1220. It fell under the power of the Marquis of Montferrat in 1292 and later became the capital of the marquessate. In 1536 it passed to the Gonzagas of Mantua. During the Gonzaga ruling the town was fortified. Vincent I ordered the building of a large star-shaped citadel, in 1590, in order to defend the town from Savoy's increasing power. In 1600 Casale resisted against all the Spanish, Savoyards and Imperials attempts to seize its citadel. The impregnable citadel of Casale was mined and destroyed in 1795 following the terms of a truce-treaty.In town remained only its old castle: the castle of the Paleologi (Palaiologos), an imposing 15th century military construction with a hexagonal plan with four angular towers and an encircling moat. Its civic tower, square in plan and made of bricks, 60 metres high, was built in 1510 with an attached bell tower. In 1799 Casale was other than an useful fortress, but rather a good point to cross the river Po.

The French Line

The army remnants had followed Moreau until the Valence bridge, the only one existing over the Po since river Sesia until Turin, and found it burnt out, as often happened during those extraordinary (and unfortunate) measurements so frequent during the armies withdrawals. Furthermore, the boats-bridge, which the French had close to Pavia and which General Moreau had ordered to dismount, the same day of the Adda clash, was not available, in order to try to envoy on right bank of Po what French had of artillery. Moreau was forced to march in a hurry and to pass the river at Turin. Thus he went towards the capital city with the Grenier division and some remains of the Serrurier division which had reached the main column from the Novara's higher territories. That walk of an army part to Turin had the advantage of making the enemy uncertain of our projects, that of covering the large parks of the army and of protecting the retreat from Milan, now occupied by Austrians.

After having made moving, to mount Cenis and to Coni, all that he had out of artillery and parks, and after having ensured the re-entry in France of the administrations and civil "commissaires", with all the non-combatants which were with the army, and after having given the necessary orders for Turin and its citadel, General Moreau went back to Alexandria to meet there the divisions of Victor and Laboissière. The Coalized army somewhat pursued the French army, after Ticino crossing. They crossed the Sesia only three days after Moreau, and, when its vanguards appeared in front of Turin, there were only ten or twelve French left behind.

The army gathered under the Alexandria walls, strong about 23000-24000 men, took its position at Bassignana, supporting its rear line at Alexandria, its left at Valence and Casale, with "eclaireurs" outpost on the left Po bank until Verrua (in front of Crescentino), and along the Bormida until Acqui. As known, the Russians occupied the Lomelline and the Austrians rambled between Voghera and Tortone. General Moreau sent consequently some battalions in Liguria, where there were too few French troops and which could be attacked from one moment to another. It gave the command of this country to general Pérignon. As told, the spreading of the insurgencies obstacled the general Grouchy call-at-arms of April 30, ending with a totally insufficient effect. Apart from few hundred French, Grouchy could only count on 2 line battalions plus an artillery company in Alessandria (II/1a Aosta, II/3a Queen), and the other troops listed in the rest of Piedmont. Casale was garrisoned with two battalions (mainly conscripts) of the 106th Line infantry. The Alessandria garrison was sent forward to defend the Po line between the village of Pecetto and Bassignana followed by a Swiss Legion's battalion.

In the meanwhile, Count Colli Ricci of Felizzano, already at disposition of the French from March and charged of the Alexandria defense against the Strevi rebels, was named Chef-de-brigade and had the task to reconstitute the French 14th Line demi-brigade, with Piedmontese volunteers. The personal prestige of the Piedmontese commander, in effects, attracted many veterans already under him during the Alps war of 1793-96. The 14th Line, officially, depended on the brigadier general François Jean Baptiste Quesnel du Torpt, but, on May 8, Colli Ricci had to replace him because of his temporary incapacity to combat. The 14th Line was sent between Pecetto and Bassignana, until the confluence of the rivers Tanaro and Po, where already the 3 battalions of the former Alessandria garrison stood, one Helvetian and two Piedmontese (II/1a and II/3a).

Armée d'Italie HQ at Valenza

Comm. In Chief: General de Division Jean Victor Marie Moreau
* NOTE: this hypothetical French Order of battle is remodeled by books and literature.
Division General Paul Grenier HQ at Valenza
Cavalry

6th Hussar Regiment Chef Jean-Baptiste-Gregoire Delaroche
13th Rgt Chasseurs à Cheval Chef Bouquet (?)
24th Rgt Chasseurs à Cheval
9th Régiment Chasseurs à Cheval Chef Claude Matthieu Gardane [33]

Arriere Garde Detachment Chef de Brigade Louis-Stanislas-Xavier Soyez
At Verrua and Casale

106th Line Demi Brigade II btn Chef Jean Claude Roussel [34] - III Btn. with Masséna in Switzerland
18th Light Demi-Brigade remnants of the I – II and III Btn – Chef Louis-Stanislas-Xavier Soyez

AvantGarde (Brigade) Chef de Brigade Louis Garreau [35]

68th Line demi-brigade II Btn - Chef de Brigade Jules-Alexandre Leger Boutrouë [36]
The I btn was with Montrichard, the III btn was in Turin
106th Line Demi Brigade I Btn. Chef de bataillon Dupellin [37]
63rd Line Demi Brigade I-II-III btns Chef-de-Brigade Villaret [38]

Brigade Général François-Jean-Baptiste baron de Quesnel du Torpt [39]
Chef (Général) de brigade Luigi Leonardo Antonio Colli-Ricci Marchese di Felizzano [40]

17th Light Demi Brigade Chef de brigade Dominique Honore Antoine Marie Vedel [41] - I-II Btns.
14th Line Demi-brigade - Chef de Brigade Jean-Claude Moreau (RESERVE)

Brigade Général count Louis Partounneaux

24th Line Demi Brigade – I , II and III Btns. Chef de Brigade Guinet ?
33rd Line Demi Brigade – I , II Btns. Chef de Brigade Roguet

Division General Claude-Victor Perrin
At Alessandria

Brigade Général baron Charles-Louis-Dieu Donné Grandjean [42]
Brigade Général comte Henri-François-Marie Charpentier [43]
Brigade Adj-Général Claude-Joseph Buget [44]

Infantry (on Pecetto road)

3rd Line Demi Brigade - Chef de Brigade Georges Mouton
5th Line Demi-brigade Chef de Brigade Louis-Hyacinthe Le Feron
21st Line demi-brigade Chef de Brigade Robert [45]
39th Line Demi-brigade Chef-de-brigade Antoine-Louis Popon de Maucune
92nd Line Demi Brigade Chef Bruno-Albert-Joseph Duplouy - I II III Btns.
93rd Line Demi-brigade Chef-de-brigade a.t.p. Charles-Sebastien Marion [46]
99th Line Demi-brigade Chef-de-brigade Pierre-Joseph Petit

Cavalry

15th Chasseurs à cheval Chef-de-Brigade Louis Lepic
18th Rgt. de Cavalerie (4 sqns) Chef Denis Terreyre
3rd Régiment Chasseurs à Cheval Chef François-Alexandre Grosjean

AvantGarde (Brigade) General Gaspard-Amédée Gardanne [48]
At Pecetto and Bassignana. It acted as division Grenier Reserve.

II Btn Aosta - 1st Piedmontese demi-brigade
II Btn Regina – 3rd Piedmontese demi-brigade
Btn Suisse 1ᵉ Legion
Piedmontese artillery coy
1st Hussars Régiment - Chef de Brigade Joseph-Denis Picard [49]

THE BATTLE OF BASSIGNANA

The May 12 morning General Chubarov with infantry and artillery, passed across the Po at Bassignana, and, as soon as the Cossacks saw these soldiers on the other side, they dashed into the river and swam over followed by one battalion of the Rozenberg vanguard, which was arriving at Borgo Franco. Other two Russian battalions were sent towards Frascarolo under Colonel Shukov, to control Valenza. In order to avoid strong French reactions, Vukassovich was sent forward to bombard Casale from the opposite Po bank. The main attack group had crossed the Mugarone pathway during the previous night: three Grenadiers battalions, three Jäger coys, two Cossacks pulk, one Dragoons squadron and two artillery coys. The first Russian infantry column (Dalheim brigade), arrived at 5.00 PM of May 11, put into requisition some boats rowing to the Mugarone island. The Cossacks of Semjornikov passed through swimming with the horses. General Miloradovich and Grand Duke Constantin also crossed by night. Came close to the French, without glowing any lights, binding the horses' mouths with ribbons to avoid their whinnies and, above all, without any fire shot, they waited for the dawn at a distance of 100-200 meters from the French lines. The place of the attack, chosen, probably, by general Rozenberg himself, was mostly unfavourable to the Coalition's troops. The right (French) bank of Po dominated the opposite (Russian) bank, which was low, swampy and passable only on sand dikes (chaussées). The nocturn advance had the task to mask the Russian moves, in the hope to find a comfortable fording point to cross the last branch of Po, after Mugarone island. It was impossble to keep a bridgehead on the large island for its too soft ground but the fording attempt would have been protected by trees and bushes, which covered the French riverside.

Avantgarde Brigade general-major Nikolaj Andrejevich Chubarov	
Imperial Russian 8th Jäger Rgt. Major General Chubarov	708
Chief from May 13: GM Ivan Ivanovich Miller – I Btn Lieut.Colonel Ivan Fjodorovich Wrangel. II Btn.	
Don Cossacks Rgt. Semjornikov (Semernikov)	438
K.k. 4th Light Dragoons Rgt. GM Andreas Frh. von Karacsaj de Vale-Sakam 1 Sqn.	150

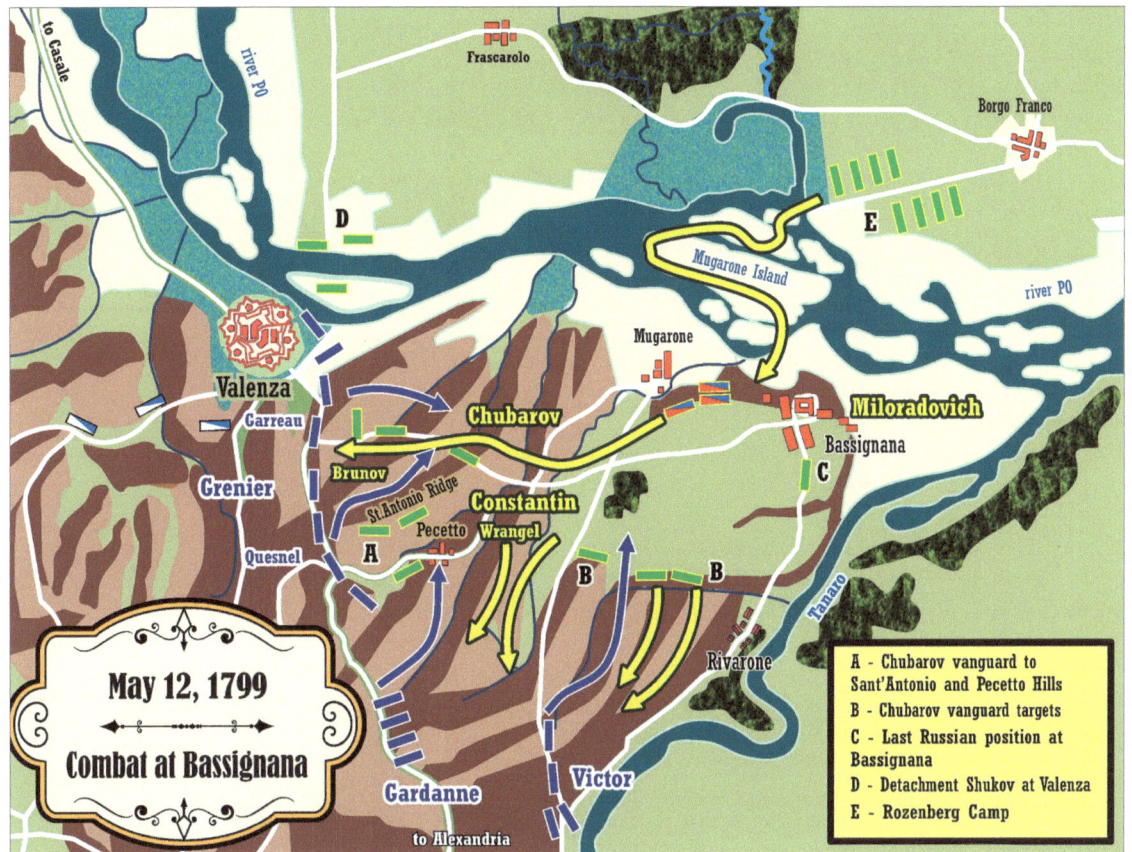

May 12, 1799 — Combat at Bassignana

A - Chubarov vanguard to Sant'Antonio and Pecetto Hills
B - Chubarov vanguard targets
C - Last Russian position at Bassignana
D - Detachment Shukov at Valenza
E - Rozenberg Camp

Detachment Colonel Shukov	
Imperial Russian Musketeers rgt. GM Baron Ivan Ivanovich Dalheim – I btn	719
Imperial Russian Grenadier Btn (GB) Sanajev Butyrsk and Archangelgorod Coys	599
K.k. 4th Light Dragoons Rgt. GM Andreas Frh. von Karacsaj de Vale-Sakam 1 Sqn.	157

Brigade General-major Ivan Ivanovich Dalheim 5°	
Imperial Russian Musketeers rgt. Young-Baden or molodo-Badensky – one battalion	690
Imperial Russian Musketeers rgt. GM Tuyrtov or Tug'lsky (Tula) – one battalion	719
Cmdr.: Major Ivan Fjodorovich Golovin	

General-major Constantin Pavlovich Romanov Grand Duke of Russia	

Moreau, thinking such kind of operation imprudent and dangerous, gave orders to avoid the resistance at the outpost; this would have attracted the whole Rozenberg division into the cauldron. The French retreated along the road to Alessandria and took new positions at Pecetto (near Valenza). They deployed the line behind a ravine with the left wing entrenched in Sant'Antonio, a village on the hills, which was defended with the artillery. The Grenier division occupied the front from Pecetto (right) to the Po (left), with Quesnel brigade at the engagement point. Victor was ordered to march forward from Alessandria in order to intercept the Russian flank. When Moreau heard news of the Russians passage he ordered Grenier to stand firm, renewing Victor to march in great haste from Alessandria. General Moreau, who was into Valenza, personally deployed his right wing. After having retreated the Bassignana detachment, as told, he took position on Pecetto heights, extending the left wing until the Po, with Valenza behind the line. The battle was received there, the French occupying higher positions. On May 12, morning, Chubarov Vanguard concentrated on Mugarone island, beginning to ford the last branch of the Po. The Russians found Bassignana free of French; the Cossacks patrols sent forward referred the Republicans were on Pecetto heights. General Chubarov, there, had ready only 3 ½ battalions with the Cossacks (about 2500 men). He advanced on two columns:

- the left one under Colonel Brunov had two Young-Baden Musketeers coys and one Jäger battalion tried to control their left flank but were sent, with Chubarov, against Sant'Antonio;

- the right one under Lieut. Colonel Wrangel attacked Pecetto with the other Jäger battalion and two coys of Sanajev Grenadiers (led by Grand Duke Constantin Pavlovich).

At about one o'clock the fight began; the Grand Duke Constantin with his sword led his troops against the village of Pecetto, which the French held. Chubarov, after having reached San Antonio and Pecetto town, deployed his charging-columns. They tried several times to push the French downhill, but were always repulsed by the Quesnel brigade. The Russian reinforced the right flank of Chubarov sending two coys of Tytrov Musketeers and the following units:

General-major Mihail Andrejevich Miloradovich 1st	
Imperial Russian Grenadier Rgt. GdI Rozenberg or Moskowsky (Moskow) one battalion	670
Imperial Russian Musketeers rgt. GM Mihail Andrejevich Miloradovich one battalion	725
Imperial Russian Musketeers rgt. LG Povalo-Shveikovsky (Smolensk) – one battalion	700

The extreme right wing of the Russian deployment was defended by Semjornikov Cossacks, reinforced with other two Tujrtov Musketeers Coys. But it was too late.

In the meantime, Victor, arriving from Alessandria, had become very close. From the heights, on which they were fighting, the Russians observed the long columns of the advancing French and the order of retreat was issued. They went back towards Bassignana to return on "friendly" river Po bank. But the misfortune reserved other surprises and the disengagement transformed itself into a real disaster.

While, when the Russian had disembarked at Bassignana, the Piedmontese inhabitants welcomed them with high "hurrays", in that return, instead, they were received with resentment and feelings of treachery. The peasants began to damage the carriages and the boats, most of which were unfastened and left free at the stream. Many of the Russian soldiers were obliged to retire into the Mugarone island but the flying bridge they established at this point having broke, they had to pass the night in the middle of the Po, under the bombardment of the French guns and very reactive against the several assaults the Victor Vanguard, Gardanne, incessantly ran. During the late night some ferries were repaired and many soldiers did reach the left Po bank. Unfortunately the main group of the wounded was left behind with some detachments. When the French arrived, a large portion of the Imperials were forced to lay down their arms, while many others drowned into the Po, trying to swim till the opposite bank.

Other two Russian probe attacks had the same bad luck. Colonel Shukov tried to cross the Po by boats. He reached an island in front of Valenza were he was pinned, because of a strong musketry (the 63rd demi-brigade on the opposite bank), and the attack aborted. Also Vukassovich passed the Po with some detachments, during the Casale bombardment. However the ferries, overrun by the strong stream, were lost and a strong French attack destroyed the raiding party.

The Russians lost in this fight 1200-1500 men, dead, wounded and prisoners, with four guns. General Chubarov (for many sources, he was killed there) [51], however he was only wounded. Wounded were also Colonels Passek and Brunov, Lieut. Colonel Wrangel, Majors Kochanowsky, Moller, Marchenko, Golovin, Korf with other 50 superior Officers. Colonel Tatarinov and other 6 Officers died. [52]

The French had about 600 men out of combat, including General Quesnel, who was wounded. This General was quickly replaced. Count Colli Ricci of Felizzano who, from March already at disposition of the French and charged of the Alexandria defense against the Strevi rebels, had been named Chef-de-brigade, had the task to reconstitute the French 14th Line demi-brigade [53], after the battle, with Piedmontese volunteers. The personal prestige of that Piedmontese commander, in effects, attracted many veterans, who were already under him during the Alps War of 1793-96.

Approaching the Great Citadel

Being Bassignana a sole Russian defeat, this made someone pleased at Vienna and, conversely, disturbed the Czar in Moscow. The Emperor tried to suggest a possible solution stating that, if Suvorov would think general Rozemberg too much tired for the campaign fatigues, he had at his disposition a good replacement in Derfelden (the Grand Duke Constantin's tutor). In every case the defeat in the "demonstrative" attack had to be rapidly forgotten and the Russian army had to drive deeply into Piedmont to redeem itself. The important fortress of Alexandria (Alessandria) had been approached just before Bassignana, on May 10; Cossacks regiments Denissov, Molchanov and Grekov, supported by Kalemin Grenadiers, had cleared the French outpost in Marengo, while the Coalized army was reaching the village of San Giuliano with the Austrians (HQs at Torre Garofoli) and Novi with Bagration's vanguard.

On May 13 the Austrians left Torre Garofoli moving northwards in direction of Sale and the Po; they also transferred their HQs from Torre Garofoli to Castelnuovo Scrivia, leaving to the Tortona siege group the task to control the Genoese roads. Avantgarde Group Bagration was ordered to leave Novi and to march towards Cambio, an hamlet on the right Po bank 3 km north of Sale and 12 km east of Bassignana (by road). Sending this order to Bagration, Suvorov extended his "At the Po!" call also to general Seckendorff. Most likely, the Russian Field Marshal had in mind something similar to a second "revenge" attack against Valenza.

At Cambio the river Po presented a singular group of large islands, however each smaller than Mugarone, and the point could have been selected as a safe fording point, having, on the left bank, a good road connection from Cairo (Lomellina) to Lomello. The Russians Musketeers battalions, not involved in the Bassignana affair, were, in a great hurry, gathered under general Förster and sent towards Cambio to ford the river, waiting for the general. At Frascarolo, general Tuyrtov took the Rozenberg's place in order to control the front of Valenza.

Valenza Observation Group General-major Jacob Ivanovich Tuyrtov	
Imperial Russian Musketeers rgt. GM Tuyrtov or Tug'lsky (Tula) – one battalion	632
Imperial Russian Musketeers rgt. GM Mihail Andrejevich Miloradovich one battalion	686
Don Cossacks Rgt. Semjornikov (Semernikov)	416

Division Lieut. General Ivan Ivanovich Förster	
Imperial Russian Musketeers rgt. Lieut. General Förster (Tambov) - one battalion	757
Imperial Russian Musketeers rgt. GM Mihail Andrejevich Miloradovich one battalion	686
Imperial Russian Musketeers rgt. Young-Baden or molodo-Badensky – one battalion	618
Imperial Russian Musketeers rgt. GM Baron Ivan Ivanovich Dalheim – one battalion	734
Imperial Russian Musketeers rgt. LG Povalo-Shveikovsky (Smolensk) – one battalion	719
Imperial Russian Grenadier Btn (GB) Sanajev 2 Coys	280

However it was not yet possible to ford the river at Cambio. So Förster left his HQs at San Nazzaro de' Burgondi that May 13, passed the Po at the boats-bridge of Mezzana Corte, reached Pontecurone on the following day and, on May 15, entered Castelnuovo Scrivia ending their march at the Sale camp.

The intention to revenge Bassignana, if any, was early abandoned and Suvorov ordered a general march towards the Lomellina, leaving back only some siege groups; actually a strange provision which seemed to leave the way open to Moreau army linking together with Macdonald. However the opportunities to seize Casale and Valenza from the rear and to take the capital Turin, mixed with some worries about the St. Gotthard struggles in southern Switzerland and the necessity to stay closer to Milano, determined Suvorov's decision. The new deployment had to begin on May 16 afternoon, but something different happened.

BATTLE AT SAN GIULIANO (OR FIRST MARENGO)

As Gachot told, on May 16, to harass the Coalition's left flank, Moreau sent forward a strong task-force (of about 6000 men) to probe the enemy's intentions. The column, central, engaged the Austrians at San Giuliano vecchio (old) where they found troops already in "order of battle". Chasteler, for Gachot, had given orders to deploy to his divisions (Bagration, Lusignan, Fröhlich and Lobkowitz ??).[54] The French divisions Victor and Grenier were to weak to bring a decisive attack by initiative but, actually, the Coalition's troops were almost taken by surprise. The Republicans had built a temporary bridge (a "pont volant") over the Bormida at the position named "I Cedri" (the Cedars). They passed the bridge and divided themselves into two columns, at 8.00 AM, along the main road, taking covers from the small stone walls: the left towards the Cascina Pietrabona (or Pederbona), the right towards la Cascina Stortigliona (names which will be renowned on the following year).

Left Wing Brigade Général Luigi Leonardo Antonio Colli-Ricci Marchese di Felizzano

17th Light Demi Brigade Chef de brigade Dominique Honore Antoine Marie Vedel - I-II-III Btns.
68th Line demi-brigade II Btn - Chef de Brigade Jules-Alexandre Leger Boutrouë
14th Line Demi-brigade - Chef de Brigade Jean-Claude Moreau
1st Hussars Régiment - Chef de Brigade Joseph-Denis Picard [55]

Right Wing Brigade General Gaspard-Amédée Gardanne

18th Light Demi-Brigade remnants of the I – II and III Btn – Chef Louis-Stanislas-Xavier Soyez
II Btn Aosta - 1st Piedmontese demi-brigade
II Btn Regina – 3rd Piedmontese demi-brigade
Btn Suisse 1e Legion
15th Chasseurs à cheval Chef-de-Brigade Louis Lepic

Brigade provisional Général de Brigade Louis Garreau (Center)
Two battalions probably deployed to watch the bridge over the Bormida in front of Alexandria

106th Line Demi Brigade I Btn. Chef de bataillon Dupellin
20th Light demi-brigade Chef-de-Brigade Lucotte (blocked in Ancona) – one battalion ?

At 9.00 in the morning the French engaged the enemy, overrunning the weak outpost in Marengo, but the first strong musketry began at 10.00 AM, with some Austrian detachments repulsed away from Marengo, Spinetta and Cassina Grossa by the 74e demi-brigade, which led the advance.
Avantgarde detachement Rousseaux (from Gardanne brigade?)

74th Line infantry Demi-Brigade Chef Antoine-Alexandre Rousseaux

In Line between San Giuliano Vecchio and San Giuliano Nuovo, around 800 mt far from Alexandria road, advanced the Jäger regiment Bagration and two Musketeers regiments. The left wing, beyond the "chaussée" behind Cascina Grossa, was hold by two Russian battalions. At the two extreme wings the Coalized Army had two divisions of Lobkowitz Dragoons and the artillery. The Centre was organized with 6 battalions of the Fröhlich division (being the Grenadiers Korherr and Weber, the first line) by the right side of the road, while former Fiquelmont Grenadiers with the fusiliers battalions Stuart along the left side. In the rear were the other two battalions (Grenadiers Paar and Stentsch) with 5 squadrons of the Lobkowitz Dragoons, far around 200 mt from the first line. There was also a skirmisher screen organized taking 10 soldiers from each first line coy.
Behind Cassina Grossa the armies clashed together. The artillery was kept on wings. The right Coalition's wing, led by Prince Bagration, repulsed the second French assault to the houses of San Giuliano. Then the Prince counterattacked with his Cossacks (Molchanov and Grekov) pushing general Colli back till the Tanaro river. The left wing and the Center of the Coalition's line, otherwise, began unbalanced; at 12.00 o'clock some of the Coalized

troops began to withdraw, also if supported by Cossacks raids (General Suvorov's report declared other two Cossacks attacks directed by Field-Atamans Molchanov and Grekov, in which the riders destroyed a squadron of the 1st Hussars and then captured 78 men).

As for the orders it had to leave Novi and march quicly through San Giuliano to Cambio. There it had to pass the Po to continue the march until Breme (near Frascarolo). Prince Bagration was caught into the clash while marching towards Sale. His Avantgarde deployed at San Giuliano while the rearguard of the march column stopped near Cassina Grossa.

After the San Giuliano battle, the orders chamged and Bagration was forced to wait at Gerola for the first occasion to pass through the Po (a stream less swollen) and to march along its left bank.

Avantguard Division General Prince Petr Ivanovich Bagration	4877	4161
units	Listed	Fit
Imperial Russian 7th Jäger (Jeghersky) Rgt. GM Bagration – 2 Btns	703	624
cmdr.: Gen. Petr Ivanovic Bagration		
Imperial Russian Musketeers rgt. GM Baranowsky II – I Btn.	799	698
Imperial Russian Grenadier Rgt. GdI Rozenberg II Btn.	763	627
Imperial Russian Grenadier Btn (GB) Lomonosov	585	501
Imperial Russian Grenadier Btn (GB) Dendrjugyn	566	453
Don Cossacks Rgt. Molchanov	496	435
8th Don Cossacks Rgt. Grekov	488	414
6th Don Cossacks Rgt. Pasdejev	477	409

Austrian Units with outposts at Marengo, Spinetta, Castel Ceriolo. In all „after battle" reports (Melas, Lusignan and Bagration) there was no mention about Karacsaj units, other than the weak outposts in Marengo. It seemed they did not participate at the battle, after the first skirmishes.

Avantgarde Brigade Generalmajor Andreas Freiherr Karacsaj de Vale-Sakam	
K.k. IR 28 Rifle Rgt. Freiherr Michael von Fröhlich I and II Btns.	1641
(the former Rgt Wartensleben) Cdr.: Oberst Franz Eder von Hartenstein	
K.k. IR 8 Rifle Rgt. (former Huff Rgt)	2695
Cmdr. Obst Johann Schröckinger von Heidenburg (I-II III Btns)	
K.k. 4th Light Dragoons Rgt. GM Andreas Frh. von Karacsaj de Vale-Sakam	935
Had 6 sqns. Cdr.: Oberst Joseph Graf Nimptsch.	

Central Division Generalmajor Freiherr Michael von Fröhlich		
Under provisional command of Generalmajor Franz Joseph Marquis de Lusignan		5374
units	Listed	Fit
Brigade Oberst Franz Xavier Weber von Treuenfeld		3398
K.k. hungarian Grenadier battalion Major Joseph Korherr ObstLeut. Johann Pértussy		618
K.k. Grenadier battalion Oblt Franz Xavier Weber von Treuenfeld		457
K.k. IR 18 Rifle Line Inf. Rgt. Graf Patrick Stuart		1741
Cmdr. Obst Franz Weber von Treuenfeld - I and II Btns		
K.k. Grenadier battalion Graf Joseph Fiquelmont Count Johann Morzin		582
Brigade Generalmajor Marquis Hannibal Sommariva		1976
K.k. Grenadier battalion FML Karl Graf von Mercandin Graf Carl Paar		520
K.k. Grenadier battalion Freiherr Georg von Stentsch Graf Anton Schiaffinati		620
K.k. 10th Light Dragoons Regiment Joseph Fürst Lobkowitz		836
(had 6 sqns. on 3 divisions I II and III) Cdr.: Oberst Marquis Hannibal Sommariva – Second Oberst and Commander Max Joseph Fürst Thurn und Taxis. II Div. ObstLt. Alois Graf Harrach – III Div. Major Ignatz Molitor		

Suvorov, fearing he was on the point to lose another battle, rode among his troops trying to rally those retreating. He stood, erect, on his horse wavening the sabre and cursing those fugitives. The Centre was heavily supported by general Sommariva, which gave time to Lusignan to come from Torre Garofoli with all his battalions and squadrons, which were deployed in front of San Giuliano vecchio. In the early afternoon moved forward also the 4800 men of Kaim's division, reinforcing the left wing. At 4.00 PM, general Moreau, observing the new situation, gave the withdrawal order. The French returned to their single bridge in good order. In the late afternoon the troops of division Kaim took possession of the battered line and hold it until night. Moreau, having realized the overwhelming superiority of the Coalition's troops, organized the withdrawal leaving Gardanne and Colli brigades as Arriere-Garde. The village of Marengo was left behind with all the wounded soldiers gathered there. The village was abandoned at 5.00 PM and, an hour after, all French soldiers had passed the Bormida backwards. The Cedar's bridge was dismantled and at 6.30 PM the first Austrians were seen on the Bormida's bank, in reconnaissance.

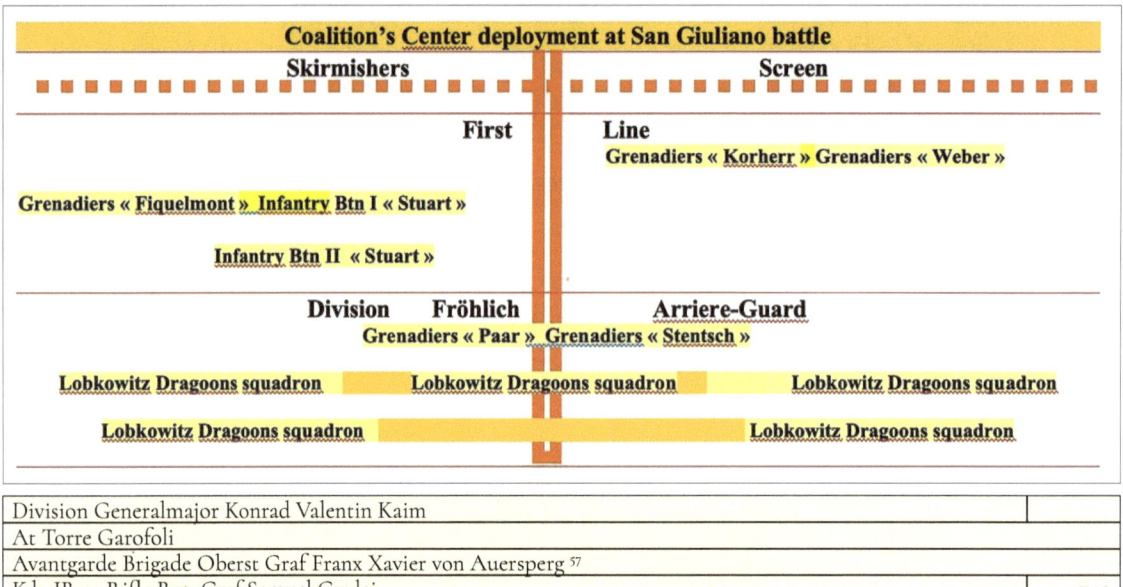

Division Generalmajor Konrad Valentin Kaim	
At Torre Garofoli	
Avantgarde Brigade Oberst Graf Franx Xavier von Auersperg [57]	
K.k. IR 32 Rifle Rgt. Graf Samuel Gyulai	740
Cmdr. Oberst Franz Posztrehowsky von Millenburg - (I- Btn) III btn to Mantua	
K.k. IR 36 Rifle Rgt. Fürst Carl Fürstenberg III Btn.	858
K.k. 1st Light Dragoons Regiment "Emperor" Kaiser Franz II 1 squadron	169
Brigade Generalmajor Graf Joseph Mittrowsky	
K.k. IR 32 Rifle Rgt. Graf Samuel Gyulai II Btn	742
K.k. IR 36 Rifle Rgt. Fürst Carl Fürstenberg (I-II Btn) Cmdr. Oberst Conrad von Thelen	1718
K.k. 1st Light Dragoons Regiment "Emperor" Kaiser Franz II	846
They had 6 sqns. on three divisions. Cdr.: Oberst Franz Freiherr von Pilati. II Div. ObstLt. Baron Karl Kölbel – III Div. Major Bernard Kees	

The French lost 569 men (dead and wounded) while the Coalized army 720 men (43 dead, 404 wounded and 273 missing) [58]; Prince Bagration was awarded with the Order of Aleksandr Njevsky for his bravery. The French retreat opened the doors of southern Piedmont. On May 18 the Russians entered Valenza and occupied Casale while Seckendorff and Shvejkowsky remained to siege Alexandria. Now the way to Turin was definitevely free. The Coalition's troops not involved in the San Giuliano battle were:

Infantry-general Andrej Grigorjevich Rozenberg Corps		

Rallying on the right Po bank

Avantguard Brigade general-major Nikolaj Andrejevich Chubarov	1328	1070
units	Listed	Fit
Imperial Russian 8th Jäger Rgt. Major General Chubarov	725	555
Chief from May 13: GM Ivan Ivanovich Miller – I Btn Lieut.Colonel Ivan Fjodorovich Wrangel. II Btn.		
Imperial Russian Grenadier Btn (GB) Sanajev Butyrsk and Archangelgorod Coys	603	515

On the left Po bank

Division Lieut. General Jacob Ivanovich Povalo-Shvejkovsky 1st	4550	4029
Imperial Russian Grenadier Rgt. GdI Rozenberg or Moskowsky (Moskow) I battalion	763	628
Imperial Russian Musketeers rgt. GM Baranowsky II – II Btn.	798	698
Imperial Russian Musketeers rgt. LG Povalo-Shveikovsky (Smolensk) – one battalion	767	719
Imperial Russian Musketeers rgt. Young-Baden or molodo-Badensky – one battalion	703	618
Imperial Russian Musketeers rgt. GM Baron Ivan Ivanovich Dalheim – I battalion	777	734
Imperial Russian Musketeers rgt. GM Tuyrtov or Tug'lsky (Tula) – one battalion	742	632

At Frascarolo (Valenza Observation Group)

Brigade General-major Jacob Ivanovich Tuyrtov	1977	1734
units	Listed	Fit
Imperial Russian Musketeers rgt. GM Tuyrtov or Tug'lsky (Tula) – one battalion	742	632
Imperial Russian Musketeers rgt. GM Mihail Andrejevich Miloradovich one battalion	749	686
Don Cossacks Rgt. Semjornikov (Semernikov)	486	416

At Sale Camp (Reserve Group). These troops, led by the same Suvorov, left Sale in the May 16 afternoon to reinforce Bagration's group. In the evening they returned to Sale without having shot a single bullet.

Division Lieut. General Ivan Ivanovich Förster	3615	3337
units	Listed	Fit
Imperial Russian Musketeers rgt. LG Povalo-Shveikovsky (Smolensk) – one battalion	767	719
Imperial Russian Musketeers rgt. GM Mihail Andrejevich Miloradovich one battalion	749	686
Imperial Russian Musketeers rgt. Lieut. General Förster (Tambov) - I battalion	770	757
Imperial Russian Musketeers rgt. Young-Baden or molodo-Badensky – one battalion	704	618
Imperial Russian Grenadier Btn (GB) Kaljemin	625	557

At Tortona Camp (together with Seckendorff)

Brigade Colonel Stepan Nikolajevich Castelli	1771	1631
units	Listed	Fit
Imperial Russian Musketeers rgt. GM Baron Ivan Ivanovich Dalheim – II battalion	777	734
5th Don Cossacks Rgt. Denissov	493	432
2nd Don Cossacks Rgt. Sujchev	501	465

With Prince Viktor Rohan

Imperial Russian Musketeers rgt. Lieut. General Förster (Tambov) - II battalion	770	757

Tortona Belagerungsgruppe

Brigade Generalmajor Friedrich Freiherr von Seckendorff	
K.k. IR 19 Rifle Rgt. Freiherr Jozsef Alvinczy de Berberek	1654
K.k. IR 34 Rifle Rgt. (future Freiherr Kraj de Kraiova)	1074
(former Esterházy) (I-II Btns) Cmdr. Oberst Johann Hillinger	
K.k. 5th Hussar Rgt. 4 sqns	826

Detached to the Russians

K.k. 14th Light Dragoons Rgt. Franz Freiherr von Levenehr 6 sqns.	850
Cdr.: Oberst Joseph Zinn. (it had 6 Sqns. On 3 div. I – II - III)	
II Div. ObLt. Josef Prohaska – III Div. Major Franz Graf Latour	

The Coalized army formed three columns which marched eastwards. They all camped at Casteggio, in the evening of May 17. On May 18 Bagration column established a boats-bridge near Bastida, followed by Fröhlich and Lusignan. On May 19 this little army passed over the Po, on 20 arrived at Mortara and on the following two days they rested there. On May 23 they formed two columns marching westwards through Vercelli, Santhià, rebuilding the Dora bridges, and arriving at Chivasso very tired. A second column (general Kaim) marched from Valenza to Casale and followed the right Po bank until Verrua and Turin. With San Giuliano was lost the last hope of General Moreau to link with Macdonald and Masséna (Switzerland) occupying a central position in Piedmont. He had too few men and had to reach Genoa to defend the old Sardinian border. Moreau divided his army in two columns: the two divisions. Victor (7200 men of which 200 were cavalrymen or 10 battalions and 4 squadrons) was sent to Savona, through Acqui and Cairo, in order to reinforce the link with the arriving Macdonalds army. It was a good example of how the French moved on that defenseless territory. Victor had to pass the Tanaro line, in Liguria, with 10 battalions in order to link with the armée de Naples. On May 19, passing near Acqui the column was attacked by insurgents. Chef-de-bataillon Raoust, leading the Vanguard and the 99th demi-brigade was wounded, 5 officers were killed. Victor, not having guns, did not react. He withdrew by night, fording the Bormida river, and reached Dego. There

▲ French infantry man in 1799 Italian campaign

he was again attacked by peasants and his exasperate soldiers began to plunder hamlets and to put houses in flames. Then he tried to reach the Cairo's depots, but was again attacked by insurgents, armed with rifles. He reached Genoa without any baggage and artillery, left behind him during the troubled march. Grenier led his 8000 men to Asti (12 battalions, 24 squadrons or the whole cavalry, all artillery) leaving 3000 men behind to seize the Citadel of Alexandria. Moreau and Grenier sent vanguards until Carignano and Moncalieri but the movement towards Turin aborted. There were some reasons to avoid such a movement but, above all, said Grouchy: *"had become essential to reduce the Piedmont insurrections which set ablaze all the country; Piedmontese guides and Savoy Officers, who, in spite of bright services, were expelled from our ranks, about 616, under pretext they were emigrated, guided by these officers, the Insurgents cut all the communications of the army with France (we remained nearly five weeks without receiving news), removed its means of subsistence and its convoys..."*

1799 FATE OF THE GREAT CITADEL: ALEXANDRIA

Alexandria (Alessandria) a walled town on Tanaro river, where it received, in the middle of a large marshy plain, the river Bormida; 27,000 inhabitants, to the South-East of Turin. It had, on the left Tanaro bank, a great Citadel linked to the town with a stone bridge and defended by fortification "à corne". The Citadel formed an elongated hexagon, with bastions, was armed with about 300 guns and could contain a garrison of about 6000 men; the hospital, the barracks and other military buildings were armored. All the fortifications were improved by French, making Alessandria one of the stronger fortresses in Europe; in 1814 the Austrians dismantled them. Town's foundation has been dated as being the year 1168, when the inhabitants of the villages of Rovereto, Marengo, Bergoglio, Gamondio, Solero, Foro, Oviglio and Quargnento joined forces to form a town called Alessandria in honour of Pope Alexander III. In 1706 ended the Spanish domination, with the arrival of the Savoy troops in Alessandria; the Treaty of Utrecht dated 1713 ratified the end of the Spanish war of succession, and the transfer of the lands of Alessandria to the Duke of Savoy and subsequently to the Kingdom of Sicily. During the 1700's the strategic role played by Alessandria was further confirmed in the defence of the Monferrato district, and the Savoy family further highlighted its importance by building a major fortification system, which involved

▲ The Russian artillery in 1799.

the destruction of the ancient hamlet of Bergoglio in 1728 and the building of an imposing hexagonal citadel, designed by the engineer Ignazio Bertola. The inhabitants of Bergoglio moved to the villages of San Michele, Valmadonna and Valle San Bartolomeo, while the aristocracy moved to the other side of the Tanaro river, towards the town.

The fortifications of Alessandria, played an important role in the 18th century conflicts, especially during the Austrian war of succession, in which the Savoy family allied with the Austrians in order to defend the local area against the supremacy and attack of French and Spanish troops.

The fortress is located North-West of the city of Alessandria, from which it is separated by the river Tanaro. It is the lowest zone of the piedmont region, about 90 metres above sea-level; this region was named 'Mesopotamia' by humanists and destined to be always a borderland. The Citadel is a huge fortress that spreads over 20 hectares and is in the shape of an elliptical hexagon, whose longer side (1 : 1,235) is parallel to the axis of the river. Its hexagonal shape is due to the need of defending the long borderline. The Citadel is a perfect example of *modern-type* fortress and consists of six bastions called by the names of the patron saints and was surrounded by moats to be flooded by the river's water. The city-entry was through a long stone-bridge leading to a huge place surrounded by multi-storey buildings placed according to Bergoglio's previous building axes, all covered by resistant vaults and built between 1749 (quarter of San Tommaso) and 1831 (warehouse of fortifications). The construction and state of conservation of Napoleonic buildings are unique. In the first months of 1799 the garrison, until his commitment to the Po survey on April, was under command of :

Général de brigade Bertrand Clauzel [59]	1422
Citadel commander chef-de-brigade Vital	
24e demi-brigade de ligne (1 btn other two at Verona)	
68e demi-brigade de ligne III btn (later attached to Montrichard division)	
12th Dragoons Rgt. 2 sqns	
National Cisalpine Guard 1 btn	

After the Bassignana and Marengo battles, into Alexandria was left Général Gardanne with his garrison of about 3000 men, tired by the heavy combats of May.

Citadel Garrison	3000
14e demi-brigade de ligne rests – Chef Jean-Claude Moreau	
63e demi-brigade de ligne – III battaillon	
II Btn Aosta - 1st Piedmontese demi-brigade	
II Btn Regina – 3rd Piedmontese demi-brigade	
Combined Cisalpine Btn Miloshevic former 3rd Cisalpine demi-brigade 400 Chef-de-Brigade Andrea Miloshevic and chef-de-bataillon Ippolito Guidetti	400
National Cisalpine Guard 1 btn	
Btn Suisse 1e Legion	400
2 Piedmontese artillery coys	

General Gaspard-Amédée Gardanne Place Commander

May-June 1799

Valenza and Casale, dismantled by the French, were abandoned. So, on May 21, general Jacob Ivanovich Povalo-Shvejkovsky 1st entered Alessandria beginning the Citadel siege.

May, 23rd 1799 Alessandria Austro-Russian siege group

Division Lieut. General Jacob Ivanovich Povalo-Shvejkovsky 1st	
Brigade Generalmajor Friedrich Freiherr von Seckendorff	
K.k. IR 34 Rifle Rgt. (future Freiherr Kraj de Kraiova) (former Esterházy) (I-II Btns) Cmdr. Oberst Johann Hillinger	926
K.k. 5th Hussar Rgt. 5 sqns	700
K.k. 14th Light Dragoons Rgt. Franz Freiherr von Levenehr 2 sqns	266
Brigade Generalmajor Nikolaj Andrejevich Chubarov	
8th Jäger Rgt. Major General Chubarov– I - II Btns	555
chief from 13 May: GM Ivan Ivanovic Miller - sent to Tortona during the Trebbia days	
Don Cossacks Rgt. Semjornikov.	416
Brigade Lieut. General Jacob Ivanovich Tuyrtov	
Imperial Russian Musketeer Rgt. Lieut. General Jacob Ivanovich Tuyrtov I - II Btns or Tug'lsky (Tula) –cmdr Major Ivan Fjodorovich Golovin	1264
Don Cossacks Rgt. Molchanov	435
6th Don Cossacks Rgt. Pasdejev	409

Brigade Generalmajor baron Ivan Ivanovich Dalheim	
Imperial Russian Musketeer Rgt GM Baron Ivan Ivanovic Dalheim – I and II btns. or Archangelogorodsky (Archangelsk). Chief from June 26th General Major Nikolay Mihailovic Kamensky 2nd Cmd: Colonel Stjepan Nikolajevic Castelli	1640
Imperial Russian Musketeer Rgt. Young-Baden or malado-badensky – I - II Btns alias Butyrskowo (Butyrsk) –Cdr. Lieutenant General Karl Ludwig Prince of Baden - (after may 18 renamed as GM Mihail Mihailovic Veletsky Rgt its former commander)	1236

June, 4th 1799 Alessandria Austro-Russian siege group

Division Lieut. General Jacob Ivanovich Povalo-Shvejkovsky 1st	
Imperial Russian Musketeer Rgt. Young-Baden or malado-badensky – I - II Btns alias Butyrskowo (Butyrsk) –Cdr. Lieutenant General Karl Ludwig Prince of Baden - (after may 18 renamed as GM Mihail Mihailovich Veletsky Rgt its former commander)	1236
II btn. Imperial Russian Musketeer Rgt. LG Povalo-Shveikovsky or Smolensky (Smolensk) cmd: Colonel Grigoriy Dimitrjevich Kasahovsky - * 1 coy was at Casale Monferrato	719
Imperial Russian Musketeer Rgt. Lieut. General Jacob Ivanovich Tuyrtov I - II Btns or Tug'lsky (Tula) –cmdr Major Ivan Fjodorovich Golovin	1264
II btn. Imperial Russian Musketeer Rgt GM Baron Ivan Ivanovich Dalheim or Archangelogorodsky (Archangelsk). Chief from June 26th General Major Nikolay Mihailovich Kamensky 2nd Cmd: Colonel Stjepan Nikolajevich Castelli was at Tortona with I btn.	734
8th Jäger (Jegherski) Rgt. Major General Chubarov– I - II Btns chief from 13 May: GM Ivan Ivanovich Miller - sent to Tortona during the Trebbia days	555
Don Cossacks Rgt. Semjornikov.	416
Don Cossacks Rgt. Molchanov	435
6th Don Cossacks Rgt. Pasdejev (written Posdeev)	409

Brigade Generalmajor Friedrich Freiherr von Seckendorf	
II btn K.k. IR 19 Rifle Rgt. Freiherr Jozsef Alvinczy de Berberek	859
K.k. IR 34 Rifle Rgt. (future Freiherr Kraj de Kraiova) (former Esterházy) (I-II Btns) Cmdr. Oberst Johann Hillinger	926
K.k. 5th Hussar Rgt. 7 sqns	918

July, 23 1799 Alessandria Austrian Citadel garrison (after capitulation)

K.k. IR 8 Rifle Rgt. (former Huff Rgt) Cmdr. Obst Johann Schröckinger von Heidenburg (I-II Btns)	1500

CAPITULATION OF ALESSANDRIA – JULY 21, 1799

CAPITULATION de la citadelle d'Alessandrie entre le Lieutenant-General Comte de Bellegarde au service de S. M. l'Empereur et Roi et le Genérat François Gardanne, Comandant de la Citadelle d'Alessandrie.	
L'ARTICLE 1.	ARTICLE 1.
La garnison sortira avec tous les honneurs de la guerre par la porte d'Asti, tambours battants, drapeaux déployés, mèche allumée, avec 9 pièces de canons et deposeront les armes sur le glacis, se rendant prisonniers gueire pour ètre conduits dans les Etats des de S. M. 1'Empereur.	La garnison de la Citadelle d'Alessandrie sortira par la porte d'Asti avec les honneurs de la guerre, tambours battans, drapeaux déployés, méche allumée, trainera avec elle 2 pièces de 4 avec leurs caissons et attelages ainsi que les munitions compétentes à ces pièces, de même que leurs Artilleurs. La garnison se formera sur le glacis de la porte d'Asti jusqu'à la porte d'Alessandrie, ne déposera point les armes et rentrera en France et ne servira contre les armées de S. M. l'Empereur et ses Aliiés jusqu'à change qui aura lieu le premier et par préférence coutre les prisonniers Autrichiens et Russes, excepté ceux désignés par l'article 2 qui ne seront pas prisonniers de guerre.
L'ARTICLE 2.	ARTICLE 2.
Mr. le Commandant, ainsi que Mr. 1'Adjudant-Général Louis avec les Aides-de-camp et Adjoints et tout l'Etat major, suivront le sort de la garnison	Ne seront point prisonniers de guerre le Général de Brigade Gardanne commandant de la Division du Tanaro, l'Adjudant-Général Louis, les Aides-de-camp et Adjoints, de méme que tous les officiers composant l'Etat major et 300 militaires choisis dans la garnison par le Général Gardaune

L'ARTICLE 3. Les officiers supérieurs, savoir Mr. le Général Gardanne, Mr. Général l'Adjudant-Louis, le Chef du Génie, celui de l'Artillerie les autres chefs de corps, conserveront leurs épées, et tous les officiers en général, conserveront leurs chevaux et équipages effets et proprietes; les soldats garderont leurs sacs, ainsi que les employés à la suite de l'armée leurs chevaux et equipages. Au reste on aura soin de fournir des chevaux sur la route à ceux qui n'en sont pas fournis. Les Piémontois, Cisalpins et Helvétiques sont prisonniers de guerre comme les François.	ARTICLE 3. Tous les officiers garderont leurs épées, leurs chevaux et équipages militaires, effets et propriétés, les soldats leurs sacs, les employes attachés à la suite de l'armée, de même leurs chevaux et équipages. On fournira d'étapes en etapes des chevaux aux militaires, autres officiers ou autres convalescents, ainsi qu'à ceux qui ayant droit à des chevaux et qui seroient démontés. La garnison Piémontoise, Cisalpine, Helvétique, faisant partie intégrante de l'armée Françoise, jouiront des avantages du meme article concernant les troupes françoises.
L'ARTICLE 4. Les équipages et propriétés et effets étant accordés à un chacun, cet article cessa de soi même et il s'entend que toute caisse militaire ou autres, magazins, dépôts, plans, archives, artillerie, munitions, attirails de guerre et tous effets de quelque dénomination qu'ils puissent être appartenauts au Gouvernement François, Piémontois ou autres, seront rendus fidèlement.	ARTICLE 4. Il sera accordé dix chariots couverts partant les effets de l'Etat-Major de chaque corps et la caisse-militaire; dans le cas où les fourgons et chevaux n'existeroient pas dans les corps, il en sera fourni par l'armée Autrichienne d'étape en étape jusqu'à la frontière de Gènes.
L'ARTICLE 5. Les malades et blessés sont prisonniers de guerre et seront traités avec l'humanité qui nous est propre. On y laissera de la garnison de la Citadelle les chirurgiens et gardes-malades nécessaires, et on choisira un lieu convenable pour l'établissement de l'hôpital.	ARTICLE 5. Les malades et blessés seront humainemeut traités dans les hôpitaux d'Alessandrie. On y laissera les chirurgiens et gardes-malades nécessaires dont on fixera le nombre, et après leur guérison ils jouiront égale ment des articles de la Capitulation; de même ceux qui pour des affaires devront rester à Alessandrie, auxquels on délivrera les passeports nécessaires lorsque leurs affaires seront terminées et les malades ne seront point prisonniers de guerre.
L'ARTICLE 6. Trois heures après la signature les troupes de S. M. l'Empereur occuperont la porte intérieure (l'Asti, ainsi que la garde avancée de cette porte.	ARTICLE 6. Trois heures après la signature de la Capitulation on remettra aux troupes Autrichiennes la garde avancée de la porte Vigne, celle de St. Michel et celle de St. Antoine. L'entrée de la Citadelle ne sera permise qu'aux Commissaires Autrichiens et à ceux qui seront envoyés par le Commandant de l'armée de siège. L'armée Autrichienne n'entrera dans la Citadelle que lorsqu'elle sera évacuée par la garnison Françoise.
L'ARTICLE 7. Accordé.	ARTICLE 7. Dans le cas où l'armée Françoise ne seroit plus sur la frontière de Gènes, on permettra d'envoyer un officier au Général en chef à son quartier-général avec la Capitulation.
L'ARTICLE 8. On conviendra en ce cas d'une manière loyale.	ARTICLE 8. S'il se trouvoit un Article douteux dans la Capitulation qui pourroit donner lieu à des contestations, il sera expliqué en faveur de la garnison
L'ARTICLE 9. La garnison aura une escorte suffisante d'après le sens de la Capitulation et son entière sécurité.	ARTICLE 9. Il sera, fourni une escorte suffisante pour la garnison et une particulière pour le Général Gardanne jusqu'à la frontière de Gènes.

ARTICLE ADDITIONEL.

D'abord après la signature de la Capitulation les otages Piémontois retenus à la Citadelle, seront rendus avec les effets à eux appartenants. On échangera réciproquement deux otages, consistant de chaque part d'un officier d'Etat-Major et d'un Capitaine, jusqu'à l'entière exécution de cette Capitulation. Aussitot après la signature l'armée Autrichienne enverra un officier de Génie, un officier d'Artillerie et un Commissaire, auxquels on remettra tous les magazins, plans, dépôts, etc. sans qu'il eu soit détourné ou détérioré la moindre chose, ainsi que les Caisses et autres effets militaires appertenauts aux gouvernements respectifs. Les chevaux de Cavalerie, d'Artillerie et autres appartenans au Gouvernement François ou autres, seront délivrés. La garnison sortira par la porte d'Asti demain 22 de juillet à 4 heures après midi; il s'entend que ceux qui doivent rester dans la Citadelle pour la remise des effets, resteront jusqu'à ce qu'ils auront terminé leur besogne. On fera une liste séparée des non-combattans qui seront rendus à l'armée Françoise. Au reste on rendra tous les chevaux et autres effets appartenants à à S. M. l'Empereur ou aux officiers Autrichiens et Alliés de Sa Majesté ou servant aux armées.

En foi de quoi on a dressé deux exemplaires pour être signés et échangés réciproquement.
Au camp devant la Citadelle d'Alessandrie le 21 Juillet a 10 heures du soir 1799.

LE COMTE DE BELLEGARDE	Le Général de Brigade Lieut.-Général Gardanne.

The race to the Sea

Also the important fortress of Ceva had fallen into insurgents hands, blocking the vital way which linked Piedmont with Savona on the sea.

Ceva, during the middle ages was a strong fortress defending the borders of Piedmont towards Liguria, but the fortification on the rock, above the town, were demolished in 1800 by the French, to whom it had been ceded in 1796. In that year, Napoleon, after having left behind Ceva and after having conquered the Bicocca of San Michele and the Bricchetto of Mondovì, found the way to Piedmont opened and carried his HQs to Cherasco. From it he sent an arrogant message to the fort of Ceva governor, Count of Tornafort, imposing him to surrender within 24 hours; on the contrary the fortress and its passages would have been destroyed by batteries fire. His aide-de-camp, Marmont, carried the letter, making all attempts in order to enter by the garrison; but he did not succeded. In 1800, Napoleon gave the order us to dismantle the Fort; six months were employed to prepare mines and charges, finally a simultaneous explosion of one hundred devices made the task out.

On May 18, Moreau knew this bad new at Asti: the Ceva's commander had given up without any resistance. The insurrection at Ceva and Mondovì had begun on May 6 when a great bunch of rioters had forced the republican garrisons to close themselves into the fortresses. Two large columns of armed civilians led by Francolino, former Sardinian Lieutenant, and the other by Doctor Cerrina, a surgeon, besieged the fortress. From May 8 to 11 the fort was bombarded by rebels and, on May 14, the fortress capitulated after a night attack of the insurgents, who destroyed a fortress door. The French commander, Maris, surrendered and was left free to reach Mondovì. Here the whole garrison was disarmed by other rioters and the French were allowed to reach Coni. Maris had a subsequent trial for indignity and the Court Martial comdemned him to death by shooting. Losing Ceva, the French lost the quickest way to reach Genoa. Moreau immediately activated two "mobile" columns and give their command to the brigadier, "provisional", Garreau and to the adjudant-général Jean Mathieu Seras, a Piedmontese born in Osasco, who had served only in the French armies. Every column had two battalions; they had to force the march and seize Ceva, but river Tanaro had a flood and the columns did not pass through, so being forced to march along its rough right bank. During the same days also Mondovì fell into Insurgents hands forcing the Coni garrison to try its capture. Moreau did not lose his self-control. He camped at Poirino and Villa-Nuova, while ordered to adjudant-général Drouot to escort baggages, artillery and ammunitions to France, through Fenestrelle pass.

Moreau waited at Savigliano the results of Garreau endeavours (which had rallied at Coni the "mobile" columns of Seras and Fressinet). He occupied Mondovì but, fearing to lose the communications with the main army, returned to Coni, where an angry Moreau changed his orders. Grouchy, and 8 battalions, were sent forwards to open the road to the sea, after having reunited all the "mobile" columns. The advance into the Insurgents' territory was followed also by Moreau, who brought his HQs at Coni. The Grouchy vanguard, led by Adjudant Garreau, and 1300 men strong, entered Mondovì engaging the Royalists. During that struggle chef-de-brigade Lacalle was killed and 330 French died or were wounded. Mondovì was occupied, the enemies retreating into Ceva fortress. Having known the victory of Garreau, Grouchy brought 4 battalion to Lesegno, near Ceva, clearing the location from a bunch of 8000 peasants, badly armed. However the strong fortress resisted and the French decided to leave general Quesnel (recovered from the wound) and 2700 men to begin a blockade. But, about May 28, the rebellion of the mountain territory was softened and the French did deploy on the Appennini Ridge.

▲ French drummer in 1799 Italian campaign

Really in that period, around May 30, the Coalition's Army reinforced itself gaining a new right wing under general Bellegarde, with 18 battalions and 4000 cavalrymen. Moreau did not pass the Appennines through Col di Tenda, because this could had separated his troops from Victor and Macdonalds. After a recoinnassance he decided to pass through Garessio and the Col du Saint-Bernard, a secondary causeway which had become renowned in 1795, with the Sérurier action during the Loano battle. The causeway was bettered in three days with the help of 2000 workers, directed by Adjudant Guilleminot. When the road was "artillery-fit", general Quesnel left the Ceva siege and camped at Murialdo, to control the withdrawal passage. Musnier abandoned Coni marching with the garrison (3000 men) towards Mondovì.

A parte of the Grenier division remained in Arriere-garde at Mondovì, the right wing detached along the Tanaro valley. The main army marched towards the mountains, with all materials and artilleries. On June 6 they safely reached Loano, while the cavalry reached Finale and Savona. This ended the long march after the San Giuliano battle.

The new French deployment of June 1799 was the following:

Division Laboissière was at Genoa with the Lapoype Division;

Division Victor guarded the Toscana's borders at Pontremoli, and in Taro and Magra valleys;

Division Grenier controlled the passes at Savona (Cerisola, Bardineto and Carpi with Partonneaux brigade, linked on its right with Quesnel brigade at Altare and Mallare; the Adjudant Piedmontese Campana stood at San Giacomo del Segno while Adjudant Garreau remained in the hills near Cadibona pass, at Torre and at Madonna di Savona.)

THE COALITION'S ARMY PIEDMONT'S OCCUPATION

After the fall of the Citadel, the Coalized army enlarged their occupation reaching all the farthest Piedmont's territories, the French being on the other side of the mountains until Autumn's last combats. From June 1, the Austro-Russian moved forward. General Seckendorff blocked Montenotte and the road to Savona, Vukassovich took the control of Ceva and Mondovì, blocking the Col du Tende road, Fröhlich, before his commitment in central Italy, with the 1st brigade occupied Coni, with the 2nd Brigade Lusignan tried to win the resistance of Fort Fenestrelle, but the French garrison resisted. Pinerolo (or Pignerolo) was abandoned by its commander, the Swiss Colonel Zimmermann, place commander, in spite of a winning action against a Russian regiment led by Count Zuccato [60]. Prince Bagration cleared the Susa valley, the important road which led to the Montcenis and Montgenevre passes. An utter brigade blocked the Canton Valais passes, impeding to Masséna to send reinforcement from Switzerland and, finally, general Hadik controlled the St. Gotthard and the Lecourbe troops.

Piedmont Coalition Army – June 4-9, 1799

Turin (Torino) HQs with Division Generalmajor Conrad Valentin Kaim

Corps Infantry-general Andrey Grigorjevich Rozenberg

Russian Corps Artillery	
Artillery Btn. Lieut. General Ejler	632
(with 1st Artillery Coy Ivanov and 2nd Artillery Coy Kuzmin)	
Divisional (regimental) Light Artillery	672

Division Lieut. General Ivan Ivanovich Förster (alias Ferster in Russian)

Brigade general-major Mihail Semenovich Baranovsky 2nd	
Imperial Russian Grenadier Rgt. GdI Rozemberg or Moskowsky (Moskow) – I-II btns	1255
cmd. (until June 7) Colonel Petr Petrovich Passek [61] then provisionally led by Rozenberg and Colonel Kushnikov	
I Btn. Imperial Russian Musketeers rgt. Förster (Ferster) or Tambowski (Tambov)	757
cmdr Lieutenant Colonel Zaltser [62]	
II Btn. Imperial Russian. Musketeers rgt. LG Povalo-Shveikovsky or Smolensky (Smolensk)	719
cmd: Colonel Grigoriy Dimitrjevich Kasahovsky [63]	
Brigade general-major Mihail Andrejevich Miloradovic 1st	
Imperial Russian Musketeers rgt. Generalmajor M. Andr. Miloradovic or Apsheronsky (Apsheron)	1372
cmdr Lieut. Colonel (from 3.10.1799 Colonel) Stepan Timofejevich Karlov. – I and II Btns.	
II Btn. Imperial Russian. Musketeers rgt. GM Baranowsky II or Nizowski Musk. Rgt.	698
Combined Imperial Russian Grenadier Btn Sanajev	515

Pinerolo (or Pignerolo) and Susa valley

Pinerolo, town at the head of the Chisone valley, had about 8000 inhab. Ist fortifications were destroyed by

French after 1796-97 campaign. Likewise at Pinerolo, all Piedmontese border Forts (Susa and Chisone valleys) were designated to be demolished, as dangerous for the République. This was the destiny of Exilles in the Susa Valley, Bard in the Aosta Valley, plus those of Ceva, San Giorgio and Demonte, the great Fortress of Fenestrelle; all were considered to be dangerous for France and listed for demolition. Fenestrelle, however, was maintained and changed in a French prison. To save the Fort many villages of the valley were forcibly taxed to cover the cost of this, Meano, Roure, Mentoulles, Fenestrelle, Usseaux and Pragelato being among them. About 14,000 lire were collected (a considerable sum for the time).

Russian Avantgarde Brigade Generalmajor Petr Ivanovich Bagration

Pinerolo Detachment General Major Gheorgy Gavrilovich Zukata	
7th Jäger (Jeghersky) Rgt. General Major Prince Petr Ivanovich Bagration [64]	624
– I and II Btn cmdr.: Gen. Bagration	
Combined Imperial Russian Grenadier Btn (GB) Lomonosov	501
8th Don Cossacks Rgt. Grekov	414
2nd Don Cossacks Rgt. Sujchev	465

Suse (Susa), encircled by walls and towers was (is) at the Mont Cenis feet where streams Cenise (Ginicia) and Dora-Riparia join together. The fortress, one of the most important military buildings, was destroyed by Napoleon's will in 1796 (treaty of Cherasco). Its name was Forte della Brunetta and it was more than a simple fortress. It was the result of the hard digging of a whole hill (80 years of work) with the target to block the Mont Cenis pass road (from France). It was linked with the old Fort of Santa Maria by a long and well hidden passage. The Paris Treaty of 16 May 1796 imposed to the Sardinian King the demolition of the Fort della Brunetta (Brunette) together with other fortresses like Exilles.

Val di Susa Detachment Colonel Vassilj Aleksejevich Chvitzky	
Combined Imperial Russian Grenadier Btn Dendrjugyn	453
5th Don Cossacks Rgt. Denissov	432

Exilles, on the Dora-Riparia, in Exilles valley, blocked the causeway from Suse to Briançon through the mont Genévre pass. The place, important for its fortifications, had the shape of a lozenge with the long sides watching over the road and the river. It had about 800-1000 inhabitants. The Exilles Fort, one of the oldest monuments in the Susa Valley, now is a rare example of a "street castle", a defensive structure with several walled circuits in defense of an internal core and an external barrier. Exilles guaranteed the strategic control of the ground axis that went from Piedmont to France through Mont Génevre. At the beginning of the 17th century, the fort was modified from its earlier structure into one fortified with ramparts. During the years 1681 to 1697, it is said the mysterious person known to history as the "Man with the Iron Mask" lived among these walls. In the first years of the 1700's, the Exilles fortress underwent major reconstruction and modernization, including the renovate of the defensive front facing France. Ruined by the French after the Treaty of Paris in 1796, the Fort was rebuilt to its present structure between 1818 and 1829 by the King of Sardinia, who had taken back his lands.

Lanzo Detachment Colonel Mihail Aleksejevich Chitrov	
I Btn. Imperial Russian Musketeers rgt. GM Baranowsky II or Nizowski Musk. Rgt.	698
cmdr Colonel Mihail Aleksejevich Chitrov	
Avigliana Detachment Colonel Kalemin	
Combined Imperial Russian Grenadier Btn Kalemin	557

Chisone valley

Fenestrelle, on Chisone stream, had a significant strategic impact. Anciently its name was Fort du Moulin, which could have had a garrison of about 1000 soldiers. During the Moreau retreat of May-June 1799 it served also as depot for the artillery park of general Debelle, after the departure from Turin. With the Restoration, (after having obtained an evil reputation as French prison), at the place of the abandoned Fort du Moulin, was built a totally new fortress, which blocked the road of the Pràgelato valley. It was on the right bank of the stream and was commanded by an other fortress built on the left bank: San Carlo. San Carlo, with the Tre Denti and Valli fortresses, were placed on rocky crests, almost inaccessible, which ended to the Catinat camp. At its end was the fort Sant'Elmo which, for its own, commanded San Carlo. All that fortresses were linked together with battlements and tunnels.

Brigade Generalmajor Franz Joseph Marquis de Lusignan	
K.k. IR 18 Rifle Rgt. Graf Patrick Stuart	1627
Cmdr. Obst Franz Weber von Treuenfels I-III btns Bellegarde Corps - Piedmont -	
K.k IR 28 Rifle Rgt. Freiherr Michael von Fröhlich	1619
former Rgt Wartensleben – I-II Btns) Cmdr. Oberst Franz Eder von Hartenstein – III Btn at Piacenza	
K.k. 14th Light Dragoons Rgt. Franz Freiherr von Levenehr 6 sqns	841
Cmdr. Oberst Joseph Zinn, (6 sqns.)	

Cuneo (Coni)

Coni, situated between two small streams, and though neither very large nor populous, was significant for the strength of its fortifications. Its name ("wedge") is due to its position on a hill between the two streams, the Stura and the Gesso. It was honoured with the title of the Maiden-Fortress (Virgin), because though several times besieged, it was never taken. The prince of Coni invested it in the war of 1744; but he was obliged to raise the siege. The place was gallantly defended by the baron Leutrum, a German protestant, the best general in the Sardinian service: but what contributed most to the miscarriage of the enemy, was a long tract of heavy rains, which destroyed all their works, and rendered their advance impracticable.

That important fortress was ceded by the treaty of Cherasco (1796), with Ceva and Tortona, to the French. In 1799 it was taken of ter ten days' bombardment by the Austrian and Russian armies, and, in 1800, after Marengo, the French demolished the fortifications.

Division Generalmajor Freiherr Michael von Fröhlich	
Grenadiers Brigade	
K.k. Grenadier Btn Graf Carl Paar (former FML Karl Graf von Mercandin)	477
K.k. Grenadier Btn Graf Johann Morzin (former Graf Joseph Fiquelmont)	476
K.k. Grenadier Btn Oblt Franz Xavier Weber von Treuenfeld	397
K.k. Grenadier Btn Oblt Johann Pértussy (former Major Joseph Korherr)	526
K.k. Grenadier Btn Graf Anton Schiaffinati (former Freiherr Georg von Stentsch)	615
K.k. 10th Light Dragoons Rgt. GdC Joseph Fürst Lobkowitz	793
(6 sqns.) Cmdr. Oberst Max Joseph Fürst Thurn und Taxis.	

Higher Bormida valley

Brigade Generalmajor Friedrich Freiherr von Seckendorf	
II btn K.k. IR 19 Rifle Rgt. Freiherr Jozsef Alvinczy de Berberek	859
K.k. IR 34 Rifle Rgt. (future Freiherr Kraj de Kraiova)	926
(former Esterházy) (I-II Btns) Cmdr. Oberst Johann Hillinger	
K.k. 5th Hussar Rgt. 7 sqns	918

Higher Tanaro valley

Mondovì originated on the hill where several rural communities and other little villages sought to free themselves from feudal domination, subject to the emperor and executed by the bishop of Asti. The community spread out at the hill foot due to the settlements that would originate the most ancient quarters of Mondovì. The weakness of Mondovì, in particular in the military field, did not allow it to remain autonomous, especially in external relations. In 1415 the *Statuta Civitatis Montisregalis*, i.e. the rules of the town, were drawn up in order to establish "defined rules" regarding government and civil life, also with respect to the Savoy. Since then, and especially in 16th cent., Mondovì developed till it became the most populated town in Piedmont. It had a Citadel. This was a military fortification, built between 1572-1574 on the orders of Emanuele Filiberto of Savoy on the ruins of the Renaissance cathedral. The term Mondovì is related to the Napoleonic Period, particularly to what is known as the battle of Mondovì, which took place on 21 April 1796. Napoleon defeated the Austro-piedmontese forces, thus preparing the Armistice of Cherasco and the later victories against Austria.

Avantgarde Brigade Generalmajor Freiherr Josef Philipp von Vukassovich

II Btn Grenzregiment of Banat (or I btn. 13th GrenzRgt)	837
III (VI?) Btn Grenzregiment of Banat (or II btn. 12th Deutschbanater GrenzRgt) Major Zedzwitz	682
K.k. Light Btn. N. 2 Oberst Carl Prince of Rohan	526
KK IR 52 Rifle Rgt. Erzherzog Palatin Anton Viktor	1292
I – II btns. cdr.: Graf Johann Nepomuk Khuen de Belasi	
K.k. 9th Hussar Rgt. FML Johann Nepomuk Graf Erdödy de Monyorókerek	466
(Erdödy Husaren) 3 Sqns.	
K.k. 7th Hussar Rgt. 6 sqns	773

NOTES

32 **Generalmajor Andreas (András) Karacsaj Graf de Válje-Szaka** was born at Kostanicza (Banal-Militärgrenze) on November 30, 1744 and died at Wiener-Neustadt on March 22, 1808. Son of an old nobility of Croatia, which distinguished against the Turks, had one brother, the younger, Kasimir (b. 1746) who died in 1793. He took the Service in 1758, 15 years old, as cadet of the Banal regiment, during the Seven Years war. He passed then to serve as Guard in the hungarian Leibgarde of Prince Esterházy, as captain and then, as Oberlieutenant, was in the regular army at the Carabiniers regiment Archduke Albert. There he became Rittmeister (the regiment having taken the name of Chevauxlégèrs Hesse-Darmstadt, then Levenehr). He distinguished himself at Praussnitz and Keul against the Prussians, and was promoted to Major. In 1787 he was in the Turks War at Chotym participating in many actions, after which he became Oberst. Finally leading a battalion of IR Kaunitz with 7 squadrons he went in campaign reaching Mohila Robea in Bessarabia. In 1789, at Walleszaka (April 19) with his battalion, 6 squadrons and 4 guns, he fought against a siege corps of about 5000 Turks, bringing himself in the attention of Russian General Suvorov. After that period he was awarded by the Emperor himself. On August 13 he was promoted Generalmajor, had the Ownership of the 4th Dragoons regiment and, in December, obtained the Maria-Theresia Knight Cross (in December 1790 he was also Commander of the Order and had the Great Cross of St.Anne's Order, from the Czarine Kathrine). The French Revolutionary wars caught him at Lemberg (L'vov) as Brigadier. In 1794 he fought in Germany with hard engagements until 1795, when he, 51 years old, began to suffer from "war fatigue" often becoming ill. So he decided to retire from Duty and to live with his family and children, at Lemberg and, then, at Pest. During the Italian campaign of 1799 was his friend, Fieldmarshal Suvorov, who recalled it on duty. Karacsaj followed his regiment and was employed as Brigadier at the Trebbia, during the siege of Alessandria, at Novi and at Bosco in Autumn. After Suvorov departure, he remained in the Italienische Armée and fought in the second Novi battle. Now Field Marshal, Karacsaj ended the campaign in Italy and followed Kray to Germany. He was at Engen (May 1800) where he received two balls in the abdomen; this was the first and the last wound. He recovered at Wiener-Neustadt where his four sons were studying at the Military Academy and where he died at the age of 64. So died one of best cavalry general of the Austrian army.

33 **Chef Claude Mathieu Gardane** Born in Marseille on 1766. Aged 14 he was Sous-lieutenant in the 1st Chasseurs regiment, Lieutenant on January 21, 1792, Captain on 1793 and chef d'escadron on 1794. Named by Directoire, on 14 prairial an IV, chef de brigade, had the command of 9th regiment of chasseurs à cheval. Moreau, général in chief of the armée d'Italie, witness oh his valour at Bassignana (23 floréal an VIII), named him général de brigade on the battlefield, rank confirmed on 27 vendémiaire an VIII. Had several wounded and was at the siege of Genoa in 1800 where he suffered a bad shot in the left leg.

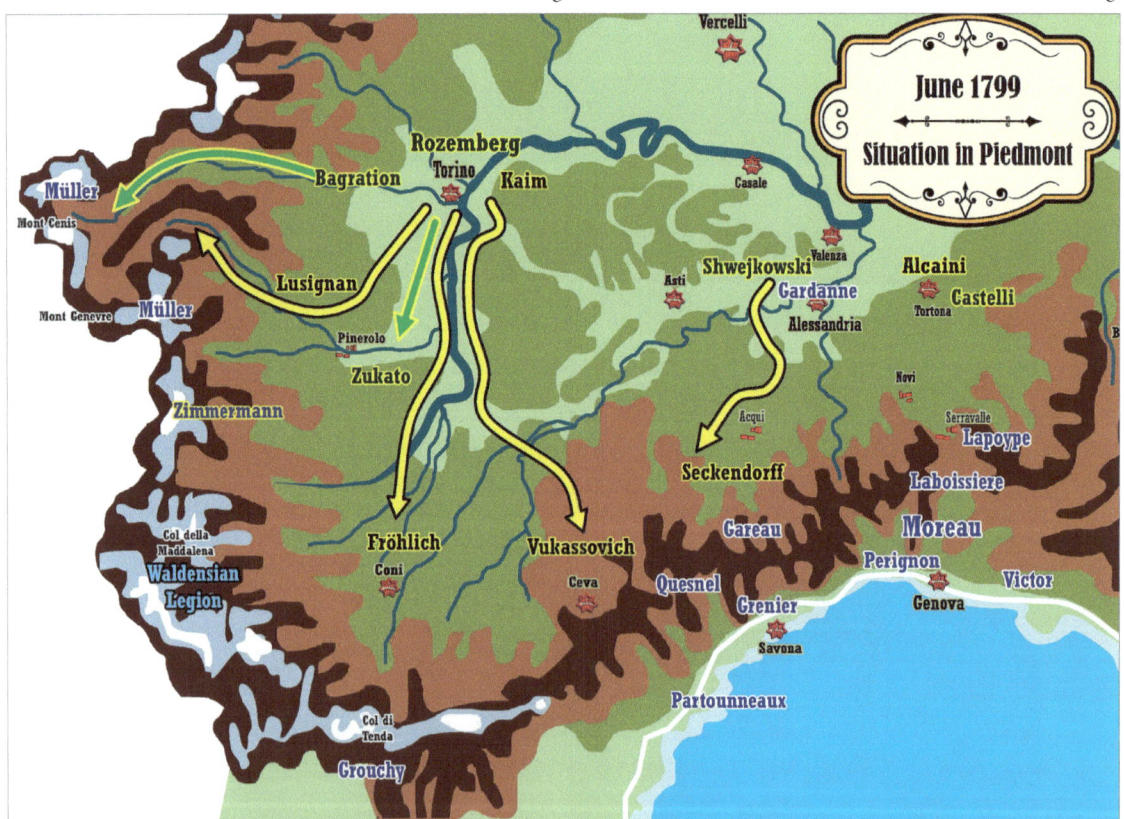

He was also Gouverneur des Pages on 1805, and aide-de-camp of Napoleon, with whom was ta Austerlitz, Iéna and Eylau. When King of Persia, Feth-Aly-Schah, wanted an alliance with France against Russia and England, Napoléon named him "ministre plénipotentiaire en Perse", on May 10, 1807. Returned in France on 1809 he was made Count of the Empire and sent to Spain as brigade general, first with the VIII corps and after with the IX. There he was suspended from the duty for having not obeyed to an order to move a force into Portugal. This fact caused the loss of trust of Napoleon and he was no more employed. King Louis XVIII recalled him on duty on June 12, 1814, but when he reached his command in the duke of Angoulème division, Napoleon was returning from Elba and he reached his Emperor. Napoleon forgave him and placed him at the Somme defences. On September 4, 1815 gardane retired and died on January 1818.

34   **Jean-Claude Roussel,** Born: 25 September 1771 - Chef-de-Brigade: 16 December 1799 - General-de-Brigade: 10 March 1809 - Commander of the Legion d'Honneur: 27 July 1809 - Baron of the Empire: 6 October 1810 - Died: 26 July 1812 (killed at Ostrowno)

35   **Adjutant-Général Louis Gareau** (or Garreau 28.05.1769-30.05.1813). He was transferred (1799) to the Italy's Army, with the Serurier division, and later with general Grenier. On 30th March passed the Adige at Polo's bridge leading the Piedmonteses. Pescantina was occupied but disorder among ranks of Meyer brigade leaded to a disaster. Serurier losses at Polo: 1500 prisoners. Gareau was named general de brigade on May 13, a provisional charge after the Bassignana battle. In October 10, 1799 he was transferred to the French maltese garrison where (1800) he was taken prisoner by the British and then released "on parole".

36   **Chef de brigade Jules-Alexandre-Léger Boutrouë**, born at Chartres, on April 20, 1760. He was on duty by the infatry regiment Rohan-Soubise, as a simple soldier, and remained there in the period 1778, 1779 et 1780, in the Église company. Retired in 1780 he began to study Law when the Revolution outbroke. He enrolled again as Aide-major in the National Guard (Ferté-Bernard), becoming a Captain of the Chasseurs de la Garde nationale of Mans. On September 3, 1791, he went to war as volunteer and captain of 1er bataillon Voluntaires de la Sarthe. From January 1792 he was at the 33e régiment d'infanterie, the old regiment Touraine, where he was named First.Lieutenant (June 15, 1792). In 1794 he led a battalion (1er bataillon du Mont Terrible) as Chief and, in the same year, he was named Chief of the 65e demi-brigade, which became the 68e (27 floreal an II). At the end of 1795 he was wounded and captured on the Rhine front, at Kehl. The following year he was released by exchange. Called to Italy he was under Grouchy in Piedmont and took part in the battle of Novi, where he was again taken prisoner. In 1804 he became Colonel of the 56th Line infantry and Knight (first) Commander (after) of the Legion d'Honneur. He had also the honorary command of the 2e régiment des Grenadiers d'Elite (reserve of the Army of England). He fought his last campaign in 1805 with Massena. Near Caldiero, the Colonel had a leg truncated by a cannon ball, while he was leading the 1st brigade of the 2nd division (in the place of general Brun, mortally wounded during the second day of the battle). The brave Colonel Boutroue died in Verona on December 4, 1805, after having suffered two amputations. He was 45 years old, the older Colonel in the Army.

37   **Chef de bataillon Jean Dupellin o Duppelin**. Born on April 3, 1771 in Phalsbourg (Meurthe). On 4 messidor an IV, he was named chef de bataillon in the 106e demi-brigade de ligne and was in Italy from 1799 to 1803. During the siege of Genoa (1800) he was wounded four times on the Montefaccio, and had an award. In 1806 he was Colonel of the 85e regiment de ligne He died on the battlefield a Thorn (Prussia), on January 25, 1813.

38   In the place of **Chef-de-Brigade Antoine-Francois Brenier de Montmorand**, wounded at Verona on April 4 and after Magnano on April 17, (subsequently named General-de-Brigade for merits on the battlefield on June 15, 1799) the demi-brigade was led by :**Chef-de-Brigade Villaret** (died in 1800) a poorly known Officer. He was renowned as one of the most reliable Officers of the Army of Italy. He died on April 15, 1800, during the assault of the Hermette mountain, replaced by Captain Blanc.

39   **François-Jean-Baptiste Quesnel baron du Torpt** (1765-1819) He was recalled at the armée d'Italie (17 pluviôse an VIII). Quesnel was on Verona battlefield and later had the left arm wounded at Bassignana. The pain of the fracture forced him to ask a rest period in 1800.

40   **Colli-Ricci Marchese di Felizzano Luigi Leonardo Antonio Giuseppe Gaspare Venanzio**, b. 23 March 1756, Alessandria d. 31 March 1809, Alessandria. Born in a family of the ancient nobility (in 1757 or 1760, according to some sources). He began his military service as an ensign in the regiment of Monferrato on 10 June 1773. He was second lieutenant aide-major on 10 June 1774, lieutenant on 20 July 1775, captain-lieutenant on 2 May 1781, captain in the regiment of Pignerol on 8 May 1782, transferred to the regiment of Acqui on 27 June 1786, became 1st Major of the regiment of Mondovì on 13 March 1793, major commanding the 2nd battalion of chasseurs on 10 April 1794, lieutenant-colonel on 2 March 1795, colonel of infantry on 5 December 1795, colonel of a corps composed of the 1st and 2nd battalions of chasseurs on 20 March 1796. After the peace he became chief of staff to an auxiliary division gathered at Novara, commander of light troops on 10 March 1797, adjutant-general in the French service on 12 December 1798, general of brigade on 5 May 1799, wounded and captured at Pasturana at the battle of Novi (15 August 1799). General of division on 14 September 1802, he commanded the 23rd military division, then the department of Liamone (Corsica). Retired on 6 June 1806. Crippled by debts, and pursued by a horde of debitors, Colli died almost in poverty ... His name is inscribed on the Arc de Triomphe on the south side. (War Archive).

His mother was a Beccaria, and his uncle was Vittorio Alfieri, the illustrious writer, who criticised him for having rallied to the French ... Colonel Marchese Colli was not related to General Baron Colli-Marchi or Marchini belonged to the Austrian army, and Colonel Marchese Colli-Ricci to the Sardinian army.

41   **Chef de brigade Dominique Honore Antoine Marie Vedel** (1771-1848) From 1799 to 1803 - Chef de brigade of the 17e Demi-brigade légère, replaced Chef Fornesy. From 1803 to 1805 - Chef-de-Brigadecommander of the 17e regiment of Light Infantry. In 1805 he was named general-de-brigade (24.12.). In 1806 he led the 3rd brigade (1st Inf. division – V Corps). Later commander of the place of Magdeburg (28.02.); on November 3, 1807 he was general-de-division. In 1808 he was named count of the Empire leading the infantry division of the II Observation Coros of the Gironda. With this he was at Baylen 1809. Returned in France he was arrested and emprisoned (until 1811).

42   **Baron Charles-Louis-Dieu Donné Grandjean** Born in Nancy on December 29, 1768. Named adjudant-général chef de brigade. With this rank he was at Pastrengo, as provisional brigade general from March 26th, where he attacked the entrenched camp taking prisoners 1,200 austrians near the Adige, being promoted to the rank of général de brigade on the battlefield. Then he fought at the Trebbia battle where he was wounded two times.

43   **comte Henri-François-Marie Charpentier** (1769-1831): Born at Soissons (Aisne) on June 23, 1769. During the years VI and VII Charpentier was in Italy as Chef-de-bataillon of 94th Line infantry. Employed as Adj. Général he was also named provisional Général de brigade from April 5, 1799 (Magnano battle) and definitively named brigadier on July 30, 1799, after the Trebbia battle where he had two horses killed under himself and where he was wounded at the abdomen. He distinguished himself at Novi and, in 1800, at Marengo. As Général-de-brigade he had Chief of Staff duties under Moncey and Jourdan and, in 1804, he had the Commander Cross of the Legion d'Honneur. On February 16, 1804 he became Général de division.

44   **Claude-Joseph Buget** Born in Bourg,on september 10 1770. Son of a chief surgeon of the Bourg Hospital, would have had to make the priest or a clerical career; but the revolution advised to leave the Catholic School for the army. Left like soldier, it had the nomination to second lieutenant on April 25, 1793, in a regiment of the armée du Nord, and was assigned to the General Staff of Dugommier, charged to besiege Toulon. Buget was distinguished in siege obtaining the nomination to adjudant-général, chef de bataillon. On November 20, 1798 was sent as adjudant-général to the armée d'Italie transferred from the Armée de Mayence. On June 13, 1795 became Adjudant General Chef de Brigade. He received his first wound on March 26 (6 germinal) under the walls of Legnago, and on the following May 16 (27 floréal) was wounded again at Marengo (San Giuliano). For the merits acquired at Pastrengo he received the gift of the Honour Sabre and a complimentary letter from the Directory on 4 floréal an VII. The First Consul wanted personally to award him with the rank of général de brigade (10 July 1799). Baron of the Empire: 26 October 1808. On October 2nd, 1839 he died at Perpignan.

45   **Chef Robert** was severely wounded in the 1795 Rhine campaign. So, on August 20, 1798, he was allowed to retire. In the emergencies of 1799, however, he was recalled to arms as, chef remis en activité: 6e complémentaire an VII

46   The 93e Demi brigade de Ligne came in Italy on February 1797. There it received the new flags, model "Armée d'Italie" designed by Bonaparte himself, on July 1797 at Belluno, Italy, in the Division Delmas: flags totally blank of Battle Honours. For this reason it was decided to add the phrase "Traversée du Tirol" on the flags. In 1799, the 3rd battalion of the 93th was envoyed at Mantua's garrison. There its flag was taken by Austrians when the fortress capitulated, July 30. While the Chef was **Varennes,** the most important officer of the demi-brigade was the Grenadier commander **Chef-de-Bataillon Charles-Sebastien Marion** (Born: May 7, 1758 . Chef-de-Brigade: September 6, 1799 . General-de-Brigade: August 20, 1805 . Officer of the Legion d'Honneur: June 14, 1804 . Baron of the Empire: September 9, 1810 . Died: September 7, 1812 (killed at la Moskowa battle).

47   **Chef-de-Brigade Charles-Augustin Salomon de Moulineuf** was substituted by Chef dB **François-Alexandre Grosjean**, promoted chef de brigade, in his place, as Salomon retired on 17 germinal an VII. (April 6, 1799) the day after Magnano.

48   **Général Gaspard-Amedée Gardanne** Born on April 24, 1758 in Solliers (Vàr), entered the service, March 1, 1779, as lieutenant in the gunners coastguard, and here remained until September 30, 1780, time of his passage in the King's Guards. He left the duty in 1784, however, when the Revolution outbroke, he was elected second major of the 1st Vàr battalion, September 16, 1791. Commander of this same battalion on November 31, 1792 he made the campaigns of the Alps. Adjudant-General chief of brigade by decree of the people representatives, on September 13, 1793, he was confirmed in this rank by decree of the 23 germinal year II, and took an active share in the operations at Toulon. Transferred at the army of Italy, the adjudant-General Gardanne distinguished at the camp of Sabion (Piedmont), near Tende pass. For this he was named temporarily brigadier general, on January 23, 1796. At the passage of Mincio he was with a bunch of 50 grenadiers to hold the Borghetto bridge. General Gardanne, defined by Bonaparte as "a Grenadier by size as by courage" put the Austrians in rout. At the battle of Castiglione, Gardanne put again in rout the enemy and contributed strongly to the success of this combat. Always with avant-guard tasks he was in Tyrol and at la Corona with Vaubois and then at the first day of Arcole, when he made 400 prisoners, at the second, when he captured other 2,300 Austrians, among whose was a general major,

taking 11 guns and 2 flags. The 27 Brumaire, when the enemy made a move to seize the bridge, general-in-chief Bonaparte gave him the order to ambush from a wood, with 2 battalions of the 32e half-brigade. As soon as the Austrians appeared, Gardanne attacked them with impetuosity; and made other 2,000 prisoners rejecting many enemies in Adige, where a great number drowned. There he was wounded by a shot, but he did continue to lead the column. Confirmed brigadier general, by decree of the Directory, on March 30, 1797, he continued the italian campaign. In 1799 he distinguished himself especially at Bassignana. Then Gardanne was blocked in Alexandria where was taken prisoner. At the beginning of the 1800 Gardanne came to Paris and took a very-active part with the events of 18 brumaire. Bonaparte, become first Consul, did not forget the services of Gardanne; he named him division general on 15 nivôse year VIII. Called at the command of the 6th infantry division of reserve army he was at Marengo where he obtained his greatest glory.

Gardanne still contributed, under the orders of Brune, at the Mincio, Brenta and Adige passages. Returned to France he was named commander of the 20th military division. In 1801 the first Consul entrusted to him the command of the French troops employed in the republic of Genoa, and in 1802 he charged him with the comamnd of all French Corps stationed in the Italian republic. He continued to exert his functions until 1805 when he passed to the command of one divisions of the army of Italy under Masséna. Gardanne distinguished himself in the combat of Caldiero. Transferred in 1806 to the 9th army corps, he made the campaigns of Prussia and Poland. After the peace of Tilsit, he returned to France by Silesia, when was ill by a pernicious fever in Breslau, and there he died on August 14, 1807.

49 **Chef de Brigade Joseph-Denis Picard** – (Born: July 23rd, 1761 - Chef de Brigade of 1st Hussars: January 8th, 1797 former adjudant général, future général, promoted chef de brigade with Patent 7 pluviose an VI (January 26, 1798) - Brigade General : February 26th, 1803 - Legion d'Honneur: December 11th, 1803 - Commander of the Legion d'Honneur: June 22nd, 1804 - Baron of the Empire: June 1st, 1808 - Died: January 20th, 1826).

50 **Baron Ivan Ivanovich Dalheim,** from April 28, 1798, was General-Major. Previously he was the Colonel commander of the Grenadier regiment of Astrakhan. Until June 28, 1799 he led the Musketeers regiment of Archangelogorod.

51 The French said, in a Bulletin, they had found a corpse with a brilliant uniform, and they were sure being the general Chubarov. Jomini confirmed this in his "Histoire des Guerres de la Révolution" (XI vol. p. 294), however he presented again Chubarov, alive, in the Trebbia battle (XI vol. p. 359). In a successive Report Chubarov was killed a second time at Pistoia (June 24, 1799). At least, at the time the French re-occupied Constance (October 7, 1799) the sergeant-major Heyberger killed Chubarov for the third time (from War Archives). Actualy, this three time dead man returned in Russia with Suvorov at the end of the campaign.

52 Bagration gave these details: Dead (1 Staff Officer, 6 Officers, 326 NCOs and soldiers); wounded (1 general, 8 Officers, 50 inferior Officers, 600 NCOs and soldiers).

53 At Bassignana, the 14th Line, officially, depended on the brigadier general François Jean Baptiste Quesnel du Torpt, wounded during the combats. It was sent between Pecetto and Bassignana, until the confluence of the rivers Tanaro and Po, where already the 3 battalions of the former Alessandria garrison stood, one Helvetian and two Piedmontese (II/1a and II/3a). After Bassignana, Colli Ricci had to replace Quesnel because of his temporary incapacity to combat.

54 Other sources said that the Austrians were totally surprised and the new of approaching French was received at 9.00 AM into the Torre Garofoli camp by general Lusignan. A sudden War Council with FML Kaim, arrived at Torre Garofoli during the early morning, left Lusignan alone to engage the enemies, being Kaim's troops too tired to fight. The French had overrun the Austrian outpost of general Karacsaj at Marengo and were advancing in line towards San Giuliano vecchio. Bagration was caught by musketry during his march towards Sale and deployed his units in order of battle at the left wing. This second version seems more reliable.
As for Coalition's troops ready for battle, it was a situation totally in contrast with the Suvorov's marching orders.

55 **Chef de Brigade Joseph-Denis Picard** – (Born: July 23rd, 1761 - Chef de Brigade of 1st Hussars: January 8th, 1797 former adjudant général, future général, promoted chef de brigade with Patent 7 pluviose an VI (January 26, 1798) - Brigade General : February 26th, 1803 - Legion d'Honneur: December 11th, 1803 - Commander of the Legion d'Honneur: June 22nd, 1804 - Baron of the Empire: June 1st, 1808 - Died: January 20th, 1826).

56 **Antoine-Alexandre Rousseaux,** born on September 17, 1756 ; soldier on October 1, 1775; sergeant on July 17, 1779; adjutant on May 10,1789. He was caught by the Revolution outbreak amd began the Officer career as second-lieutenant (29.10.1790), firts-lieutenant (16 december 1790); captain (25 february 1792). In 1794 he was named Adjutant-général chef-de-brigade and in the following year he was chef-de-brigade.

57 **Oberst Franz Xavier Johann Sarkender Alois Priskus Graf von Auersperg** was born on January 19, 1749 and died at Przemysl on January 8, 1808. He was Major in the IR 36 Fürst Carl Fürstenberg and in 1793 was named Oberstleutnant. In 1796 he reached the rank of second colonel in the regiment. As IR 36 Oberst he made the 1799 campaign in Italy distinguishing himself at Novi. After that battle he received the provisional rank of brigadier (October 2) and was confirmed

Generalmajor on November 18, 1799, after having fought with bravery the Savigliano battle. In 1800 he was at Mondovì and at Lesegno clash (October 26). In 1802 he had the Cross of Maria Theresia and on April 1807 he was named Feldmarschall-leutnant. He became the Owner of the K.k. IR 37 and Territorial Division commander at Kaschau (Kosice). He died in the fortress of Przemysl.

58   Suvorov's report declared 2500 French dead and 200 taken prisoners (he often overestimated the enemy's losses). The Field Marshal told that the Coalition lost 27 dead (one being Officer) and around 80 wounded. A memoir told about 180 dead (6 Officers) and 250 wounded for the Austro-Russians. Melas' report of July 11 declared 97 dead and 286 wounded (11 Officers) with 115 French taken prisoners. Lusignan's report of July 9 declared about 300-400 French prisoners.

59   **Général de brigade Bertrand Clausel** (more correctly Clauzel, Count) (1772-1842), marshal of France, was born at Mirepoix (Ariege) on the 12th of December 1772, and served in the first campaign of the French Revolutionary Wars as one of the volunteers of 1791. In June 1795, having distinguished himself repeatedly in the war on the northern frontier (1792-1793) and the fighting in the eastern Pyrenees (1793-1794), Clausel was made a general of brigade. In this rank he served in Italy in 1798 and 1799, and in the disastrous campaign of the latter year he won great distinction at the battles of the Trebbia and of Novi. In 1802 he served in the expedition to S. Domingo. He became a general of division in December 1802, and after his return to France he was in almost continuous military employment there until in 1806 he was sent to the army of Naples. Soon after this Napoleon made him a grand officer of the Legion of Honour. In1808-1809he was with Marmont in Dalmatia, and at the close of 1809 he was appointed to a command in the army of Portugal under Massena.
Clausel took part in the Peninsular campaigns of 1810 and 1811, including the Torres Vedras campaign, and under Marmont he did excellent service in re-establishing the discipline, efficiency and mobility of the army, which had suffered severely in the retreat from Torres Vedras. In the Salamanca campaign (1812) the result of Clausel's work was shown in the marching powers of the French, and at the battle of Salamanca, Clausel, who had succeeded to the command on Marmont being wounded, and had himself received a severe wound, drew off his army with the greatest skill, the retreat on Burgos being conducted by him in such a way that the pursuers failed to make the slightest impression, and had themselves in the end to retire from the siege of Burgos (1812). Early in 1813 Clausel was made commander of the Army of the North in Spain, but he was unable to avert the great disaster of Vittoria. Under the supreme command of Soult he served through the rest of the Peninsular War with unvarying distinction. On the first restoration in 1814 he submitted unwillingly to the Bourbons, and when Napoleon returned to France, he hastened to join him. During the Hundred Days he was in command of an army defending the Pyrenean frontier. Even after Waterloo he long refused to recognize the restored government, and he escaped to America, being condemned to death in absence. He took the first opportunity of returning to aid the Liberals in France (1820), sat in the chamber of deputies from 1827 to 1830, and after the revolution of 1830 was at once given a military command. At the head of the army of Algiers, Clausel made a successful campaign, but he was soon recalled by the home government, which desired to avoid complications in Algeria. At the same time he was made a marshal of France (February 1831). For some four years thereafter he urged his Algerian policy upon the chamber of deputies, and finally in 1835 was reappointed commander-inchief. But after several victories, including the taking of Mascara in 1835, the marshal met with a severe repulse at Constantine in 1836. A change of government in France was primarily responsible for the failure, but public opinion attributed it to Clausel, who was recalled in February 1837. He thereupon retired from active service, and, after vigorously defending his conduct before the deputies, he ceased to take part in public affairs. He lived in complete retirement up to his death at Secourrieu (Garonne) on the 21st of April 1842.

60   **General Major Gheorgy Gavrilovich Zukata or, in Italian, Zuccato** (Цукато) – a Russian count sort, begun general-major, descendant of an ancient Venetian family which left the service at the Württemberg Court and entered Russian service in 1788. He participated in the Second Turkish war, distinguishing himself at the assault of Prague. During Suvorov's Italian campaign was at the Trebbia and Novi battles. In 1809 - 1810, sent for a command in Little Walachia, organized a regular cavalry regiment from the Serbian cossacks. He died in 1810.

61   **Colonel (Polkovnik) Petr Petrovich Passek (Пассек)** was promoted General-major on June 7, 1799. From July 16, 1798 to that date he had led the Grenadier regiment of Moscow (Rozenberg Grenadiers). From June 7, 1799 to August 6, 1803 he became the Owner of the Grenadier regiment of Kiev, which he commande from 1803 to November 15, 1804. In 1807 he became the Owner of the Musketeers regiment of Mogilev..

62 Former **Major Zaltser** was promoted Lieutenant Colonel on May 6, 1799, after the Adda battles, and became Colonel on September 11, 1800. He led the Tambovsky regiment until February 7, 1806.

63   **Colonel Grigoryi Dmitrjevich Kasahovsky** (Касаговский) became General Major on February 16, 1800 when he left the command of the Smolensk Musketeers Regiment becaming the Chief of the Vitebsk Musketeers Regiment.

64   From May 17, 1797 until March 8, 1800 its official number was the 6th Jäger (6-й Ерерский полк – Jeghjerskyi). Only after 1800 it assumed the number 7th; otherwise in all sources it was always related as 7th regiment. Its commander was also its Owner till September 20 (to December 31) when it was under Colonel Vassiliy Aleksejevich Chvitzky who was at Susa with the Prince.

▲ A portrait of Russian general Suvorov paint by by Schteiben

www.ingramcontent.com/pod-product-compliance
Lightning Source LLC
Chambersburg PA
CBHW041521220426
43667CB00003B/58